Illustration from Cotton Nero A.x—The Dreamer at the Stream

The Signifying Power of *Pearl*

This book enhances our understanding of the exquisitely beautiful, fourteenth-century, Middle English dream vision poem *Pearl*. Situating the study in the contexts of medieval literary criticism and contemporary genre theory, Beal argues that the poet intended *Pearl* to be read at four levels of meaning and in four corresponding genres: literally, an elegy; spiritually, an allegory; morally, a consolation; and anagogically, a revelation. The book addresses cruxes and scholarly debates about the poem's genre and meaning, including key questions that have been unresolved in *Pearl* studies for over a century. Noting that the poem is open to many interpretations, Beal also considers folktale genre patterns in *Pearl*, including those drawn from parable, fable, and fairy-tale. The conclusion considers *Pearl* in the light of modern psychological theories of grieving and trauma. This book makes a compelling case for re-reading *Pearl* and recognizing the poem's signifying power. Given the ongoing possibility of new interpretations, it will appeal to those who specialize in *Pearl* as well as scholars of Middle English, Medieval Literature, Genre Theory, and Literature and Religion.

Jane Beal is Associate Researcher in the Department of English at the University of California, Davis, USA.

Routledge Studies in Medieval Literature and Culture

1. **Biblical Paradigms in Medieval English Literature**
   From Cædmon to Malory
   Lawrence Besserman

2. **Sin and Filth in Medieval Culture**
   The Devil in the Latrine
   Martha Bayless

3. **Cultural Difference and Material Culture in Middle English Romance**
   Normans and Saxons
   Dominique Battles

4. **Mary Magdalene in Medieval Culture**
   Conflicted Roles
   Edited by Peter V. Loewen and Robin Waugh

5. **The Signifying Power of *Pearl***
   Medieval Literary and Cultural Contexts
   for the Transformation of Genre
   Jane Beal

The Signifying Power of *Pearl*
Medieval Literary and Cultural Contexts for the Transformation of Genre

Jane Beal

LONDON AND NEW YORK

First published 2017 by Routledge

2 Park Square, Milton Park, Abingdon, Oxfordshire OX14 4RN
52 Vanderbilt Avenue, New York, NY 10017

Routledge is an imprint of the Taylor & Francis Group, an informa business

First issued in paperback 2019

Copyright © 2017 Taylor & Francis

The right of Jane Beal to be identified as author of this work has been asserted by her in accordance with sections 77 and 78 of the Copyright, Designs and Patents Act 1988.

All rights reserved. No part of this book may be reprinted or reproduced or utilised in any form or by any electronic, mechanical, or other means, now known or hereafter invented, including photocopying and recording, or in any information storage or retrieval system, without permission in writing from the publishers.

Notice:
Product or corporate names may be trademarks or registered trademarks, and are used only for identification and explanation without intent to infringe.

Library of Congress Cataloging-in-Publication Data

CIP data has been applied for.

ISBN: 978-1-138-67807-1 (hbk)
ISBN: 978-0-367-87864-1 (pbk)

Typeset in Sabon
by codeMantra

We lost you– for how long a time–
true *Pearl* of our poetic prime!
We found you, and you gleam, re-set
in Britain's lyric coronet.

—Alfred Lord Tennyson,
Quoted in Marian Mead, trans., The *Pearl* (v)

In the course of theoretical work over the last century, the term genre has been invested with many different kinds of significance. Tzvetan Todorov, for instance, argued that a contemporary debate about genre is an "anachronistic pastime" and that such discussions belong to "the good old days of the classics." However, in my opinion, the concept of genre is an important tool for anyone who wishes to clarify – and, as a result, to simplify to a certain degree – the main differences between *Pearl* and the texts of the contemplative writers. As Alastair Fowler pointed out, one of the main benefits of the concept of genre is that it provides a "communication system, for the use of writers in writing, and readers and critics in reading and interpreting." However, it is important to strike a balance between acknowledging the uniqueness of a work and assigning it to a particular type, and to be aware of the relative instability of each genre.

—Annika Sylén Lagerholm,
Pearl and Contemplative Writing (23)

The *Pearl*, finally, is an elusive poem.

—Edward Vasta,
"Introduction," The *Pearl*, trans.
Sister Mary Vincent Hamilton (ix)

In loving memory

of my sister, my Pearl-Maiden:
Asya Pleskatch
(1983–2003)

scio enim quod redemptor meus vivat
et in novissimo de terra surrecturus sim

Job 19:25 (Vulgate)

Contents

List of Illustrations	xiii
Preface	xv
Acknowledgments	xxiii
Introduction: Signifying	1
1　Literal Sense: Desiring the Beloved	20
2　Allegorical Meaning: Rejoicing in Salvation	43
3　Moral Purpose: Consoling the Heart	66
4　Anagogical Revelation: Imagining Spiritual Marriage to Christ	85
5　Beyond the Four Levels of Meaning: Folktale Genre Patterns in *Pearl*	107
Conclusion: Remembering	137
Bibliography	155
Index	169

List of Illustrations

Manuscript Illustration from Cotton Nero A.x—The Dreamer at the Stream   i
1.1   Medieval Hood   41
C.1   Layers of Memory in *Pearl*   139
C.2   Memorial Processes   151

Preface

Entering into the study of *Pearl* is like entering into the cathedral of memory. The idea that the poem is like an architectural edifice is not new.[1] Neither have literary scholars failed to notice that the poem is memorial or that medieval people conceived of their memory as the carefully wrought and framed, interior architecture of the soul.[2] Indeed, the ornate structure of *Pearl* has led to several comparisons between it and many other things: cathedral,[3] chantry chapel,[4] rose-window,[5] saint's reliquary,[6] rosary, ecclesiastical chandelier, royal crown,[7] the microcosm of a human body with a heart at its center,[8] the macrocosm of a *mappamundi* with Jerusalem near its center,[9] and (of course) a pearl.[10] But it seems to me that *Pearl* is especially like a cathedral of memory. How is *Pearl* like a memory-cathedral, and what can readers of the poem learn from such a comparison?

Answers to these two questions emerge gradually from sustained consideration. They require a deeper understanding of the structure of *Pearl* itself and of the poem's signifying power, which intersects with medieval art, architecture, glassmaking, liturgy, devotional practices, literary forms, medicine, and science. The interdisciplinary study of *Pearl*, and the fields of human knowledge and culture to which it pertains, makes the poem meaningful to many different kinds of readers today.

The Cathedral of Memory

Pearl is a narrative poem of 1,212 lines that are divided into 101 stanzas of 12 lines each.[11] The stanzas are grouped into 20 sections, each unified by a concatenation word used in the opening line and closing line of the stanza, usually with a varied meaning each time the word occurs. There are five stanzas in each section, with the exception of XV, which contains six.[12] The poem has been compared to art forms like the diptych and the triptych because the sections can be divided like a diptych, with two sections facing one another (10-10),[13] or a triptych, with two outer panels turned inward toward a central one (4-12-4).[14] One scholar has argued that the poet makes use of "the golden section" (phi), which was used by classical poets such as Virgil and Horace to structure their poems (the *Georgics* and the *Ars poetica* respectively), in order to demonstrate a relationship between the finite microcosm of the poem and the infinitely expanding macrocosm of the universe.[15]

This level of structural complexity, layering the building blocks of words on lines, lines on stanzas, stanzas on micro-sections, and micro-sections on macro-sections, suggests that the poet saw himself as the master-builder of a cathedral of memory.[16] In the Middle Ages, the understanding of the cathedral space—or, indeed, any church or chantry chapel—was closely linked to the biblical conceptualizations of Noah's Ark and the New Jerusalem.[17] Its floor plan was linked to the shape of the Cross, upon which medieval Christians always remembered Christ's body, and so the idea of the cathedral was also connected to the idea of the human body.[18]

When the *Pearl*-poet depicts the Dreamer's journey through the poem, it is as if the shape of a cathedral forms the subtext for the shape of his journey. He begins in a garden, which resembles a church graveyard, and then rises into space as if climbing the stairs to enter the cathedral doors. He processes through the blue columns of the trees on either side of him to the cross-bar of the stream that separates him from the Pearl-Maiden. She stands like a pearlescent window, around and through whom shines the bright light of God's truth and the Church's right teaching, until the Dreamer lifts his eyes to behold—as if between the two of them or in the space above them (or both)—the vision of the great high priest of all believers, the Lamb in the New Jerusalem.[19] There he again sees the Pearl-Maiden, who processes behind the Lamb in company with other virgins as if in a choir, and the sight drives him nearly mad with longing.

The three places in the poem where the Pearl-Maiden exists, first in the garden, then on the opposite bank of the stream in the dreamscape, and finally in the heavenly procession with saints following the Lamb, inevitably invoke her as the patron-saint of the Dreamer's cathedral. She may be buried outside of it, but she is also enshrined within it. For saints could be memorialized within an ecclesiastical edifice, at the front of chapel, church, or cathedral, in various ways: their entire bodies could be buried in the altar, or under it in the crypt, or bits of their bones could be enclosed in a reliquary.[20] If the body of the saint could not be obtained, then a saint's statue or a window might stand in place of the actual body. But whether the literal body or a figure of it lay (or stood) at the front of the church, and even if it were recognized as a site at which miracles were performed at times of special visitation, medieval people were still taught to believe that the spirit of the saint had departed from the bones and existed apart in heavenly places until the general Resurrection when body and soul would be reunited. Like the saint in the cathedral, the Pearl-Maiden in the poem exists in more than one place at one time: in the earth, in the Dreamer's memory, and in God's own heaven. The loss of the beloved Pearl-Maiden, which has brought about the split realities of her postmortem existence, is the grief with which the Dreamer is trying to come to terms.

The poet represents the narrator-dreamer of the poem as himself, remembered at an earlier stage of spiritual development, and his creation of the lyrical *Pearl* poem is not only like building a cathedral, but also like singing a song. But there is an innate tension in the singing, an implied question: does the poet sing an old song or a new one? A song motivated by carnalitas or caritas? Augustine wrote in his sermon-commentary on Psalm 95:

> Cantate Domino canticum novum, cantate Domino omnis terra. Si canticum novum cantat omnis terra; sic aedificatur, cum cantat: ipsum cantare, aedificare est; sed si non vetus cantet. Vetus cantat cupiditas carnis: novum cantat caritas Dei.[21]

> (Sing to the Lord a new song; sing to the Lord all the earth. If all the earth sings a new song, it is thus built when it sings: to sing this song is to build! But not so if the old song will sing out. The desire of the flesh sings the old song; the love of God sings the new song.)

So when the Dreamer takes his journey through the poem, which is, at some level, like a meditative walk through the interior of a cathedral, the poet is singing into poetic and textual existence the memory of his transformative experience: a new song that gradually overcomes the old. The song, the psalm of *Pearl*, moves from lament to praise.

Because readers and hearers of the poem journey with the Dreamer, through the poet's powerfully reconstructed cathedral of memory, it is as if they traverse the interior of a sacred space as well: hearing the song of the poet like a liturgy and, just as importantly, seeing what the Dreamer sees. *Pearl* is a highly imagistic poem, and each image appears in the poem like an icon or a stained glass window in a cathedral, inviting meditation and rumination. These images serve to cue, orient, and shape the readers' memory.[22] Because the readers do what might be called "memory work" in the process of imagining the poem's images, they, too, become like builders and singers.[23]

Many passages in *Pearl* paraphrase the very same scriptures that were sung and read in the liturgical celebrations that took place within medieval cathedrals. These would inevitably echo in the minds of medieval readers, resonating with the same texts they heard in their chapels, churches, and cathedrals at specific times throughout the liturgical year.[24] These were meant to change the people that heard them. As Ann Meyer observes, "church buildings, as they were defined by the liturgies celebrated within them, are complex programs of transformation in which the observer's longing for perfection and sanctity finds direction and focus."[25]

Medieval Literary and Cultural Contexts for the Transformation of Genre

The idea of a cathedral of memory provides a way into the poem and a deeper understanding of it. Extant medieval art and architecture do provide key contexts, certainly, but they are not the only ones needed for understanding *Pearl*. Interpreting *Pearl*, in its fullest sense, requires knowledge of additional medieval literary and cultural contexts.

The signifying power of *Pearl* is revealed, in part, by its many connections to other medieval texts and contexts. *Significatio* is a technique of medieval rhetoric, in which any given word may have more than one sense (a form of punning or *double-entendre*), and the *Pearl*-poet works this technique masterfully in his poem.[26] Part of the way he does so is by resonance and filiation: by using words that echo familiarly within the associative memory of his readers and by connecting images they know from their other visual experiences to the narrative he is writing. Much of what was common literary and cultural knowledge in the late-fourteenth century is lost on modern readers, so it requires explanation to show how *Pearl* could have affected medieval readers and can affect modern ones who regain what time and translation have erased.

In a sense, the purpose of this book is to re-inscribe memory and illuminate understanding of *Pearl*. In various chapters, I explore the relationship between *Pearl* and other texts and contexts, in an effort to show how the poet wrote a poem that is not only literally, an elegy; spiritually, an allegory; morally, a consolation; and anagogically, a revelation, but also a poem intended for common speakers of the English language, living in late-medieval England, who had listened throughout their lives to the folktales of their time: parables, fables, and fairy-tales. By writing a poem with many levels of meaning, the poet appealed to a wide audience, part of which was learned in the traditions of the four-fold interpretation of scripture and another part of which was less learned, but nevertheless could grasp the plot and much of the point of his story emotionally and spiritually. The conclusion of the book, like this preface, is concerned with the memorial process involved in writing, reading, and remembering *Pearl*.

The literary and cultural contexts relevant to the understanding of *Pearl* include medieval love lyrics, both sacred and secular, and the practice of allegoresis, on not only biblical texts, but also classical poetry. This practice was a strategy for reading and for writing new works of literature, especially in vernacular languages. The liturgy of the church, which influenced every believing person who attended Mass throughout the year, influenced the *Pearl*-poet and the shape of his poem, too. He was aware of the symbolic significance of many images and material objects in his culture, which appear in his poem, foremost among these the pearl itself. He also paid attention to the symbolic development of other images and things in his poem, especially birds, which he associated with their consolatory function. Certainly the literary genre of dream vision, alongside the visionary experiences medieval contemplatives had in prayer, also help to explain why he crafted such a highly visual poem, one closely affiliated with the biblical book of Revelation, and expected what he was doing to be understood by his readers.

The poem essentially fulfills a combination of literate and aural expectations, for beyond (or within) the four-fold layers of meaning, there lies a series of folk-tale motifs taken from parables, fables, and fairy-tales. If modern readers learn how these types of tales circulated in the late-medieval period, in both spoken and written forms, with wide-ranging (but not truly unlimited) variations and commentaries, the sense of the allusions and metaphors in *Pearl* emerges more clearly.

Medieval texts and contexts give the insight needed for interpretation, but so too do medieval literary criticism and modern genre theory. In this study, I look closely at interpretive cruxes in *Pearl* scholarship in order to find a plausible middle way through the debates. The definitions of genres, developed and applied in modern criticism, have helped this endeavor as has the gradual acceptance of the idea among critics that *Pearl* participates in more than one genre—and in none exclusively. For the poet is in fact in the business of transforming genre and the generic expectations of his readers through his unique work.

Literary theory makes some important contributions to the development of my arguments, especially those theories concerned with human psychology, grieving, and trauma, notably in the second chapter and the conclusion. Traumatic memory is better (if still imperfectly) understood today than it was in the past. When the occurrence of post-traumatic stress disorder became widespread among "shell-shocked" soldiers in World War I, modern people—veterans and their families—needed ways to survive and heal while their medical caregivers needed ways to diagnose and treat. The DSM eventually provided guidelines. But of course the psychological stages of grieving and the more intense form of grieving occasioned by traumatic loss— PTSD—existed in medieval times, even though it did not go by that name, and many medieval poems depict the psychologically wounded soldier / knight who goes mad in the forest though he has no visible, physical injury. The Dreamer is certainly grieving, and he may also be traumatized, and it can be helpful to examine his experience through both a medieval and a modern lens.

Indeed, we never learn from the poem exactly how the Pearl-Maiden died, or was lost to the Dreamer, suggesting an unwillingness on the Dreamer's part to remember the details of his loss even in the face of a very great need to do so. But he remembers many other things practically and symbolically connected to his loss, and gradually his memory is illuminated. This process, as the *Pearl*-poet represents it, is emotional and theological at the same time. However, the poet is careful to demonstrate, through the Dreamer's journey, that knowledge of Christian doctrine is not enough without someone willing to enter into the suffering of the one who is bereft. For the Dreamer, that someone is first the Pearl-Maiden herself and then the Lamb of God. His healing process takes place in the context of the Christian communal memory of things that were, are, and (especially) will be. Indeed, the Dreamer's healing takes place in the context of a shared hope in a redemptive future for all Christians: the New Jerusalem of heaven, revealed within his cathedral of memory, and the Eucharist.

My approach to understanding *Pearl* thus relates to many disciplines. Among these disciplines are literature, folktale studies, biblical studies, literary criticism and theory (especially psychology and trauma theory), cultural studies, medieval history and theology, translation studies and translation theory, and individual and cultural memory studies. It is hoped that this book will therefore appeal to many different types of students and scholars.

Invitation

The existence of *Pearl* in a single manuscript, Cotton Nero A.x, is something of a miracle. There are no other copies of the poem known to be extant, and the one book in which it appears survived a fire that broke out on October 23, 1731, at Ashburnham House, Westminster, where it was being temporarily stored with other Cotton manuscripts.[27] Readers today are fortunate indeed to be able to read the poem.

The original book is small, and though its existence was noted by the seventeenth century in at least one record, it was only edited and published for the first time in the nineteenth century. As such, it is a curiosity, but it wouldn't seem to demand our attention, given its humble origins. Yet *Pearl* is in content a masterpiece, an extraordinary poem of great beauty and startling insight.

Ann Meyer has written that "*Pearl*, one might say, is a poem about the devastating limitations of human love and our yearning for it to be otherwise."[28] This was certainly what drew me, so intensely, into the world of the poem in the first place, but it has stayed with me for many more reasons than this. I invite all readers to re-read *Pearl*, as they read this book, and to discover, again, what the poem signifies and why it matters to them.

Notes

1. Drawing on earlier work by Elizabeth Salter (namely, her essays "Alliterative Revival I" and "Alliterative Revival II") and Barbara Nolan in *The Gothic Visionary Perspective* (1977, repr. 2016), Ann Meyer developed the most sustained argument in *Pearl* studies comparing the poem to cathedral and chantry chapel, looking at specific ecclesiastical edifices in England and Europe. See *Medieval Allegory and the Building of the New Jerusalem* (Woodbridge: D.S. Brewer, 2003). See also Lucy Anderson, *The Architecture of Light: Color and Cathedral as Rhetorical Ductus in the Middle English Pearl* (Diss., New York University, 2009), who argues that the form of *Pearl* is a deliberately fictive or imaginary cathedral.
2. See Mary Carruthers, "Invention, Mnemonics, and Stylistic Ornament in *Psychomachia* and *Pearl*," in *The Endless Knot: Essays on Old and Middle English in Honor of Marie Borroff*, ed. by M. Teresa Tavormina and R.F. Yeager (Cambridge and Rochester, NY: D.S. Brewer, 1995), 201–14.
3. See Salter, Nolan, and Meyer (as cited in n1 above).
4. Meyer, *Medieval Allegory and the Building of the New Jerusalem*, chapters 3–6.

5. Kevin Marti, *Body, Heart, and Text in the Pearl-Poet*, Studies in Mediaeval Literature 12 (Lewiston, NY: The Edwin Mellon Press, 1991), 83.
6. Seeta Chaganti, *The Medieval Poetics of the Reliquary: Enshrinement, Inscription, Performance* (New York, NY: Palgrave Macmillan, 2008), 95–130, that is, chap. 4, "Enshrining Form: *Pearl* as Inscriptional Object and Devotional Event."
7. Ian Bishop, *The Pearl in its Setting* (Oxford: Blackwell, 1968), 30–31. John Bowers and John Gatta have also compared *Pearl* to a crown. See Bowers, *The Politics of Pearl: Court Poetry in the Age of Richard II* (London: Boydell and Brewer, 2001), 108, 134 and Gatta, "Transformation Symbolism and the Liturgy of the Mass in *Pearl*," *Modern Philology* 71 (1974): 243–56.
8. Marti, *Body, Heart, and Text*, 83.
9. Meyer, *Medieval Allegory and the Building of the New Jerusalem*, 179.
10. Dorothy Everett, *Essays on Middle English Literature*, ed. P.M. Kean (Oxford at the Clarendon Press, 1955), 88. This was one of the earliest studies demonstrating how the circularity implied by the poem's concatenation words, linking the end to the beginning, is like the central image of the poem, the pearl. Bishop later argued that this "endlessly round" structure was intended to represent the perfect sphere of the heavenly kingdom. See Bishop, *Pearl in its Setting*, 29. For a complementary interpretation, see also the conclusion of this book, "Remembering."
11. On the significance of the "twelveness" of *Pearl*, see Susanna Greer Fein, "Twelve-line Stanza Forms in Middle English and the Date of *Pearl*," *Speculum* 72 (1997): 367–98.
12. Even in this exception, there is a clear marriage of structure and theme: the concatenation phrase in section XV is "never the less."
13. Harwood, Britton, "*Pearl* as Diptych," in *Text and Matter: New Critical Perspectives of the Pearl-Poet*, ed. Robert J. Blanch, Miriam Youngerman Miller, and Julian N. Wasserman (Troy, NY: Whiston, 1991), 61–78. In *The Politics of Pearl*, Bowers has compared the poem to the Wilton Diptych specifically.
14. This comparison was suggested early in *Pearl* studies by Charles Grosvenor Osgood. See Osgood, "Introduction," *The Pearl: A Middle English Poem*, ed. Charles Grosvenor Osgood (Boston and London: D.C. Heath and Co., 1906), lviii, n 1.
15. Edward Condren, *The Numerical Universe of the Gawain-Poet: Beyond Phi* (Gainesville, FL: University Press of Florida, 2002).
16. Given that the *Pearl* poem can be compared to a cathedral, the *Pearl*-poet himself can be compared to a metalworker, a mason, and a master-builder. Carruthers calls him a "master jeweler," noting that while the Parable of the Merchant, from which so much of the poem is elaborated, might lead us to expect the narrator to compare himself to a merchant, instead he compares himself to a jeweler: the poem thus transforms the protagonist of the parable from merchant to maker. See Carruthers, "Invention, Mnemonics, and Stylistic Ornament," 201–02.
17. On the connections between cathedral structure and Noah's Ark, see Stefaan Van Liefferinge, "The Geometry of Rib-Vaulting at Notre-Dame of Paris: Architectural or Exegetical Space?" in *Space in the Medieval West: Places, Territories, and Imagined Geographies*, ed. Meredith Cohen and Fanny Madeline (Dorchester: Ashgate, 2014), 37–50, esp. 38–40. To make his argument, Van Liefferinge draws on the description of Noah's Ark by Hugh of St. Victor, which appears in English translation in *The Medieval Craft of Memory: An Anthology of*

Texts and Pictures, ed. Mary Carruthers and Jan Ziolkowski (Philadelphia, PA: University of Pennsylvania Press, 2002), 41–70. On the connections between cathedrals and the New Jerusalem, see Ann Meyer, *Medieval Allegory and the Building of the New Jerusalem*, 94–97, which explains Abbot Suger's dedication of St. Denis and the goal of re-creating the Heavenly Jerusalem on earth.
18. Cf. John 2:21.
19. On the use of glass imagery in *Pearl*, see Heather Phillips, "Medieval Glass-Making Techniques and the Imagery of Glass in *Pearl*," *Florilegium* 6 (1984): 195–215.
20. The classic study on these cultural phenomena is Peter Brown, *The Cult of the Saints: Its Rise and Function in Latin Christianity* (Chicago, IL: University of Chicago Press, 1982).
21. Augustine, "In Psalmum 95: Enarratio: Sermo," http://www.augustinus.it/latino/esposizioni_salmi/esposizione_salmo_116_testo.htm (accessed 15 March 2016). The translation given is my own.
22. Cf. Carruthers, "Invention, Mnemonics, and Stylistic Ornament," 204.
23. Carruthers has noted that "any person thinking is fundamentally a craftsman, like a builder – or a jeweler" (203), that thinking is constructive (not merely reiterative), and that the *Pearl*-poet is teaching his thinking readers, essentially, to "think in pearls."
24. For more on this liturgical echoes in *Pearl*, see chap. 2 of this book.
25. Meyer, *Medieval Allegory*, 147.
26. For a discussion of medieval rhetorical terms and their application to *Pearl*, see Sylvia Tomasch, "A *Pearl* Punnology," *JEGP* 88 (1980), 1–20, esp. 2.
27. "History of the Cotton Library," http://www.bl.uk/reshelp/findhelprestype/manuscripts/cottonmss/cottonmss.html (accessed 15 March 2016).
28. Meyer, *Medieval Allegory and the Building of the New Jerusalem*, 154.

Acknowledgments

In Matthew's Gospel is recorded a parable of Jesus known as the Parable of the Pearl of Great Price: "Again, the kingdom of heaven is like a merchant in search of fine pearls, who, on finding one pearl of great value, went and sold all that he had and bought it." This pearl is a symbol of salvation, the gift of the God who opens the kingdom of heaven to those in search of it and his righteousness. The parable and its central symbol greatly inspired the medieval English poet who wrote *Pearl*, and his poem, in turn, inspired this book. I am deeply thankful to this unknown poet, whose dream vision has consoled me many times in my life. To many others—teachers, students, colleagues, editors, reviewers, and my friends and family—I am also thankful, for they have made *Pearl* more meaningful to me as we have shared this poem together in communities of learning.

    I first encountered *Pearl* through Marie Borroff's modern English translation in a course on medieval literature taught by Professor Helen Dunn at Sonoma State University. While completing my Master's degree in English literature, I studied the poem in the Middle English edition of Malcom Andrew and Ronald Waldron in a graduate seminar on authorship and late-fourteenth century literary careers with Professor Anne Middleton at UC Berkeley. At UC Davis, where I completed my doctorate, I studied *Pearl* in a graduate seminar taught by Professor Caron Cioffi on medieval gardens. I am thankful to these three professors for the insights they shared with me when I was first learning about the poem, and I am also thankful to the translator and editors who first provided me with the texts that allowed me access to the language and imagination of the *Pearl*-poet.

    I am thankful to my students at Wheaton College, Colorado Christian University, and, most recently, the University of California at Davis, who have compelled me to study the poem so as to become a more effective teacher of it myself. My students asked me many questions, in a variety of different classroom contexts, that prompted me to explore and explain *Pearl* further. Courses in which I taught *Pearl* have included survey and special topics courses for undergraduates, such as Introduction to Literature, Literature of the Western World, Classical and Early British Literature, British Literature I, Poetry Seminar, Spiritual Autobiography, and the Mythology of J.R.R. Tolkien, as well as creative writing classes. Because of my increasing interest in teaching the poem well, I eventually began translating and annotating parts of it for my students when the existing translations and editions did not address specific questions or issues. I am thankful to my student, Jessica Thennisch, who asked me to complete a dual-language of the entire poem, which I subsequently did: *Pearl: A Medieval Masterpiece in Middle English and Modern English*.

Seeing the effort entailed in teaching *Pearl* in different types of courses, in relation to different kinds of texts, I was motivated to reach out to many colleagues who teach the poem at the university level. With the help of my co-editors, Ann Meyer and Mark Bradshaw Busbee, this effort eventually produced the volume, *Approaches to Teaching the Middle English* Pearl. I learned a great deal from my fellow teachers and writers through that project, many of whom I knew through sessions held by the *Pearl*-poet Society and other groups that meet annually at the International Congress on Medieval Studies at the University of Western Michigan each May. I am thankful to them and to the organizers of the Congress, who help to make such fruitful exchange of knowledge possible.

I want to mention my special thankfulness for my colleague, Dr. Kimberly Jack, who was particularly helpful at the 2015 *Pearl*-poet Society Congress session on "Approaches to Teaching *Pearl*." She shared with me her insights on the Dreamer's hood, which is depicted in the first illustration of the manuscript, and her knowledge of medieval textiles was quite relevant to interpretation. I was glad to learn from her and incorporate her knowledge into the first chapter of this book.

I am thankful to colleagues in the field of *Pearl* studies who have edited, translated, and interpreted the poem so well; to the reviewers who have helped me to refine my interpretations of *Pearl*, including Joseph Wittig, and to the editors who have published my work on *Pearl* in the past, especially Edward Donald Kennedy, James H. Forse, Michael Boecherer, Nicola Masciandaro, and Karl Steel. I am thankful to my fellow scholar-poets, Cynthia Kraman and Adrienne Odasso, too, for their insights on *Pearl*. Librarians at the Shields Library of UC Davis, the Fowler Library of Colorado Christian University, and the Buswell Library of Wheaton College have helped me in my research. I am thankful to all of them, especially Roberto Delgadillo at UC Davis.

My editorial colleagues at Ashgate Publishing and Routledge have been very helpful to me in the process of improving this manuscript. Ann Donahue, acquisitions editor at Ashgate, first expressed interest in this book, requested it, and sent it out for review. I am very appreciative of her help and insight. I received helpful suggestions through the anonymous review process as well: to those who advocated for the publication of this book, blessings be upon your heads! After Ashgate joined Routledge, I began to work with acquisitions editor Elizabeth Levine, her fellow editors Polly Dodson and Emma Sudderick, and editorial assistants Alexandra (Allie) Simmons and

Erin Little; they provided valuable guidance through the process of bringing this book to publication, including help with permissions, images, and copy-editing, for which I am very thankful.

I also sincerely appreciate Assunta Petrone and my anonymous copyeditor at CodeMantra for their diligence and hard work, and Lindsey Cannan, my collaborator on the index to this book, for identifying the pages of the proofs in which each of the indexing terms appear.

Marcella Mulder, an editor of mine from Brill, granted permission to reprint several paragraphs in chapter four of this book from my essay, "Moses and Contemplative Christian Devotion," which appears in a volume I edited, *Illuminating Moses: A History of Reception from Exodus to the Renaissance* (Leiden: Brill, 2014). Malcolm Andrew and Ronald Waldron, editors *of Poems of the* Pearl *Manuscript*, 5th ed. (Liverpool University Press, 2007), and LUP gave permission to quote lines from *Pearl* that appear in this book. I am thankful for the generosity of everyone involved in the permissions process, and especially for the collegiality and kindness of Malcolm Andrew, who corresponded with me about the matter.

I have tried to read every edition, translation, and critical study of *Pearl*, and I have gained at least one new insight from each one. I greatly enjoy reading not only *Pearl* itself but all of the scholarship on this poem, for both are uniquely beautiful. So I am indebted to a number of scholars I have never met, or only met in passing, whose ideas have fascinated me. Their names can be found throughout this book.

My mother and step-father, Barbara and Rudy Holthuis, helped to support me in 2013–2014 as I completed the first draft of *The Signifying Power of* Pearl. Professors Margaret Ferguson and Liz Miller at the University of California, Davis, nominated me for the position of Associate Researcher in the Department of English for 2015–2016, which gave me access to library resources that I needed to complete the revisions to this book. In 2016, I also received a research grant for teaching a seminar for the UC Davis Center for Excellence in Teaching and Learning (now the Center for Educational Effectiveness) on "The Mythology of J.R.R. Tolkien," in which I once again had opportunity to teach *Pearl* in translation. For all of this support, I am truly grateful.

On a more personal note, I would like to add that I am thankful for the life of my sister Asya, my Pearl-Maiden, whose death in a car accident at the age of 20 in 2003 compelled me to re-read *Pearl* many times for its multiple meanings. I am also thankful for Anil Agnello Comelo, once my Dreamer, with whom I had many conversations about the Lamb of God, and for my dearest friend, Jennifer Franet, my Beatrice, who died in a car accident at the age of 33 on Christmas Day 2008. I will never cease to be thankful for my life-long friend Stacey, who survived brain surgery intended to treat hydro-cephalus in 2009; for my mother, my Phoenix, who recovered from cancer in 2011; and for my sister Alice who survived, unharmed, a car accident in

December of 2014. To my friend and prayer partner when I was teaching at Wheaton College, Dr. Gary Thomas LaVanchy: thank you for giving to me the gift of listening to my life.

In the week when I was making a few final (but nonetheless, time-consuming) changes to *The Signifying Power of* Pearl, I was also serving on a stage design team for University Covenant Church in Davis, California. The upcoming sermon series focused on the theme of "grace raining down," and our team had the responsibility of creating a picture of this idea at the front of the church. So we took multi-colored blue banners and brought them swooping down from the ceiling on one side to connect to a tall, wooden cross on the other side. Down and around the cross flowed extensions of the blue banners, and they connected to the baptismal, over which ivy vines were hung. The flowing blue fabrics were then spread down the stairs and covered with green plants and white flowers, including little marguerite daisies. I am thankful to the church worship director and pastor, Rev. Josh Anway, for inviting me to be a part of the team that designed this stage, for I could not help but remember when I looked at it what the *Pearl*-poet writes: "þe grace of God is gret inoghe."

Jane Beal, PhD
Casita Pomelo
Davis, CA
February 2016

Introduction
Signifying

For many years, and with great pleasure, I have been reading *Pearl* in Middle English editions and Modern English translations, and I have been reading about *Pearl* in the scholarship and literary criticism of diverse colleagues in America, Britain, and around the world. *Pearl* is my favorite poem, and I have never grown tired of studying it. It seems to me to be an almost inexhaustible source of beauty, wisdom, and strength in times of loss or sorrow. It may be that I perceive the poem this way because it is an intrinsically Christian work of art, and I admire it for the way that it makes me, a woman of faith, see truth again from new angles.

In addition to reading *Pearl*, I have taught the poem and written about it, actions that have compelled me to think deeply about the poem and the relationship of my own work to the historical development of scholarship about it. This process is, of course, on-going, for there exists a veritable cornucopia of interpretive work on *Pearl*. I knew this, but I experienced it in a new way while in the process of co-editing another book, *Approaches to Teaching the Middle English* Pearl, which is forthcoming from the MLA in the Approaches to Teaching World Literature series.[1] For that book, one of my many responsibilities included writing what is called the "Materials" section, in which I give an overview of the history of the scholarship of the poem.

To date, there are eleven printed editions of *Pearl* in Middle English,[2] eight dual-language editions,[3] and fifteen complete, modern English translations in verse as well as two in prose.[4] Numerous partial editions and translations exist, including translations in German, Frisian, Italian, and Japanese.[5] Some of the partial modern English translations appear in anthologies of medieval literature.[6] There are various commentaries on the poem, such as a recent volume of *Glossator*, which has 20 articles on the poem—one on each of the poem's 20 sections.[7] There are also four book-length collections of critical essays, one of which is pedagogical;[8] eight substantial introductions to the life and works of the *Pearl*-poet;[9] and, published between 1918 and 2015, roughly 25 academic books that interpret the works of the *Pearl*-poet (though only some are on *Pearl* exclusively).[10] There are also approximately 40 dissertations on *Pearl*, the *Pearl*-poet, and/or the other works attributed to the poet: *Patience, Cleanness, Sir Gawain and the Green*

Knight, and *Saint Erkenwald*. There are nine bibliographies or bibliographic essays surveying editions, translations, and academic studies (books, articles, dissertations, theses, and so on), including my own "Materials."[11] Counting published essays and articles on *Pearl*, there are well over a thousand works of scholarship on the *Pearl*-poet in print.[12] Meanwhile, the multimedia age has made the poem and many studies of it available via the Internet.[13]

Pearl-poet studies have not yet reached the epic proportions of Chaucerian studies. It is still possible, with a critical reception history that essentially began in 1864 with the first edition of the poem for the Early English Text Society, to read everything on *Pearl*, given, as Andrew Marvell might say, "world enough and time." However, as Marvell's fellow Cavalier poet Robert Herrick once observed, "Old Time is still a-flying." Very soon, it will not be possible for a single scholar to master all that has been written on *Pearl*. There is simply too much to read.

Given this impending reality (which, of course, is really a gift demonstrating how inspiring the *Pearl*-poet has been to so many readers and writers), it becomes necessary to analyze, organize, and simplify the received wisdom of *Pearl* scholars: to identify major trends in the scholarship, including key debates and shifts in the wider realm of scholarly perception of the poem, in order to contextualize new work. The work of medieval literary scholars has a tendency to resist easy categorization and to fit comfortably into more than one category, so simplifying proves challenging. Nevertheless, some order has to be imposed or new and old scholars alike will never be able to grasp even most of the interpretive possibilities (to say nothing of "all").

In his 1975 article, "The State of *Pearl* Studies Since 1933," Laurence Eldredge surveyed the development of literary criticism on *Pearl* since René Welleck's 1933 essay that undertook the same task (covering the time period from 1864 to 1933). Whereas Welleck concluded that three outstanding debates remain—whether *Pearl* is elegy or allegory, whether it is theologically heretical or orthodox, and what the meaning of its symbolism may be—Eldredge considered subsequent criticism in these three categories, setting aside editions and translations, and added two more categories: debates about the authorship and historicism of the poem. Forty years after the publication of Eldredge's essay, I surveyed materials pertaining to *Pearl*, including versions of the poem (editions, translations, etc.) and literary criticism of it. However, like Eldredge, I was faced with the necessity of being selective.

Certainly the early debates have held my attention, but *Pearl* scholars have largely moved on (albeit in different ways) from the binaries implied by the summaries of Welleck and Eldredge. With the advent of literary theory, new modes have been applied to interpretation of the poem, with often striking results. However, it must be said that, while *Pearl* scholars use many interpretive tools in their analyses, including contemporary theoretical approaches, they rarely disregard philological, paleographical, codicological, cultural, historical, and theological contexts—though they may differ in how they see those contexts. They also like to blend their theoretical approaches, so that "feminist and psychoanalytic approaches interpenetrate; new historicist and material culturist analysis overlap; interpretations utilizing the concepts of allegory and ineffability both converge and diverge."[14]

It is not my intention to repeat here more of what I have written elsewhere, for that would be redundant, but rather to indicate where this book, *The Signifying Power of* Pearl, fits in the overall development of scholarship on the poem. For it does seem to me that an on-going conversation has been unfolding in my lived experience, the poem called *Pearl*, and my readings in the field of *Pearl* studies. As a result of this conversation, and contemplation of it, I have gained a deepening understanding of the poem over time.

At the simplest level, my original intellectual understanding and analysis of the poem grew out of the need to resolve, at some logical level and in some coherent way, the competing interpretations I read in the criticism about whether *Pearl* was an elegy or an allegory. Like many other scholars, I concluded that these two ways of reading did not need to be mutually exclusive. However, at first, I was persuaded that an elegiac reading was both more probable and more palatable. It was only the wisdom of Joseph Wittig, who served as a reviewer for *Studies in Philology* when our mutual friend and colleague, Edward Donald Kennedy, was editor of that fine journal, that persuaded me to leave the question of genre quite open at the end of my first published article on *Pearl*, "The Pearl-Maiden's Two Lovers."[15]

In the process of looking very closely at the language of *Pearl*, in an attempt to "solve" the "problem" of "genre" (and, yes, I use quotations to call into question each term, for I no longer regard the plethora of generic elements in *Pearl* as a problem in need of solution), I realized the poet's deliberate, linguistic ambiguity never allows a careful reader to assume she can know what the exact relationship between the Dreamer and the Pearl-Maiden is: never once does he identify the two as father and daughter, though it has been quite common in scholarship to identify the two protagonists in this way since Richard Morris, the original editor of the poem, first read the relationship as familial.[16] I was encouraged by the insights of Mother Angela Carson,[17] which had been dismissed by Eldredge,[18] that there might be another way of seeing the two figures: not as relatives, but as lovers, not in some carnal sense (the Pearl-Maiden is clearly virginal), but in an intimate, emotional sense. For the Middle Ages did have at least two models for this type of relationship: unconsummated courtly love in secular circles, on the one hand, and spiritual friendship between contemplatives in monastic circles on the other.

My study necessarily caused me to engage with scholarship from feminist and psychoanalytic criticism, which was then current and has continued to flourish in the development of the interpretation of the poem. These theoretical approaches do indeed repay the careful reader when studying *Pearl*.[19] Like some other medievalists, I admit, I can feel uncomfortable when these modes are applied in ways that do not seem consonant with the historical and cultural contexts that, beyond any doubt, helped to shape *Pearl* through the genius of the poet.[20] I feel equally uncomfortable when late-medieval historical facts seem taken out of context and misapplied to interpretation of the poem.[21] I am not, in the end, persuaded by such arguments, though I am always interested in them. I also know, of course, that my own arguments for interpretation may be measured by a similar yardstick—and found wanting. So I do not judge too harshly. In fact, I normally hold my judgment back and keep considering those parts of any given colleague's case that make sense to me.

That being said, *Pearl* is a poem that is uniquely coherent and structured—so much so, that it is fair to say that there is no other late-medieval English poem that can compare to it in this regard. So I have always thought that any interpretation of it must ultimately be similarly coherent and structured. Here the work of Alastair Minnis and Ian Johnson, co-editors of *The Cambridge History of Literary Criticism, Vol. II: The Middle Ages*, has proven helpful to me.[22] Their volume demonstrated that the Middle Ages had literary theories of its own, perhaps best exemplified in the *Divine Comedy* of Dante and best expressed in his letter to Can Grande, which emphasizes the four-fold method of interpretation. It was clear to me that the *Pearl*-poet had at his disposal the vast resources of the tradition of the four levels of biblical interpretation, that he used these to compose *Pearl*, and that he could have had a reasonable expectation that the more educated members of his lay audience would, by all means, understand the possibilities of such an approach on the poet's part and on their own part as listeners, readers, and interpreters. So another essay came about, "The Signifying Power of *Pearl*," which has been revised for inclusion as the second chapter in this study and which shares its title with this book.

Later, working with my friend and colleague Ann Meyer on our co-written piece on allegory and symbolism in *Pearl* further reinforced my understanding that the four-fold approach was not a closed system, a didactic insistence by the poet that his audience read his work in a singular way. Instead, it was an open invitation to participate in the process of interpretation. As Ann wrote so beautifully, in our essay:

> … multiple meanings are not mutually exclusive. Rather, many meanings are both correct and simultaneous. For an audience to engage in the process of interpretation, then, is to participate in the divine visions of dreamers themselves. The reader or allegorical interpreter is the soul always in motion on spiritual pilgrimage.[23]

This is a powerful idea. Allegory is not static; it is not mere personification; it does not convey a one-to-one correspondence between signifier and signified. Rather, it is a genre that invites allegoresis and readerly participation in the creation of meaning. This is not meant to imply that any meaning will make sense, for there are limits to allegory, however wild and out of control it may seem to modern sensibilities at times. Yet allegory is very much like an open door. In walking through it, readers discover possibilities that literal readings would never suggest. For there were (and still are) multi-layered contexts of texts that vividly existed in medieval readers' minds, especially biblical texts and interpretations of them and images of them by which readers were surrounded.

In the process of discovering my own allegorical reading of *Pearl*, I was influenced by my participation in a traditional, liturgical Anglican church in West Chicago, where we did not say the word "alleluia" during Lent, expressly so that we could shout it joyously at the celebration of the Easter Vigil on Holy Saturday and return to using it as a regular part of services during other liturgical seasons of the year. I researched this practice only to learn that is very old, and indeed, medieval people sometimes wrote the word "alleluia" on a scroll and buried it, on Septuagesima Sunday, in anticipation of Lent. It occurred to me that *Pearl* is a Paschal poem in many respects (and the comparison of it to a Christmas liturgy strange indeed);[24] that the Pearl-Maiden repeatedly praises God, but the Dreamer holds back (and indeed never says the word "alleluia" or the phrase "Praise God"); and that there was a way to imagine the Pearl-Maiden as a figure of the alleluia, a figure of joy, the Dreamer's "blys"—without denying a literal interpretation of her or the elegaic reality that draws so many readers to love this poem called *Pearl*.[25]

In due course, I considered *Pearl* as a consolation. This understanding of the poem's genre was first articulated by John Conley, who saw it as the third option in the binary opposition in the scholarship between elegiac and allegorical interpretations.[26] He considered the poem in relationship to Boethius and the *Consolation of Philosophy*, a comparative approach by which many subsequent scholars have been influenced.[27] I was interested in the poem not only as consolation but also as an expression of the Dreamer's emotional suffering and healing journey. In a paper I presented at the 2007 International Congress on Medieval Studies, called "*Pearl* and the Memory of Trauma," I looked at medieval consolation side by side with modern theories of grief and trauma. I also became interested in the avian imagery of the poem, and I wrote another essay on that. Revised aspects of that paper, combined with the essay, inform the third chapter of this book as well as the conclusion.

Just a few months before presenting at the 2007 International Congress, I gave a paper entitled "*Sponsa Christi*: Imagining Spiritual Marriage in the Middle Ages" at the Pruit Memorial Symposium and Lilly Fellows Program National Research Conference on "The World and the Christian Imagination" at Baylor University. In it, I attempted to place the Pearl-Maiden's marriage to Christ in the larger context of visions of spiritual marriages that medieval Christian contemplative women (like Margery Kempe and Birgitta of Sweden) had experienced and written about in their spiritual autobiographies. After writing on Moses and the contemplative tradition for a volume of essays I edited, *Illuminating Moses: A History of Reception from Exodus to the Renaissance*, I returned to develop this paper into the fourth chapter of this book.

The chapter on the anagogical sense reflects the interests that the *Pearl*-poet and I share in the medieval contemplative tradition, the stages of purification, illumination, and unification with the divine, and the visionary experiences of medieval people who have sometimes been called "mystics." It was *Pearl* that originally catalyzed my interest, and I subsequently explored that interest in essays on early medieval women writers (such as Marie de France, Julian of Norwich, and Margery Kempe) and on Moses and medieval Christian contemplative devotion, the latter the aforementioned study that I undertook for *Illuminating Moses*.[28] To come back, as it were, to the mystical beginning near the end of this book on *Pearl* was especially meaningful.

I might have finished this book with that fourth chapter, for I had, at that point, considered all four senses and made a coherent case for explaining the poem in light of the medieval "literary theory" of the *Pearl*-poet's time. However, I could not help but notice that the poet did not limit himself to composing according to the four-fold genre theory of his day. Certainly medieval approaches to scriptural exegesis shaped *Pearl*, but the poet's work was not so esoteric as to be of interest to only the clerical, monastic, or noble classes. The educated elite would probably take an interest in a poem so complicated and beautiful and could indeed be considered part of the poet's intended audience, but other readers and hearers who were less educated might be drawn to his use of folktale patterns: the motifs he used from the genres of the fable, the parable, and the fairy-tale. The fact that the poem was written in English (not Anglo-Norman or Latin) and the very ordinariness of the Dreamer-narrator, too, bespeaks of the poet's interest in a wider audience.

As scholarship on *Pearl* has developed in new directions, turning away from old debates in light of new discoveries, genre theory continues to be relevant to promote comprehension of the poem.[29] In this book, I seek to illuminate understanding of the exquisitely beautiful, fourteenth-century, Middle English dream vision poem, *Pearl*. I argue that the poet intended *Pearl* to be read at four levels of meaning and in four corresponding genres: literally, an elegy; spiritually, an allegory; morally, a consolation; and anagogically, a revelation. Using both medieval and modern genre theory, I try to address cruxes and scholarly debates about the poem's genre and meaning, including key questions that have been unresolved in *Pearl* studies for over a century: What is the nature of the relationship between the Dreamer and the Maiden? What is the significance of allusions to Ovidian love stories and the use of liturgical time in the poem? How does avian symbolism, like that of the central symbol of the pearl, develop, transform, and add meaning throughout the dream vision? What is the nature of God portrayed in the poem, and how does the portrayal of the Pearl-Maiden's intimate relationship to

God, her spiritual marriage to the Lamb, connect to the poet's purpose in writing? In my final chapter, noting that the poem is open to many interpretations, I also consider folktale genre patterns in *Pearl*, including those drawn from parable, fable, and fairy-tale. I hope that this book makes a compelling case for re-reading *Pearl* and recognizing the poem's signifying power.

Overview of Literary Claims and Interpretations

How does *Pearl* signify? This book seeks to answer that question without foreclosing the possibilities of future interpretation. It presents inquiry about genre and layers of meaning in the poem as a means of discovery.

There is a growing consensus in *Pearl* scholarship that the early literary criticism of the poem, debating whether it is elegiac or allegorical, really presented readers with a false generic dichotomy. The poem need not be limited to one genre or interpretation when it clearly invites multiple understandings. Various scholars have argued that the *Pearl*-poet deliberately crafted a poem that could be interpreted literally, allegorically, morally, or anagogically as scripture was in the Middle Ages.[30] Taking this reading a step further, it seems that, in terms of its genre, *Pearl* is a dream vision that operates at four levels of meaning and in four corresponding genres: the literal sense makes it an elegy; the allegorical meaning, an allegory; the moral purpose, a consolation; and the anagogical unveiling, a revelation.[31] In this book, I consider the layers of meaning in *Pearl*, showing how they are in harmony, in order to reveal more of the poem's signifying power.

The first chapter, "Literal Sense: Desiring the Beloved," considers whether *Pearl* is an elegy. As many scholars, including the poem's first editor in the nineteenth century,[32] have argued, the form of *Pearl* indeed gives elegiac expression to grief, but perhaps not by a father mourning the daughter. Instead, re-examination of the evidence—the fourteenth-century illustrations provided at the beginning of the poem in the manuscript, the lines in the poem that have been used to support the father-daughter reading (which are, in fact, highly ambiguous), the literary context of medieval love lyrics and Marian hymns influenced by the Song of Songs—suggest another possibility.

As Angela Carson first suggested in 1965, perhaps the Pearl-Maiden is not the Dreamer's two-year-old child, but the young woman he loved in life then lost in death.[33] This hypothesis goes a long way toward explaining the language of courtly romance that the Dreamer uses to address the Pearl-Maiden, language that recent feminist and psychoanalytic literary critics have characterized as expressing "incestuous" desire.[34] But the Dreamer's desire is not so perverted. His spiritual struggle is to accept the will of God, not to suppress a reverse Elecktra complex. The Pearl-Maiden's love for him is pure, and his love for her is in the process of being purified through his experience in the dream vision.

The second chapter, "Allegorical Meaning: Rejoicing in Salvation," considers whether *Pearl* is an allegory. Many scholars have seen the Pearl-Maiden as an allegorical figure, but there have been many different viewpoints offered concerning what she represents.[35] Initially, *Pearl* may not appear to be complete allegory, like the *Romance of the Rose* or the *Vision of Piers Plowman*, in which allegorical figures correspond to one type of virtue or vice. But medieval allegoresis, as Ann Meyer has shown, is much more complex than personification: it is an interpretive activity, not just a form, and the dream vision can, like Dante's *Divine Comedy*, operate on both a literal and an allegorical level.[36]

Many aspects of *Pearl* suggest its allegorical nature, and this chapter explores three of these: its spiritual language, which so often has a double meaning; its use of the classical love stories of Orpheus and Eurydice and Pygmalion and Galatea, both of which have a long tradition of medieval allegorical interpretation associated with them, of which the *Pearl*-poet was apparently aware; and the use of liturgical (rather than calendrical) time in the narrative. Special attention to the Pearl-Maiden's allegorical significance in this context suggests she stands for the Dreamer's joy in salvation, which he lost, but is beginning to perceive again and greatly desires to experience once more.

The third chapter, "Moral Purpose: Consoling the Heart," considers whether *Pearl* is a consolation. Some scholars have seen the poem as such, but others have been unconvinced, especially at the poem's conclusion, that the Dreamer is consoled.[37] Yet at the moral level of meaning, the level at which truth is applied to life, it is more likely that the poet wrote with the intention of revealing through the Dreamer's spiritual journey his own consolation, which is not only theological—a recognition that the sacrifice of Christ, the Paschal Lamb, redeems humanity from sin and makes reunion with God in heaven possible—but also emotional.

This emotional consolation has been overlooked at times, but it is perceivable when the depiction of birds, avian metaphors, and the bird's eye view of the New Jerusalem (a view of the architecture of heaven made possible only if the Dreamer and the reader with him are flying above it as if on eagle's wings) are traced through the poem. These lead straight to the Lamb, whose joy, despite the suffering indicated by his wide, wet wound (described at line 1135)—his bleeding side—is revealed as an iconic image on which the Dreamer meditates. The example of the bleeding Lamb shows the Dreamer what he might be able to experience, too: joy in the midst of pain, true consolation in the face of loss. For his loss on earth is temporary, but the joy he looks forward to in heaven is eternal.

The fourth chapter, "Anagogical Revelation: Imagining Spiritual Marriage to Christ," considers whether *Pearl* is a revelation. Because the last third of the poem is devoted to the Dreamer's vision of the New Jerusalem, largely a paraphrase of John's vision of the New Jerusalem recorded in the book of Revelation, some scholars have noted *Pearl*'s revelatory and apocalyptic qualities. Recently, the poem has been considered especially in terms of Apocalypse manuscripts and medieval translations and paraphrases.[38] But the anagogical level of meaning in the poem is not exclusively or primarily about imagery. Anagogy is about last things, about things that are to come, and concerns the very nature of God.

The characteristics of God in *Pearl* (and the other poems of A.x Cotton Nero) have been debated, with some scholars seeing God as cantankerous and anthropomorphized, relating to humanity in covenantal but emotionally distant ways.[39] Yet these evaluations ignore the profound spiritual intimacy the Pearl-Maiden's marriage to her beloved Lamb implies. This loving relationship is not, in the poem, declared to be exclusive: quite the opposite! Thousands of pure brides process with the Lamb before the Dreamer's eyes, and the Dreamer himself wakes to realize that God is his friend, making him, therefore, a friend of the Bridegroom (see line 1204). The experience of God's love, the poem suggests, is for everyone, and all are invited into it. A consideration of medieval contemplative practice provides the historical context for understanding how this works in *Pearl*.

The fifth chapter, "Beyond the Four Levels of Meaning: Folktale Genre Patterns in *Pearl*," considers the poet's use of parabolic allusions, fable motifs, and fairy-tale qualities in his dream vision. Parables, especially the Parable of the Laborers in the Vineyard, allow the Pearl-Maiden to articulate a complex view of her own self-understanding. Fable motifs drawn from the well-known and oft-translated stories of Aesop, especially metaphoric comparisons of the Dreamer to hawk, quail, and doe, suggest that the Dreamer became vulnerable to doubt and the devil's deception in the midst of his grief. The Dreamer's spiritual conflict is resolved, in part, by the appearance of the Lamb of God, who, although he far exceeds any fabulous context or analogue, can nevertheless be considered *vis à vis* the Aesopian fable of "The Wolf and the Lamb," in which the lamb's innocent, truthful replies to the wolf do not save his life but do show the right response to the devil's attack. The fairy-tale qualities in *Pearl* harken back to the Cupid and Psyche myth, but the poet is intent upon overturning the Dreamer's (and his audience's) generic expectations of human love in order to point to a divine romance: it is not the Dreamer and the Maiden who represent Love and the Soul, but Christ and his Bride, of whom both the Pearl-Maiden and the Dreamer are a part.

The poet's use of folktale genre patterns in *Pearl* shows that he was not interested in using the four levels of meaning exclusively or drawing on erudite approaches to interpretation that would appeal only to the *literati* of his day. His ear was also attuned to stories told among ordinary, everyday people—parables, fables, fairy-tales—and he seemed to have an awareness of a great nexus of texts (both written and spoken) that his audience could understand. He wrote in English, not Latin, which clearly suggests he aimed to appeal to vernacular readers and listeners. These need not have been primarily of the upper class, since parables, fables, and magical love-stories were well known among virtually everyone in late-medieval, English storytelling culture. The conclusion of *Pearl* points to the Dreamer-narrator's desire (and thus, presumably, the poet's) that all of "vus" would come to see ourselves as precious pearls of the Prince.

Literary Methods and Unique Contributions

Throughout these chapters, my methods of study include asking key questions, surveying scholarly opinion, discovering philological insights, analyzing literary features, and situating the poem in relevant medieval literary and historical contexts. These means help me to best address the many cruxes and challenges to interpretation that *Pearl* presents. Yet as wise, old King Solomon once said, there is nothing new under the sun.[40] This book is part of a bejeweled net of ideas, one that I see as shimmering and illuminated and woven together with strands of thought that have occurred not only to me but to others as well.

For example, though I had read neither D.W. Robertson nor Jane Chance on using the four levels of meaning as a means of interpreting *Pearl* before the thought of reading the poem that way occurred to me, nevertheless, their work preceded mine and now informs it. In "Pearl as Symbol," Robertson argued:

> The symbol of the Pearl may be thought of on four levels. Literally, the Pearl is a gem. Allegorically, as the maiden of the poem, it represents those members of the Church who will be among the "hundred" in the celestial procession, the perfectly innocent. Tropologically, the Pearl is a symbol of the soul that attains innocence through true penance and all that such penance implies. Anagogically, it is the life of innocence in the Celestial City. The allegorical value presents a clear picture of the type of innocence; the tropological value shows how such innocence may be obtained; and the anagogical value explains the reward for innocence. To these meanings the literal value serves as a unifying focal point in which the other values are implied to one who reads the book of God's Work on the level of the *sentence*.[41]

Robertson added, "The homiletic purpose of the poem ... results from the poet's emphasis on the tropological level."[42] Years later, Jane Chance considered "homiletic purpose" in the genre of *ars praedicandi* and the use of the four levels of meaning in relation to the Pearl-Maiden whom she identifies not only as angel, but also as preacher.[43]

My contribution is to see a connection between the four levels of meaning and a way to speak to the genre debates that have raged over the poem for more than a century and a half. For I do see that the poem has literal, spiritual, moral, and anagogical levels of meaning that correspond to elegiac, allegorical, consolatory, and revelatory genres. My interpretation of how the four levels of meaning emerge in *Pearl* is unique.

In this book, many of my ideas are shared with a community of literary interpreters, which supports the probability of their accuracy. The book adds to the body of interpretation of *Pearl* through its clear and comprehensive presentation of the evidence. Through it, I hope to influence future interpretation of the poem by encouraging others to:

- read the relationship between Dreamer and Pearl-Maiden without any taint of incestuous implication;
- see the Pearl-Maiden's allegorical significance as connected to the Dreamer's joy in salvation;
- recognize that the poem is certainly intended by the poet to be consolatory, not the opposite, as the avian imagery, metaphors, and perspectives in the poem reveal;
- perceive the loving, emotionally close reality of the Divine as depicted in the dream vision; and
- consider the use of parable, fable, and fairy-tale qualities in the poem and their implications, especially the likelihood that the poet was not composing for a narrow audience of courtly elites or monastic contemplatives, but rather for a broad audience of vernacular English readers and listeners.

My interpretation of the poet's understanding of God seems to me to be particularly important: the God of Christian faith is not cruel, and the *Pearl*-poet does not represent him as such. God is Love,[44] and the *Pearl*-poet is intent upon revealing God not only as sovereign Lord, but as Bridegroom and Friend. This makes sense in the context of late-medieval affective piety.

The spiritual journey of the Dreamer is a process that modern readers often recognize as psychological. Literary critics have certainly applied the paradigms of psychoanalysis to *Pearl* from Freudian, Jungian, and even Lacanian perspectives,[45] but these older schools of psychological understanding seem to me to be less useful than more recent insights into working memory, the grieving process, and, more specifically, post-traumatic stress. Therefore, in the conclusion of this study, I move beyond considering *Pearl* in terms of its language (philology), literary features (literary analysis), and literary contexts (comparative literary analysis) and consider it in psychological terms.

For just as the Dreamer returns to earth upon awakening, so must the reader. The experience of reading *Pearl* is not meant to leave readers lingering in heaven but rather to help effect a soul-healing that strengthens them for the journey that is this life. How *Pearl* does that is always worth further contemplation.

Reading *Pearl* as Ascension through Contemplation

Pearl is a poem that rewards multiple re-readings. It enables the reader to journey with the Dreamer from the "erber,"[46] the earthly garden where he falls asleep, to the dreamscape after his spirit "springs into space,"[47] to the vision of the New Jerusalem in heaven. The poem's landscapes are like rungs on Jacob's ladder, which medieval people understood as an image of a contemplative process that begins with humility and leads from purgation to illumination, and finally, unification with God.[48]

The Dreamer is certainly in a humble place in the garden at the beginning of the poem, literally lying on the *humus* ("the ground"), in the garden where he lost his pearl:

> Allas! I leste hyr in on erbere;
> Þur3 gresse to ground hit fro me yot ...
> On huyle þer perle hit trendeled doun
> Schadowed þis worte3 ful schyre and schene. (ll. 9–10, 41–42)

The imagery used by the poet to convey the Dreamer's loss suggests descent and downward motion.[49] The Dreamer is lying on the ground, and in contemplating the loss of his beloved pearl, he sinks even lower still, mentally rolling down the hill as he remembers and even sinking, in thought, into the earth where his pearl is buried. Only as he begins to contemplate the plants and flowers springing up from the spot where she was lost does he fall asleep and reverse direction, so that his mind no longer runs downward, but instead springs into space.

In rising to the dreamscape, the Dreamer undergoes purgation through a dialogue with the Pearl-Maiden that strips away intellectual pretense and gets to the heart of the Dreamer's emotional problem: his grief has not allowed him to surrender to the will of God. The vision the Pearl-Maiden requests for him—the vision of the New Jerusalem—illuminates his understanding and raises it still higher. For when he beholds the iconic image of the bleeding Lamb, he sees that his visage, despite painful suffering, is full of gladness.

But the longing for unification, which in the Pearl-Maiden has led to a spiritual marriage to her Lord, the Lamb, in the case of the Dreamer is directed toward a creature, his beloved, rather than the Creator-Christ. So when he surges toward, the stream in an attempt to cross over to the heavenly side, he instead awakens with the awareness that he might have experienced more of the heavenly delights if he had surrendered to God's will.[50] The whole poem, the reader realizes at the conclusion, has been related by an awakened Dreamer who remembers his experience in the light of new learning. This was intimated near the beginning of the poem,[51] but it is affirmed again in the end.

Pearl and Transformation

Throughout the poem, a single symbol shines: the pearl that is transformed as the Dreamer's understanding rises from earthly to heavenly realms before returning again to the garden. The pearl first appears at the beginning of the verse narrative as the obsession of the Dreamer's memory, something he represents as almost literal, something precious that fell from him and rolled away into the grass and was lost.[52] In the dreamscape, the Dreamer encounters thousands of pearls as gravel beneath his feet. Symbolically, these grains of pearlescent sand may represent the losses of many people on earth. But the Dreamer never searches through them for his pearl.

For the Dreamer knows that his pearl is not "something" but "someone," however he may have objectified her symbolically in the opening stanzas, and when he encounters the Maiden herself, he instantly recognizes her as the pearl that he lost. The Pearl-Maiden is dressed in garments bejeweled with pearls, and she wears a pearlescent crown, and in the midst of her breast, there is another pearl: large, luminous, and undeniably beautiful. As the dialogue between Dreamer and Pearl-Maiden unfolds, it becomes clear that the pearl is a contested site of interpretation: a symbol whose meaning is understood differently by each of them. For the Dreamer, the Maiden is his pearl, but for the Maiden, the pearl is the gift of God, the symbol of salvation, just as it is in the Parable of the Merchant told by Jesus and recorded in Matthew's Gospel.[53] The two argue about symbolism, but the Pearl-Maiden makes the stronger case. How could she not? She is in heaven, and the Dreamer is on earth, even though they meet in the liminal space of dreaming.

The Pearl-Maiden reveals to the Dreamer that she is married, and she is not his pearl, but the bride of the Lamb. The pearl that the Lamb has given to her is the one, she implies, that the Dreamer should desire, for she advises him to forsake the mad world and purchase the pearl that is flawless.[54] She advises him, in other words, to become the Merchant of Christ's parable. Her counsel is reminiscent of Christ's command and concomitant promise: "Seek first the Kingdom of God, and his righteousness, and all these things shall be added unto you."[55] But the Dreamer does not desire salvation and the kingdom of heaven the way he desires the beauty of his beloved Pearl-Maiden, whom he has lost.

The Dreamer continues to regard the Maiden as his pearl, despite her revelation that there is another pearl for him. Knowing that nothing she says will persuade him—that intellectual and theological argument cannot compare to the emotional and spiritual power of revelation—the Pearl-Maiden asks that the Dreamer have a vision, a *clara visio* before his death, of heaven. As the Dreamer watches, he sees in great detail the architecture of the New Jerusalem, and each of its twelve gates is a pearl that leads into the realm of the saints, the angels, and the holy God that rules over all as Lamb and Light ("lombe-ly3t").[56] The symbolism of pearl-gates draws on John's vision from

Revelation in the Bible, but in the new context of *Pearl*, they signify by means of yet another transformation of the symbol: the pearl that has been an almost-literal gem, the Pearl-Maiden herself, and the token of Christ's peace and salvation and the kingdom of heaven is now a gate into heaven itself.

The Lamb, when he appears, has pearlescent qualities, for he is pure, white, and luminous.[57] But his horns are red and gold, signifying Christ's blood and his sanctity, and red blood pours forth from the wound in his side.[58] The pearl that symbolizes salvation participates in some of the same imagery as the representation of Lamb, yes, but the Lamb in *Pearl* is the iconic image of the Savior. The Savior, if it be possible to express this human idea in limited words, is greater even than the salvation that he brings.

When the Dreamer wakes, he recognizes that all of us, he and his readers together, are precious pearls for the Prince's "paye"[59] (for his pleasure or, read another way, for which he has paid, i.e., through his death on the Cross). In other words, at the end, the Dreamer comes back to the beginning, but now he sees that not just the Pearl-Maiden alone but every person is a pearl. We are the pearls that Christ died to save, and the pearl of salvation that Christ gives to us is a restoration of our true identity, not as sinners but as sons and daughters, brides and friends, of the Lamb of God who takes away the sins of the world.[60]

Suggestions for Reading

This book is best read straight through, from the beginning to the end, in order to get the sense of the overall argument as it develops. Having a copy of *Pearl* close by, an edition (with glossary) and more than one translation, will be helpful for comparison. For only by re-reading the dream vision, as this book encourages everyone to do, can the poem's signifying power take effect.

Notes

1. Jane Beal and Mark Bradshaw Busbee, eds., *Approaches to Teaching the Middle English Pearl*, Approaches to Teaching World Literature Series (New York: MLA, 2017).
2. The three most commonly used of these eleven are Malcolm Andrew and Ronald Waldron, eds., *The Poems of the Pearl Manuscript: Pearl, Cleanness, Patience, Sir Gawain and the Green Knight*, 5th ed. (Liverpool: Liverpool University Press, 2007); J.J. Anderson and A.C. Cawley, eds., *Sir Gawain and the Green Knight, Pearl, Cleanness, and Patience*. rev. ed. (London: Everyman, 1996; London: Dent, 1962, 1976); and Sarah Stanbury, ed., *Pearl*, TEAMS: Teaching Middle English Text Series (Kalamazoo, MI: Medieval Institute, 2001) http://www.lib.rochester.edu/camelot/teams//stanbury.htm. A new edition bound to be in high demand, in part due to its dual print and ebook formats, is Ad Putter and Myra Stokes, eds., *The Works of the Gawain-Poet: Pearl, Cleanness, Patience, Sir Gawain and the Green Knight* (London: Penguin Classics, 2014).

3. For dual language editions, see, for example, William Vantuono, ed., *Pearl: An Edition with Verse Translation* (Notre Dame, IN: University of Notre Dame Press, 1995) or Casey Finch, ed. and trans. *The Complete Works of the* Pearl *Poet* (Berkeley, CA: University of California Press, 1993), which includes the Andrew and Waldron text of the four poems of the *Pearl* manuscript with notes and Peterson's text of *Saint Erkenwald* along with Finch's translation and additional notes.
4. The two most commonly used verse translations in modern English are Marie Borroff, trans., *"Pearl": A New Verse Translation* (New York, NY: Norton, 1977), which has been reprinted in *The Gawain Poet: Complete Works; Sir Gawain and the Green Knight, Patience, Cleanness, Pearl, Saint Erkenwald* (New York, NY: Norton, 2011), and J. R. R. Tolkien, trans., *Sir Gawain and the Green Knight, Pearl, and Sir Orfeo,* ed. Christopher Tolkien (Boston, MA: Houghton; New York, NY: Del Ray, 1975).
5. For foreign language translations of *Pearl*, see, for example, in German, trans. Otto Decker (1916); in Frisian, trans. D. Kalma (1938); in Italian, trans. F. Olivero, (1936), trans. Augusto Guidi (1966), and trans. Enrico Giaccherini (1989); and in Japanese, trans. Sakyo Sekigawa, (1952), trans. Takeshi Miyata (1954), trans. Yoshio Terasawa (1960); and trans. and ed. Masaiku Naruse (1971). More detailed bibliographic information for these translations is listed in Malcolm Andrew, *The Gawain-Poet: An Annotated Bibliography*, 1839–1977 (New York and London: Garland Publishing, Inc., 1979).
6. Although *Pearl* used to be included in some of the major anthologies, such as Norton's, it has been replaced by *Sir Gawain and the Green Knight* in more recent editions. However, it does appear in Middle English in anthologies of medieval literature still used in college classrooms, including those edited by Charles Dunn and Edward Byrnes, eds., *Middle English Literature* (1973), which is organized chronologically from the twelfth to the fifteenth century; by Thomas Garbáty, ed., *Medieval English Literature* (1984), which is organized by genre (where *Pearl* is placed in the category of allegorical and religious verse alongside *Piers Plowman*), and by Ann Sullivan Haskell, ed., *A Middle English Anthology* (1969, 1985). It also appears in John Conlee, ed., *Middle English Debate Poetry: A Critical Anthology* (1991), although this book is out of print. It is now included in the *Broadview Anthology of British Literature, Vol. I: The Medieval Period*, 3rd. ed. (Toronto: Broadview, 2015) as part of the online (not the print) book.
7. See *Glossator: Practice and Theory of Commentary* 9 (2015) - http://glossator.org/volumes/.
8. The four edited essay collections are John Conley, ed. *The Middle English "Pearl": Critical Essays* (Notre Dame, Ind.: University of Notre Dame Press, 1970); Robert Blanch, Miriam Youngerman Miller, and Julian N. Wasserman, eds., *Text and Matter: New Critical Perspectives of the* Pearl-*Poet* (Troy, NY: Whitston, 1991); and Derek Brewer and Jonathon Gibson, eds. *A Companion to the Gawain-Poet* (Woodbridge: Boydell & Brewer, 1997, rpt. 1999); the pedagogical one is Jane Beal and Mark Bradshaw Busbee, eds., *Approaches to Teaching the Middle English* Pearl (New York, NY: MLA, 2017).
9. The most widely read introduction to the *Pearl*-poet is Malcolm Andrew's "Theories of Authorship" in *A Companion to the Gawain-Poet* (1997, rpt. 1999). The three most recent, book-length introductions are Ad Putter's *An Introduction to*

16 *Introduction*

the Gawain-Poet (1996), J.A. Burrow's *The Gawain Poet* (2001), and John Bowers' *An Introduction to the Gawain-Poet* (2012).

10. Most books are on the four (or five) poems attributed to the *Pearl*-poet. Recent examples include Piotyr Spyra's *The Epistemological Perspective of the Pearl-Poet* (London: Ashgate, 2014) and Cecilia Hatt's *God and the Gawain-Poet* (Woodbridge: Boydell and Brewer, 2015), both of which consider all four poems in Cotton Nero A.x. A few books that concern *Pearl* exclusively are Annika Sylén Lagerholm, *Pearl and Contemplative Writing*, Lund Studies in English (Stockholm: Almqvist and Wiksell International, 2005), Sandra Pierson Prior, *The Fayre Formez of the Pearl Poet* (East Lansing, MI.: Michigan State University Press, 1996), and Theodore Bogdanos, *Pearl: Image of the Ineffable* (University Park and London, PA: The Pennsylvania State University Press, 1983).
11. See especially Laurence Eldredge, "The State of *Pearl* Studies since 1933." *Viator* (1975): 171–94 and Robert Blanch, "The State of *Pearl* Criticism." *Chaucer Yearbook* 3 (1996): 21–33.
12. See especially Malcolm Andrew, *The Gawain-Poet: An Annotated Bibliography*, 1839–1977 (New York and London: Garland Publishing Inc., 1979).
13. For a dual-language edition of the poem online, see Bill Stanton, *This Being a Translation in Verse of the of the Middle English Poem* Pearl *by an Unknown Poet* (1995) - http://www.billstanton.co.uk/pearl/pearl_old.htm; for additional resources, see Jane Beal, "Medieval Pearl" – http://medievalpearl.wordpress.com.
14. Jane Beal, "Materials," in *Approaches*.
15. Jane Beal, "The Pearl-Maiden's Two Lovers," *Studies in Philology* 100 (2003): 1–21. A revised and expanded version of this study appears as the first chapter of this book.
16. Morris, Richard, ed. *Early English Alliterative Poems in the West-Midland Dialect of the Fourteenth Century*. EETS, OS 1. (Oxford: Oxford University Press, 1864; rev. ed., 1869).
17. See Angela Carson, "Aspects of Elegy in the Middle English *Pearl*," *Studies in Philology* 62 (1965): 17–27.
18. Eldredge wrote of Carson's essay: "this interpretation seems to me to misunderstand the courtly vocabulary and to stand the poem's imagery on its head" (174).
19. See, for example, David Aers, "The Self Mourning: Reflections on *Pearl*," *Speculum* 68.1 (1993): 54–73 and Sarah Stanbury, "The Body and the City in *Pearl*," *Representations* 48 (1994): 30–47. These two essays are widely read and cited in *Pearl* studies. See also Stanbury, *Seeing the Gawain-Poet: Description and the Act of Perception* (Philadelphia, PA: University of Pennsylvania Press, 1991).
20. Gilbert, for example, sees implications of incest in the relationship between the Dreamer and the Pearl-Maiden. See Jane Gilbert, "Gender and Sexual Transgression," in *A Companion to the Gawain-Poet*, ed. Derek Brewer and Jonathon Gibson (Woodbridge: D.S. Brewer, 1997), 53–70.
21. John Bowers, *The Politics of "Pearl": Court Poetry in the Age of Richard II* (Cambridge: D. S. Brewer, 2001). For an answer to some of Bowers' points, see Alan J. Fletcher, "*Pearl* and the Limits of History," in *Studies in Late Medieval and Early Renaissance Texts in Honour of John Scattergood*, ed. Anne Marie D'Arcy and Alan J. Fletcher (Dublin: Four Courts, 2005), 148–70.
22. Alastair Minnis and Ian Johnson, *The Cambridge History of Literary Criticism*, Vol. II: The Middle Ages (Cambridge: Cambridge University Press, 2005). Even

before this, Richter included the letter to Can Grande in the influential anthology of rhetorical and theoretical criticism, *The Critical Tradition*.
23. Jane Beal and Ann Meyer, "Allegory and Symbolism in *Pearl*," in *Approaches*.
24. Ian Bishop, *The Pearl in Its Setting* (Oxford: Basil Blackwell, 1968).
25. One of the most moving, personal yet academically informed essays I have read in this vein is Dan Kline, "The *Pearl*, A Crayon, and a Lego," *Essays in Medieval Studies* 15 (1999): 119–22.
26. John Conley, "Pearl and a Lost Tradition," in *The Middle English Pearl: Critical Essays*, ed. John Conley (Notre Dame, IN.: University of Notre Dame Press, 1970), 50–72. The essay was originally published in *JEGP* 54 (1955): 332–47.
27. It is fair to say that, since Conley's essay, along with Dante's *Divine Comedy* and *The Romance of the Rose*, Boethius's *Consolation of Philosophy* is the most frequently mentioned context for comparative textual analysis of *Pearl*.
28. Jane Beal, "Moses and the Christian Contemplative Devotion," in *Illuminating Moses: A History of Reception from Exodus to the Renaissance*, ed. Jane Beal (Leiden: Brill, 2014), 305–52.
29. For a persuasive discussion of the essential importance of medieval theories of genre and its relationship to modern understandings of genre, see, for example, Ingrid Nelson and Shannon Gayk, "Introduction: Genre as Form-of-Life," *Exemplaria* 27 (2015): 3–17. The authors comment: 1) "Perhaps because of its long history as an exception to modern genre theory, medieval literature has inspired a body of criticism that emphasizes the social and practical aspects of genre, taking into account what Fredric Jameson called "the radical discontinuity of modes of production and of their cultural expressions" (130). The critic Hans Robert Jauss's concept of medieval genre as an audience's "horizon of expectations" (76–109) inaugurated a small but incisive body of criticism that examines how genre creates and is created by social structures, use-contexts, and use-value" (4). They add, later, "genres, too, bind form and life … [they] not only reflect the lived experience of their readers but aim to shape it" (5).
30. See D.W. Robertson, "The Pearl as Symbol," *Modern Language Notes* 65 (1950): 155–61; Jane Chance, "Allegory and Structure in *Pearl*: The Four Senses of the *Ars praedicandi* and Fourteenth-Century Homiletic Poetry," in *Text and Matter: New Critical Perspectives of the Pearl-Poet*, ed. Robert J. Blanch, Miriam Youngerman Miller, and Julian N. Wasserman (Troy, NY: Whitston, 1991), 31–59, and Jane Beal, "The Signifying Power of *Pearl*," *Quidditas: A Journal of the Rocky Mountain Medieval Association* 33 (2012): 27–58, which is revised as chap. 2 of this book. For a related view, see Lawrence Clopper, "*Pearl* and the Consolation of Scripture," *Viator* 25 (1992): 231–46.
31. I first made this argument in my essay, "The Signifying Power of *Pearl*," 27. For literal interpretations, see my essay, "The Pearl-Maiden's Two Lovers," *Studies in Philology* 100 (2003): 1–21 (or the revised and expanded version of it in chapter 1), John Bowers, *The Politics of Pearl: Court Poetry in the Age of Richard II* (London: Boydell and Brewer, 2001), and Lynn Staley Johnson, "*Pearl* and the Contingencies of Love and Piety," in *Medieval Literature and Historical Inquiry: Essays in Honor of Derek Pearsall*, ed. David Aers (Woodbridge: D.S. Brewer, 2000), 83–112. For allegorical readings, see Jane Chance, "Allegory and Structure in *Pearl*: The Four Senses of the *Ars praedicandi* and Fourteenth-Century Homiletic Poetry," in *Text and Matter: New Critical Perspectives of the Pearl-Poet*, ed. Robert J. Blanch, Miriam Youngerman Miller, and Julian

N. Wasserman (Troy, NY: Whitston, 1991), 31–59, D.W. Robertson, "The Pearl as Symbol," *Modern Language Notes* 65 (1950): 44–61, Sister Madeleva, *Pearl: A Study in Spiritual Dryness* (New York, NY: D. Appleton and Co, 1925), and W.H. Schofield, "Symbolism, Allegory, and Autobiography in *The Pearl*," PMLA 24 (1909): 585–675. Ian Bishop's *The Pearl in Its Setting* (Oxford: Blackwell, 1968) is generally considered an allegorical reading of the poem. Note that Bishop also sees *Pearl* as a *consolatio*, but Davenport sees it as a *contra-consolatio* in "Desolation, not Consolation: *Pearl* 19–22," *Review of English Studies* (1974): 421–23; both views are a kind of examination of the moral sense. For interpretation of the poem as revelation, see Cynthia Kraman, "Body and Soul: *Pearl* and Apocalyptic Literature," in *Time and Eternity: The Medieval Discourse*, eds. Gerhard Jaritz and Gerson Moreno-Riaño (Turnhout: Brepols, 2003), 355–62 and Ann R. Meyer, *Medieval Allegory and the Building of the New Jerusalem* (Woodbridge: D.S. Brewer, 2003).

32. Richard Morris first edited *Pearl* for the Early English Text Society in 1864.
33. Mother Angela Carson, "Aspects of Elegy in the Middle English *Pearl*," *Studies in Philology* 62 (1965): 17–27.
34. Jane Gilbert, "Gender and Sexual Transgression," in *A Companion to the Gawain-Poet*, ed. Derek Brewer and Jonathon Gibson (Rochester, NY: Boydell & Brewer, 1999), 59 and Sarah Stanbury, "Feminist Masterplots: The Gaze on the Body of the *Pearl's* Dead Girl," in *Feminist Approaches to the Body in Medieval Literature*, ed. Sarah Stanbury and Linda Lomperis (Philadelphia, PA: University of Pennsylvania Press, 1993), 109. Catherine Cox, dealing with what she calls the "erotic language" of *Pearl* is clearly aware of the incestuous implications, and so questions the father-daughter understanding of the relationship between Dreamer and Pearl-Maiden, but does not answer the issue she notes. See "'My Lemman Swete': Gender and Passion in *Pearl*," in *Intersections of Sexuality and the Divine in Medieval Culture*, ed. Susannah Chewning (Surrey: Ashgate, 2005), 80.
35. For a summary of these views, see the first paragraphs of chapter 2 in this book.
36. See Ann R. Meyer, *Medieval Allegory and the Building of the New Jerusalem* (Woodbridge: D.S. Brewer, 2003), and Jane Beal and Ann Meyer, "Symbolism and Allegory in *Pearl*," in *Approaches to Teaching the Middle English Pearl*, ed. Jane Beal and Mark Bradshaw Busbee (New York, NY: MLA, 2017).
37. For a survey of these contrasting views, see the opening paragraphs of chapter 3 in this book.
38. See the first footnote in chapter 4 of this book.
39. For discussion, see the opening paragraphs of chapter 4 in this book.
40. Ecc. 1:9.
41. Robertson, "Pearl as Symbol," 160–61. Robertson notes his indebtedness to Sister Mary Vincent Hillmann's views in this essay. Later, Louis Blenker would also make an argument for four-fold interpretation. See Louis Blenker, "The Theological Structure of *Pearl*," *Traditio* 24 (1968): 43–75, esp. 74–75.
42. Robertson, 161.
43. Jane Chance, "Allegory and Structure in *Pearl*: The Four Senses," 31–59.
44. 1 John 4:8.
45. See David Aers, "The Self Mourning: Reflections on *Pearl*," *Speculum* 68 (1993): 53–73; Sarah Stanbury, "The Body and the City in *Pearl*," *Representations* 48 (1994): 30–47. For another interpretation by Stanbury, see "Feminist

Masterplots: The Gaze on the Body of *Pearl*'s Dead Girl," *Feminist Approaches to the Body in Medieval Literature* (Philadelphia, PA: University of Pennsylvania Press, 1993), 96–115; and George Edmondson, "*Pearl*: The Shadow of the Object, the Shape of the Law," *Studies in the Age of Chaucer* 26 (2004): 29–63.
46. *Pearl*, line 9. All *Pearl* quotations are from *The Poems of the Pearl Manuscript*, 5th ed. Malcolm Andrew and Ronald Waldron (Liverpool: Liverpool University Press, 2007).
47. My translation of *Pearl*, line 61.
48. Russell A. Peck, "Jacob's Ladder," in *A Dictionary of Biblical Tradition in English Literature*, ed. David Lyle Jeffrey (Grand Rapids, MI: William B. Eerdmans Publishing Company, 1992), 388–90.
49. As Annika Sylén Lagerholm notes, drawing on the work of G.R. Evans in his essay, "Saint Anselm's Analogies," this loss is worth considering in light of Saint Anselm's use of a "pearl analogy to describe humankind's situation. The soul of man, the pearl, fell from God's hand into the dirt of sin. God cleanses and restores it safely to the treasure-chest of heaven." See Lagerholm, *Pearl and Contemplative Writing*, 52.
50. See the penultimate stanza of the poem.
51. *Pearl*, lines 49–56.
52. I say "almost literal" because even in the opening lines, the narrator calls the pearl "hyr"; the implications of calling a gem "her" (rather than "it") are, in English, non-literal. Of course, *margarita* is a feminine noun in Latin, and the poet may have been influenced by the Latin here.
53. Matt. 13:45.
54. *Pearl*, lines 743–44.
55. Matt. 6:33.
56. *Pearl*, line 1046.
57. See A.C. Spearing, "Symbolic and Dramatic Development in *Pearl*," *Modern Philology* 60 (1962): 1–12.
58. For further discussion, see Hugh White, "Blood in *Pearl*," *The Review of English Studies* 38.149 (1987): 1–13.
59. *Pearl*, line 1212.
60. For further discussion of the Lamb in *Pearl*, see White, "Blood in *Pearl*," 1–13, Nancy Ciccione, "*Pearl* and the Bleeding Lamb," in *Approaches to Teaching the Middle English Pearl*, ed. Jane Beal and Mark Bradshaw Busbee (New York, NY: MLA, 2017), and my essay, "The Jerusalem Lamb of *Pearl*," *Glossator* 9 (Spring 2015): 262–83.

1 Literal Sense
Desiring the Beloved

Is the exquisitely beautiful, fourteenth-century, Middle English dream-vision poem *Pearl* an elegy? In 1864, the first editor of the poem, Richard Morris, said that it was. In his introduction to the Early English Text Society edition, he wrote: "the author evidently gives expression to his own sorrow for the loss of his infant child, a girl of two years old."[1] This view, that the poem elegiacally represents the relationship between the Dreamer and the Pearl-Maiden as one between a father and a daughter, was at first accepted and then hotly debated by literary critics.

In 1909, W.H. Schofield summed up the opposing argument by stating, quite correctly, that the poem lacks "any statement of the poet on which to build the prevalent notion that 'the Pearl' ... is his own child. Never once does he refer to her as such, nor does she a single time refer to him as a father."[2] Subsequently, Sister Madeleva wrote a significant study interpreting the poem allegorically, *Pearl: A Study in Spiritual Dryness* (1925). However, the elegists made more persuasive interpretive arguments of the poem than the allegorists did, in part because the elegists typically had a single reading of the relationship between Dreamer and Maiden while allegorists had many. As a result, acceptance of Morris's original interpretation spread widely among readers of *Pearl*.[3]

Though Laurence Eldredge would identify the genre debate (elegy vs. allegory) in *Pearl* studies as one still in need of resolution as late as his 1975 review of *Pearl* scholarship, A.C. Spearing's 1962 landmark essay, "Symbolic and Dramatic Development in *Pearl*," had already shifted critical opinion.[4] Spearing accepted, as a given, that the relationship between the Dreamer and the Pearl-Maiden was a father-daughter one, and he went on to show the poet's masterful skill in developing the central symbol of the poem, the pearl. When Spearing's arguments were reprinted in his 1970 book, *The Gawain-Poet*, they reached a wider audience who recognized the brilliance of Spearing's attention to symbolism (rather than allegory), and many accepted, as he did, that the poem was as an elegy representing a man mourning the death of his daughter.

At the same time that the poem's genre was being debated, interest in the poem's courtly language began to emerge. Scholars noted its allusions to the Song of Songs and the French allegory, the *Romance of the Rose*.[5] By 1991, in the fine anthology *Text and Matter: New Perspectives of the Pearl-Poet*, Charlotte Gross had written a key essay on the subject of courtly love language in *Pearl*.

Gross begins her essay by acknowledging the father-daughter relationship in *Pearl*: "When the bereaved narrator of *Pearl* at length encounters his daughter face to face. ..."[6] She goes on to evaluate the use of courtly love language in the poem, noting borrowings from the Song of Songs, medieval French vocabulary, and courtly love lyrics. She then contrasts the Pearl-Maiden's description of her mystical marriage to Christ with the Dreamer's description of the Pearl-Maiden herself, arguing that the Pearl-Maiden uses courtly love language correctly, but the Dreamer does not.

> ... while the Pearl-Maiden correctly employs courtly language as a metaphor for the ineffable, the dreamer's spiritual condition is such that he consistently misapprehends her teaching ... The dreamer-narrator's own inappropriate use of courtly language betrays his spiritual misorientation.[7]

Although Gross accepts that the Dreamer and the Pearl-Maiden are father and daughter and acknowledges the Dreamer's "inappropriate" use of love language, she does not ultimately reconcile the conflict inherent in a father addressing his daughter like a lover.

In her 1997 essay, Jane Gilbert, on the other hand, "resolves" this problem by suggesting the poem contains evidence of repressed incestuous desire. In her contribution to *A Companion to the Gawain-Poet*, Gilbert analyzes gender and sexual transgression in *Cleanness*, *Pearl*, and *Sir Gawain and the Green Knight*, and she argues that *Pearl* contains implications of incest.

> Feminist critics have long (Greer 1971) complained that women are infantilized in Western culture—that the features which are considered to constitute their sexual attractiveness are in many cases those of the child ... In *Pearl*, this combination works powerfully to emphasize the idea of incest with a very young daughter, and thus to render the desire the Dreamer expresses disturbing.[8]

Other critics, such Sarah Stanbury and María Búllon-Fernández, have also wrestled with the problem of incestuous implications in a poem infused with the language of courtly love directed, apparently, by a father toward his daughter. In "Feminist Masterplots: The Gaze on the Body of the *Pearl*'s Dead Girl" (1993), Stanbury actually states that the Pearl-Maiden *initiates* the incestuous plot.[9] In an effort to mitigate the difficulty, Búllon-Fernández suggests, "Even though from a 'realistic' point of view the daughter might have been two years old, the narrator's language reveals that he does not see her as two-years-old."[10]

22 Literal Sense

While the idea of a father-daughter relationship in *Pearl* has been generally accepted, and the use of love language generally recognized, implications of incest have not. Most scholars ignore the issue. Yet incestuous desire is, of course, a social taboo of staggering proportions, especially in a medieval Christian context: appalling and, it should go without saying, unlikely to be celebrated with the religious symbolism and theological import of a poem like *Pearl*. Such implications may remain, however, if the Dreamer is interpreted as the Pearl-Maiden's father. But is he? If the Dreamer and the Pearl-Maiden are not father and daughter, what kind of relationship might they have to one another?

Pearl is the kind of poem that prompts many answers to this question, including allegorical ones,[11] but for now I wish to suggest that the textual evidence and the literary context of the poem both support the possibility that the Dreamer was not the Pearl-Maiden's father but her lover in life who now mourns her loss in death. Mother Angela Carson first suggested this in 1965, but except for a dismissive review by Laurence Eldredge, the argument has received little or no attention.[12] In order to explore the idea of an untainted love relationship between Dreamer and Maiden, I will re-visit the textual evidence in favor of the father-daughter interpretation to show its ambiguity and then consider the illustrations from the A.x Cotton Nero manuscript that may support interpreting the Dreamer and Maiden as lover and beloved. An analysis of the Song of Songs imagery in Marian hymns and secular love lyrics will show that *Pearl*'s larger literary context supports an interpretation of the Dreamer-as-lover and the Pearl-Maiden-as-beloved. Finally, having established this possibility, I will re-read the poem with attention to the dialogue between the two protagonists in order to demonstrate its effects on interpretation of themes in *Pearl*.

The Relationship between the Dreamer and Pearl-Maiden

Certain key lines from *Pearl* form the basis of the opinion that the Pearl-Maiden is the Dreamer's two-year old daughter.

(1) At the fote therof there sete a faunt
A mayden of menske, ful debonere. (ll. 161–62)

(2) Ho watz me nerre then aunte or nece:
My joy forthy watz much then more. (ll. 133–34)

(3) Thou wost wel when thy perle con schede
I watz ful yong and tender of age. (ll. 411–12)

(4) ... To make the quen that watz so yong. (l. 474)

(5) Thou lyfed not two yer in oure thede
Thou cowthez neuer God nauther plese ne pray,
Ne neuer nawther Pater ne Crede—
And quen mad on the fyrst day! (ll. 483–86)

(6) ... And synthen to God I hit bytayt,
In Krystez dere blessyng and myn
That in the forme of bred and wyn
The preste vus shewez vch a daye. (ll. 1207–10)[13]

The first passage describes the Pearl-Maiden when the Dreamer first sees her, but before they have spoken to one another. Malcolm Andrew argues that *faunt* indicates the Pearl-Maiden is a child.

> The O.E.D. informs us that *faunt* is an aphetic form of the Old French *enfaunt*, *enfant*, compares the Italian *fant*, and glosses "infant, child, young person." In the M.E.D., three distinct senses are specified: (a) "a young child of either sex, an infant, babe," (b) "a son or daughter," (c) "*fauchun fantes*, the young of a falcon." Putting aside the highly (c)—which is clearly not relevant to *Pearl*—we are left with (a) and (b), each of which denotes both young and close relationship, and, furthermore, is illustrated by examples which have unmistakable connotations of warmth and tenderness. These could hardly be more appropriate to the situation in *Pearl*—provided the Maiden is understood literally.[14]

Andrew goes on to say that the poet uses the word specifically to indicate a child of one or two years of age. However, this assertion is problematized by three things: first, the Old English definition of "young person"; second, Andrew's later qualification that "in most of the [M.E.D. dictionary citations] the word *faunt* is used to describe a child of *unspecified* age" (my emphasis);[15] and third, line 162, which apparently defines *faunt* as "a mayden of menske, ful debonere." As Carson explains, "*Faunt* is the only descriptive phrase in the poem which might imply that the Pearl is a young child; the possible implication of the term is cancelled, however, by 'a mayden of menske, ful debonere' (l. 162) which is in apposition to it."[16] The word clearly has a range of meanings that can denote a child or a young person. While there can be little doubt that the Pearl-Maiden was young in either a literal or a spiritual sense when she died, an idea confirmed in passages three and four above by the Pearl-Maiden and the Dreamer respectively, there is no need to assume from line 161 that she was a two-year-old infant.

Passages three and four speak in general terms of the Pearl-Maiden's youthfulness, leaving her exact age unspecified and thus conveying the same ambiguity already seen in lines 161–62. It is worth noting, however, that the Pearl-Maiden's "youthfulness" at death may have been spiritual rather than literal. In the twelfth section of the poem, the Pearl-Maiden alludes to a story told in all three of the Synoptic Gospels that features the disciples attempting to prevent little children from approaching Jesus.[17] Jesus rebukes them, saying, according to the Pearl-Maiden: "Do way, let chylder vnto Me tygt;/*To suche* is heuenryche arrayed" (ll. 718–19, my emphasis). In other words, the Pearl-Maiden reinforces Jesus' point that, in order to enter heaven, a person must be child-like. So, in speaking of her "tender age" (l. 411), the Pearl-Maiden may have the sentiments of Christ's axiom in mind.

Perhaps partially for this reason, arguments in favor of the Pearl-Maiden's infancy have generally relied most heavily on the fifth passage, lines 483–86, and the Dreamer's assertions that the Pearl-Maiden "lyfed not two year in oure thede" and learned neither her Paternoster nor her Creed. Literally, "thede" means land or country. Allegorically interpreted, "thede" parallels *saeculum* and stands in contrast to the heavenly realm in which the Dreamer finds himself—hence the notion that the Pearl-Maiden lived two years on earth and then died. Yet "oure thede" could be a much more specific reference to England or to a particular part of England, such as the North-West Midlands.[18] If this were the case, then the Pearl-Maiden might have been an adult traveler, immigrant, or guest who lived less than two years in a "country" she shared with the Dreamer during a later part of her life. As Carson explains:

> A fair and possible conclusion to draw from the statement [ll. 483–86] is that [the Pearl-Maiden] came from another land. If, as the Jeweller says, the Pearl died without having learned the Pater and Creed, it does not necessarily follow that she died as a child. It is true that children were taught these prayers, but it is also true that the learning of them would be requisite for a newly baptized adult.[19]

Thus, although a first reading of lines 483–86 may suggest a convenient age for the Pearl-Maiden at the time of her death, upon closer examination, the lines prove to be ambiguous.

The *Pearl*-poet is even more ambiguous in the second passage given above, lines 233–34, when he asserts that the Pearl-Maiden was to him "nerre then aunt or nece." Although this passage is typically cited to support the argument that the Pearl-Maiden is the Dreamer's daughter, the lines obviously do not make his relationship to her explicitly clear. The passage implies a close relationship either through blood kinship or emotional intimacy or both, and it excludes the possibility that the Pearl-Maiden is the Dreamer's aunt or niece because she is "nearer" than that. The passage would seem to allow for four other kinds of roles for the Pearl-Maiden: mother, daughter, sister, or beloved.

Other passages insisting on the Pearl-Maiden's youth (passages three and four above) make it unlikely that the Dreamer refers to his mother, who could not have been younger than the Dreamer himself when she died. Looking at these lines in isolation, however, the Pearl-Maiden could be the Dreamer's daughter or sister.[20] The lines neither confirm nor deny these two possibilities. However, their context in the poem suggests the Dreamer expresses a remembered and still desired emotional intimacy with the Pearl-Maiden, comparable to that between two lovers, rather than a blood kinship.

The lines occur in a passage before the Dreamer first addresses the Pearl-Maiden but after seven stanzas in which he has deeply admired her.

> No gladder gome hethen into Grace
> Then I quen ho on brymme wore;
> Ho watz me nerre than aunte or nece:
> My joy forthy watz much the more.
> Ho profered me speche, that special spyce,
> Enclynande lowe in womman lore,
> Cagte of her coroun of grete tresore
> And haylsed me wyth a lote lygte.
> Wel watz me that euer I watz bore
> To sware that swete in perles pygte! (ll. 231–40)

The Dreamer asserts there is no happier man ("gome") than he as he watches the Pearl-Maiden bowing in a womanly fashion ("in wommon lore"). He remembers how close the two of them used to be and the joy he experienced as a result. He calls her "that special spyce," an allusion to the Song of Songs, and blesses the day that he was born because it has allowed him to converse with the Pearl-Maiden.[21] The interaction suggests an encounter between a man and a woman he loves.

In the final passage, lines 1207–10, Norman Davis sees a formula of greeting typically used in medieval letters addressed to children from their parents: "In Krytez dere blessyng and myn" (l. 1208). He therefore uses this line in conjunction with the second passage discussed above, lines 233–34, to reach the conclusion that "the poet is speaking of his child."[22] However, as Davis himself later discovered and added in an appendix to his original article when it was reprinted: "The use of the formula outside of letters is not restricted without exception to a parent addressing a child."[23] In addition, *Pearl* is not, in terms of genre, a letter, nor are lines 1207–10 formulated as a greeting. They are contained within the concluding stanza of the poem and comment upon the awakened Dreamer's willingness to commit his sorrow over his lost pearl to God.

Thus, in each of the six passages usually given in support of the argument that the Pearl-Maiden is the Dreamer's two-year-old daughter, the textual evidence proves ambiguous. The "faunt" of line 161 seems to be a "mayden of menske, ful debonere" (l. 161); the nearness of line 233 may express the Dreamer's feelings of emotional intimacy with the Pearl-Maiden; the youthfulness of lines 412 and 474 may be granted without assuming infancy, especially given that they might have a spiritual rather than literal connotation; the two years in "oure thede" (l. 483) may indicate two years in a longer life span when the Pearl-Maiden lived in a country shared with the Dreamer, and the formula "In Krystez dere blessyng and myn" (l. 1208) is not restricted to parental missives. These readings mean the relationship between the Dreamer and the Pearl-Maiden may be a courtly one.

26 *Literal Sense*

One extra-textual argument remains to be addressed, however, before this lover-beloved interpretation can be explored. Some critics have believed that the *Pearl*-poet was influenced by a passage of Augustine's *De Civitate Dei*, XXII.14, in which Augustine argues that when dead infants are resurrected at the Second Coming of Christ, they shall be in their mature, adult bodies. This argument has been taken out of context and applied to the Dreamer's vision of his supposedly infant daughter. Augustine's point has to do with the resurrection of the body at the end of time, not the appearance of children in heaven or dream visions. The fourteenth-century Italian poet Boccaccio does use the conceit of the *puella senex* in his eclogue "Olympia," in which his once five-year-old daughter appears to him from heaven on a hillside speaking in the mature language of a grown woman. But Boccaccio's Olympia clearly declares to Silvius (the name Boccaccio gives his self-representation in the narrative poem):

> Salve dulce decus nostrum, pater optime, salve!
> Ne timeas, sum nata tibi.
> (Hail, chiefest glory, dearest father, hail!
> Fear not, I am thy daughter.)[24]

Unlike Olympia, the Pearl-Maiden never identifies the Dreamer as father or herself as daughter.[25] In the case of *Pearl*, the *puella senex* argument relies on no specific textual evidence from the poem; indeed, it requires ignoring or straining to interpret other evidence that does not fit with it.

The Manuscript Illustrations of *Pearl*

The four illustrations of Cotton Nero A.x. that preface *Pearl* provide visual evidence in support of the idea that the Dreamer and the Pearl-Maiden relate to one another as a man and a woman in a courtly love relationship.[26] These pictures provide the only known contemporary medieval commentary on *Pearl*.[27] As such, they act as "glosses" pertinent to interpretation of the poem. They depict the Pearl-Maiden not as an infant or child, but as a young woman, and they position the bodies of the Dreamer and Maiden in relation to one another in a way that evokes the tension of male desire and female resistance typical of courtly love romances.

In the first illustration, viewers can see a garden setting with the Dreamer dressed in a red, loose-fitting robe with large sleeves; he has a blond beard and wavy hair. Foliage surrounds him. He is asleep in the garden beside a darkened patch that looks like a human body lying on its side, back to the Dreamer, and the Dreamer's hands are reaching out toward the lower back of this body (almost as if the two of them were in a spooning position). The pearlescent, white flowers growing out of the dark patch also draw the attention of our eyes. The tassel of the oddly-angled, blue hood wrapped around the Dreamer's neck, pulling upward through the trees toward the sky, may be the illustrator's way of envisioning the line: "my spirit sprang into space."[28] Certainly, there is tension between the hands reaching downward toward the mound and the blue line disappearing upward into a nearby tree while the thicker part, the actual hood with its five tassels, is pulling to one side.

The second illustration, which depicts the Dreamer standing beside a stream and pointing directly over a dark bush (the same color as the dark mound in the previous illustration) at a fish within it, may make viewers wonder about whether the image should be interpreted naturalistically, allegorically, or psychologically. In nature, it wouldn't be unusual for a man to see fish in a stream. However, the poem itself makes no mention of any fish, but rather emphasizes the bejeweled bed of the river when the Dreamer reaches it.[29] Interpreted allegorically, medieval Christian iconography has a long tradition of representing the fish as a symbol for Christ. Yet we know that the Dreamer feels estranged from Christ until the end of the poem— and the fish in this stream does not look like the traditional *ichthus*.[30] From a psychological perspective, is this a phallic or fertility symbol?[31] Perhaps viewers are meant to think of Peter, whom Jesus promised to make a "fisher of men,"[32] or of medieval astrology, and the twelfth sign of the zodiac, Pisces, associated with water and the beginning of spring (February and March).[33] Whatever the case may be, the fact that the picture shows the Dreamer pointing at this fish so dramatically suggests that the illustrator wanted to provoke viewers to ask questions and seek meaning.

The third illustration represents the Dreamer on one side of the stream and the golden-crowned Pearl-Maiden on the other. The dark color associated with the mound in the first illustration and the bush in the second has entirely disappeared. Instead there is a five-pointed, star-shaped flower at the Dreamer's feet with a pearlescent, white center. The Dreamer and the Pearl-Maiden contrast with one another: he in his red robe and she in a high-necked white one, gathered at the waist. Her blond hair is braided.[34] The two figures seem to be having a conversation with their hands. The Dreamer reaches out to the Pearl-Maiden, pointing at her, while she holds up the palms of both of her hands as if to ask him to halt or stop. Is this a pose that courtly lovers might take, the entreating lover and the sovereign beloved? Viewers may notice that while the Pearl-Maiden is crowned, the Dreamer is not, a symbol that implies her higher rank and authority.

Then we notice that three fish are depicted in the stream, one swimming in the opposite direction of the other two. What do these fish represent? Is this Trinitarian symbolism? Or might the three fish correspond to the three characters of the poem, the Dreamer, the Pearl-Maiden, and the Lamb? The Pearl-Maiden and her lord, the Lamb, may very well be "swimming in the same direction," but the Dreamer's conversation with the Pearl-Maiden in the poem suggests he is "swimming against the current." This interpretation may be reinforced by the fact that the gazes of the Dreamer and Pearl-Maiden do not meet; each is looking away from the other. But the Dreamer's pointing finger is just over the nose of the fish in the middle, between the other two fish, and if we follow the arc of his finger pointing across the stream to the body of the Pearl-Maiden, we find that its trajectory ends, not at the Pearl-Maiden's face or heart, but at the *mons Veneris*, which is modestly concealed by the Pearl-Maiden's white robes.

The fourth illustration shows the Dreamer and the golden-crowned Pearl-Maiden still on opposite sides of the stream, only now the Pearl-Maiden is removed behind a crenellated castle-wall decorated with eight crosses, a tower beside her and a small fortress behind her. The conversation of the speaking hands continues, with the Dreamer reaching up to her and turning his face in a painfully awkward angle to look up at her. She, meanwhile, is holding one hand to her heart while the other one is extended downward toward the Dreamer in the position a lady might employ for a suitor to take it and kiss it. The stream now has only two fish in it, much enlarged and looking somewhat ominous, again facing each other so that at least one of them is working against the current. Meanwhile, the dark color associated with the mound and the bush in the first and second illustrations, absent in the third, has reappeared in a low, dark bush near the Dreamer's feet. Is this representative of the threat of death?

Scholarship on these illustrations has primarily been concerned with evaluating their quality, whether crude or sophisticated,[35] but visual interpretation of their meaning is called for in relation to the settings, characters, and themes of the poem. While definitive decisions about what these illustrations are meant to convey may not be possible, it seems unlikely that the illustrations represent a relationship between a father and his two-year-old daughter.[36] If the only contemporary commentator on the poem, the illustrator, did not apparently think that this was the nature of the relationship between the Pearl-Maiden and the Dreamer, should we?

A medieval reader glancing at these illustrations would not suppose the Dreamer is speaking as a father to his daughter. Instead, the man's lower position in relation to the woman's elevated one might suggest a submissive lover conversing with his lady. The iconography of the Pearl-Maiden's crowned head and castle home, the Dreamer's out-stretched hands, and the garden setting all suggest *amour courtois*.[37] This is not the only possible interpretation of the poem, and modern critics might well disagree with the illustrator's understanding of it. Yet it seems, to borrow a phrase from Gross's essay on courtly language, that the illustrations evoke "the invariable triad of the courtly love-lyric: a lady identified with ideal perfection, a lover who aspires to and is ennobled by that perfection, and the inviolable distance separating the two."[38]

This effect parallels that of the love language in the poem. The language of love in *Pearl*, as I have already suggested, is contextualized by the Song of Song's influence on both Marian hymns and courtly love lyrics. An investigation of the larger literary context of *Pearl*'s love language will lend further support to the idea that the poem depicts a lover-beloved relationship between the Dreamer and the Pearl-Maiden.

Love Language in Its Medieval Literary Context

Interpretation of the Song of Songs in the Middle Ages consistently affirms that the literal, sexual use of love language was a device intended to make readers ponder the allegorical, spiritual meaning of love. As E. Ann Matter and Ann Astell have shown, beginning with Origen's *Commentarium in Cantica Canticorum* in the third century, medieval Christian commentary on the Song of Songs encouraged a spiritual rather than sensual understanding of its love language, but only with difficulty.[39] As Astell states, "The first problem arises from what the Song leaves unstated; the second from what it actually says."[40] Unlike Hosea in the Old Testament or the Apocalypse in the New, the Song of Songs does not explicitly state that the Bridegroom is God and the Bride is a figure of Israel or the Church or an individual Christian soul. Origen provides a model for all later commentators when he attempts to harmonize the apparent contradiction between the carnal love described in the Song and the spiritual love that is supposedly intended by it. In doing so, he completely subverts the literal reading in favor of the allegorical one.

> Epithalamium libellus hic, id est nuptiale carmen, dramatis in modum mihi videtur a Solomone conscriptus, quem cecinit instar nubentis sponsae et erga sponsum suum, qui est Sermo Dei, caelesti amore flagrante. Adamavit enim eum sive anima quae ad imaginem eius facta est, sive ecclesia.[41]
>
> (It seems to me that this little book is an epithalamium, that is to say, a marriage-song, which Solomon wrote in the form of a drama and sang under the figure of the Bride, about to wed and burning with heavenly love towards her Bridegroom, who is the Word of God. And deeply indeed did she love Him, whether we take her as the soul made in His image or as the Church.)[42]

Partially as a result of Origen's influence, "Medieval Latin commentary on the Song of Songs ... was always allegorical."[43]

The spiritual or allegorical understanding of the relationship depicted in the Song of Songs had three basic manifestations during the Middle Ages. Origen was the first to identify the Bride with the church or the soul. In addition to these two readings, the Bride was also identified with the Virgin Mary. Medieval commentators believed that the interaction between the Bride and the Bridegroom reflected Mary's historical relationship with Christ. These readings, together with the fact that the Song of Songs was the most frequently interpreted book of medieval Christianity, reveal a medieval fascination with the epithalamium. This fascination held throughout the Middle Ages but developed meaningfully in twelfth-century Europe when members of religious orders began to join as adults, rather than as children.

> Many were drawn from aristocratic circles; a high percentage had been married; most were familiar with secular love literature; some—notably the trouvère Folquet—had written secular love songs prior to their entrance. The spiritual formation of recruits such as these required (and inspired) a body of monastic love literature which is notably different from earlier writings on charity in its incorporation of feminine imagery and in its preferred symbolism of God's love for humanity by the love between a man and a woman—a symbolism explicitly derived from the Song of Songs.[44]

Astell's analysis reveals, in essence, that twelfth-century interpreters of the Song of Songs had a lived experience in secular society that included exposure to secular love lyrics and even sexuality itself. The secular experience of the commentators may explain the nature of their meditation on the Song, the influence of the Song on both sacred and secular lyrics, and, importantly, the soft blurring of distinctions between spiritual and sensual love language that sometimes occurred in them.[45] This blurring of distinctions also occurs in fourteenth-century English literature.

Middle English Marian hymns and secular lyrics both use the same language to express love. The influence of the Song of Songs pervades the love language used in both genres to describe devotion to either the Queen of Heaven or the "hertes quene," that is, to Mary or to the lady loved by the poet. Typically, despite similar language, the object of the poet's affections—whether the heavenly queen or an earthly one—is clear. However, that clarity is not always evident from the outset of a lyric. A close reading of key lines from three lyrics will show that the lyricists deliberately played with word choice, permitting and enjoying the resulting ambiguity about who or what was being signified. This play forms a model for understanding the language of love in *Pearl*. Although one might suppose that imagery from the Song of Songs in *Pearl* would have been interpreted by medieval readers in a spiritual sense, just as the Song of Songs itself was, the tradition of secular love lyrics shows that the meaning of love language in *Pearl* is not pre-determined.

The first lyric, "Quia amore langueo," uses the language of love in its spiritual sense and is a striking example of Marian piety. Written in the voice of Mary herself, it employs a Latin refrain taken directly from the Song of Songs: *quia amore langueo*, that is, "I languish from love." In the Song of Songs, the line occurs twice, both times spoken by the Beloved:

> Introduxit me in cellam vinariam
> ordinavit in me caritatem
> fulcite me floribus stipate me malis
> quia amore langueo (Song of Songs 2:4–5)

> (He led me into the wine cellar
> he governed love in me
> strengthen me with flowers, surround me with apples
> because I languish from love.)

And:

> Adiuro vos filiae Hierusalem si inveneritis dilectum meam ut nuntietis ei quia amore langueo (Song of Songs 5:8)
>
> (I adjure you, daughters of Jerusalem, if you find my love so that you may tell him that I languish from love.)[46]

By extracting "quia amore langueo" from the Song of Songs and re-contextualizing the phrase in a Marian hymn, the poet plays the role of commentator; his poem becomes an interpretation of the Song of Songs. The Bride is Mary who languishes because she longs for reunion with "mankinde" (l. 7). The separation between the two of them causes her profound sorrow:

> I longe for love of man my brother,
> I am his vokete to voide his vice;
> I am his moder—I can none other—
> Why should I my dere childe dispise?
> If he me wrathe in diverse wise,
> Through flesshes freelte fall me fro,
> Yet must me rewe him till he rise.
>
> *Quia amore langueo* (ll. 9–16)[47]

The poet portrays mankind collectively as Mary's son (thereby making mankind comparable to Jesus) whom she loves. Throughout the lyric, Mary speaks to her "child" and pleads with him to seek her and God, as if they were parents, asking rhetorically, "Why was I crouned and made a quene?/ Why was I called of mercy the welle?" (ll. 81–2). In the concluding stanza, however, the mother/son relationship shifts to a lover/beloved relationship. This shift perfectly demonstrates the influence of the Song of Songs, interpretative commentaries upon it, and the orthodox use of the language of love in devotional writing.

> Nowe, man, have minde on me forever.
> Loke on thy love thus languisshing;
> Late us never from other dissevere;
> Mine helpe is thine owne; crepe under my winge.
> Thy sister is a quene, they brother a kinge,
> This heritage is tayled; sone come thereto;
> Take me for thy wife and lerne to singe.
>
> *Quia amore langueo* (ll. 89–96)

32   *Literal Sense*

Mary is thus depicted as mother, sister, and beloved wife. In Mary's voice, the poet shows that man's relationship with heaven's queen parallels, and at the same time exceeds, every human relationship between a man and a woman. The relationship between the Christian and Mary is like the relationship between mother and son, sister and brother, husband and wife, but in an idealized and purified sense.

The language of love from the Song of Songs was also used in a less than ideal, pure, or orthodox sense in a secular love lyric. The first stanza from a second lyric is a fine case in point.

> O excellent sovereigne, most semely to see,
> Both prudent and pure, like a perle of prise,
> Also fair of figure and oreant of bewtye,
> Bothe cumlye and gentil, and goodly to advertise;
> Your brethe is sweeter than balme, suger, or licoresse.
> I am bolde on you, thoughe I be not able,
> To write to your goodly person which is so ameable to reason.
>   For ye be both fair and free,
>   Therto wise and womanly,
>   Trew as turtil on a tree
>   Without any treason. (ll. 1–12)[48]

Two commonplace references to the Song of Songs are apparent here: the fragrant breath of the beloved and the comparison to the turtle-dove. Later lines develop allusions to the Song of Songs; for instance, "Your chere is as comfortable as blossome on brere" and "Your necke like the lillye" together remind us of "Like a lily among thorns is my darling among the maidens" (Song of Songs 2:2). The general sentiments concerning the beauty of the beloved are also similar.[49]

However, what is perhaps most striking about the first stanza is its potential for either a spiritual or a secular reading. "O excellent sovereigne" sounds suspiciously like an address to Mary; only in later stanzas will it become clear that the lady in question could not possibly be Mary, first because the poet mentions Mary in an aside that makes it plain that she is not the object of his affection addressed here: "For Jesus' sake that bought us dere/And his moder, that meiden clere,/Helpe to comforte my careful chere ..." (ll. 33–4). Second, the poet clearly has sexual intentions toward his beloved, which he could not appropriately direct toward the Virgin Mary.

Furthermore, and perhaps more importantly, the love language of this lyric parallels similar language used by the Dreamer to describe the Pearl-Maiden. Compare, for instance, the lyric's "perle of prise" to any number of references to pearls in the longer poem; "fair of figure" to "fayre fygure" (l. 747); "oreant of bewtye" to "Perle pleasaunte ... oute of oryent" (ll. 1, 3); "free" to "frely" (l. 1155); or "wise and womanly" to "wommon lore" (l. 236). The lyric's use of "perle of prise," a phrase that alludes to the parable of the Pearl of Great Price, would particularly seem relevant to interpretation of *Pearl* since here in this secular love poem it is clearly a romantic epithet expressing an earthly desire.

The use of love language in both Marian hymns and secular love lyrics derived from the Song of Songs engenders ambiguity and questions, questions raised for readers at the beginning of hymns and lyrics that are only answered at the end of them—if at all. Who is being addressed? Mary or beloved? What kind of love is at issue? Spiritual or sensual? How can readers, medieval or modern, read love word signifiers for their correct signified referents? The following lyric raises each of these questions.[50]

> (1) Upon a lady my love is lente,
> Withoutene change of any chere—
> That is lovely and continent
> And most at my desire.
>
> (2) This lady is in my herte pight;
> Her to love I have gret haste.
> With all my power and my might
> To her I make mine herte stedfast.
>
> (3) Therfor will I non other spouse
> Ner none other loves, for to take;
> But only to her I make my vowes,
> And all other to forsake.
>
> (4) This lady is gentill and make,
> Moder she is and well of all;
> She is never for to seke,
> Nother too grete nere too small.
>
> (5) Redy she is night and day,
> To man and wommon and childe infere,
> If that they will aught to her say,
> Our prayeres mekely for to here.
>
> (6) To serve this lady we all be bounde
> Both night and day in every place,
> Where ever we be, in felde or towne,
> Or elles in any other place.
>
> (7) Pray we to this lady bright,
> In the worship of the Trinite,
> To bringe us alle to heven light.
> Amen, say we, for charite. (ll. 1–28)

As with the second lyric, which began "O excellent sovereign, most semely to see," the first line of this lyric—"Upon a lady my love is lente"—does not make the object of the poet's affections clear. It may, in fact, suggest the wrong object—but deliberately so. The author of the second lyric is at play among the words that suggest Marian devotion; conversely, the authors of the first and third are at play among the words that suggest sexual love. This third lyricist keeps his readers in suspense with regards to his object for three and a half stanzas—half of his poem—before revealing that his "spouse" (l. 9) is Mary, "Moder she is and well of all," and the lady on whom his love is settled. This play of love language has particular relevance for *Pearl*.

Pearl inherits the language of love from the Song of Songs along with everything such an inheritance implies: potential for spiritual or sensual interpretation of the primary relationship it depicts; problems, to use Astell's terms, with what is stated as well as what is unstated; and the possibility that its love language may refer to either heavenly or earthly objects of desire. When the lyricists use phrases like *quia amore langueo*, "O sovereigne quene," "perle of prise," and "spouse," the words can refer equally well to Mary or human beloved. When such love language occurs in *Pearl*, what does it signify? Seen in the historical context of the Song of Songs, Marian hymns, and secular love lyrics, *Pearl*'s love language makes it possible to read the relationship between the Dreamer and the Pearl-Maiden as one between lover and beloved. As it turns out, however, the Dreamer is not the Pearl-Maiden's only lover.

The Pearl-Maiden's Two Lovers

Pearl begins in a garden, the *hortus conclusus* of medieval love lyric, and with a lover who claims, "I dewyne, fordolked of *luf-daungere*/Of that pryuy perle withouten spot" (ll. 11–12, my emphasis). W.R.J. Barron convincingly glosses "luf-daungere" as "love frustration," and Andrew and Waldron note:

> The compound may be the poet's own, but the word *daungere* ('feudal power') signifies the power of the mistress over her suitor, specifically her power to keep him at a distance, and is so personified in the *Roman de la Rose*. ... *Luf-daungere* is here used metaphorically to suggest longing for, and separation from, any loved object, and the whole line is perhaps reminiscent of the phrase *quia amore langueo*.[51]

The garden setting and the poet's word choice suggest that the narrator is a suitor suffering the pains of love.

Once he falls asleep, the Dreamer encounters and speaks to the Pearl-Maiden. Characterized by some as a *debatio*, the conversation takes up the majority of *Pearl*'s sections (12 out of 20). It consists of 11 questions by the Dreamer and 12 responses by the Pearl-Maiden, and it develops in three stages: re-acquaintance, disagreement, and renewed desire. Excluding the Dreamer's first and final addresses to the Pearl-Maiden, each stage features three questions by the Dreamer, the third of which provokes an important revelation from the Pearl-Maiden. At the end of the re-acquaintance stage, the Pearl-Maiden reveals to the Dreamer for the first time her marriage to her "Lorde the Lombe" (l. 413).

> Bot my Lorde the Lombe thurg Hys godhede,
> He toke myself to Hys maryage
> Corounde me quene is blysse to brede
> And sesed in all Hys herytage
> Hys lef is. I am holy Hysse. (ll. 413–18)

This revelation distresses and angers the Dreamer, and it leads him to question the validity of the Pearl-Maiden's marriage: first by saying only Mary can be the queen of heaven (ll. 424–29), then by asserting the Pearl-Maiden sets herself too high in heaven, and finally by claiming her story is "vnresounable" (l. 590) because she has received a reward greater than she deserved.

The Pearl-Maiden puts an end to the Dreamer's disagreement with her by means of a re-telling and explication of the Parable of the Laborers in the Vineyard that lasts for 12 uninterrupted stanzas. At the end of the Pearl-Maiden's learned dissertation on the nature of the heavenly rewards, the grace of God, innocence, and righteousness, however, the Dreamer responds with a complete *non sequitur*.

> O maskelez perle in perlez pure,
> That berez," quoth I, "the perle of prys,
> Quo formed they thy fayre fygure?
> That wrogt thy wede he watz ful wys;
> Thy beauté com neuer of nature—
> Pymalyon paynted neuer thy vys,
> Ne Arystotel nawther by hys lettrure
> Of carped the kynde these propertéz;
> Thy colour passez the flour-de-lys,
> Thyn angel-hauyng so clene cortez. (ll. 745–54)

In other words, while the Pearl-Maiden was speaking, apparently the Dreamer was not listening to her with attention, but gazing at her with desire. He takes note of her "fayre fygure" (l. 747), her lovely clothes (l. 748), her "beauté," (l. 749), her color, which surpasses the flour-de-lis (l. 753), and her angelic bearing (l. 754). In the middle of these praises, he makes a secular allusion to Pygmalion, the sculptor of Ovid's *Metamorphoses* who fell in love with the statue he made himself. According to Ovid:

> Interea niveum mira filiciter arte
> Sculpsit ebur formaque dedit, qua femina nasci

>   Nulla potest, operisque sui concepit amorem.
>   Virginis est verae facies, quam vivere credas,
>   Et, si non obstet reverentia, velle moveri.[52]
>
>   ([Pygmalion] made, with marvelous art, an ivory statue,
>   As white as snow, and gave it greater beauty
>   Than any girl could have, and fell in love
>   With his own workmanship. The image seemed
>   That of a virgin, truly, almost living,
>   And willing, save that modesty prevented,
>   To take on movement.)[53]

The Dreamer's allusion to this Ovidian tale betrays his earthly mind-set. Like Pygmalion, he wishes to possess the beautiful woman he beholds with his eyes and, in a sense, creates according to the dictates of his own imagination. The longer he watches her, the more his desire increases.

The Dreamer's secular reference to Aristotle, like the allusion to Pygmalion, suggests earthly, even academic preoccupations. In this passage, Aristotle stands for human reasoning and the limits of "lettrure" (l. 751). He appears as a "figure of logic," emblematically implying the Dreamer's circumscribed understanding of *kynde*, an understanding that reflects "the Dreamer's unswerving faith in his own reason and in his ability to rely on observations of the phenomenal world."[54] Whereas the Pearl-Maiden has discoursed at length on the Parable of the Vineyard, very much like a preacher explicating the spiritual sense of scripture in a homily, the Dreamer has been meditating on how far the Pearl-Maiden's "propertéz" exceed those described by the Philosopher. The contrast in their meditations could not be starker, and the Pearl-Maiden recognizes this.

The Pearl-Maiden responds to the Dreamer's suit by asserting, "My makelez Lambe that al may bete … Me ches to Hys make" (ll. 757, 759). The "matchlessness" of Christ's love implies that it easily surpasses the Dreamer's; that love has won the Pearl-Maiden, and she has become Christ's "make," that is, His bride.[55] She repeats the words of love the Lord used to woo her for the Dreamer's benefit: "Cum hyder to me, My lemman swete, / For mote ne spot is non is thee" (ll. 763–64). Christ's suit is a translation of the Song of Songs 4:7–8 (Vulgate): "Tota pulchra es amica mea et macula non est in te" and represents His desire for spiritual union with the Pearl-Maiden. Re-vocalized here in her discussion with the Dreamer, Christ's words have the effect of His presence; the Dreamer and the Lord compete in their own *debatio*, mediated by the Pearl-Maiden, to love and be loved by her.

The Dreamer responds rather negatively to the reiteration of his Pearl's love affair with another suitor.

>   Why, maskellez bryd that brygt con flambe,
>   That reiatéz hatz so ryche and ryf,

> Quat kyn thyng may be that Lambe,
> That the wolde wedde vnto His vyf? (ll. 769–72)

The tone of the Dreamer's speech appears to be one not of awe, but of irony. First, he lets out an exclamation of surprise and incomprehension: *why*. Then he compliments the Pearl-Maiden by calling her an "unblemished bride," as if he accepts the marriage she has reported to him. But then he asks *quat kyn thyng*—what kind of thing—is the Lamb that he would marry the Pearl-Maiden? After asking this somewhat antagonistic question, the Dreamer concludes his address to the Maiden with another subtle compliment, calling her, "a makelez may and maskellez," that is, a matchless and flawless maid. "Makelez," or matchless, can mean both without peer and without mate. Here the pun suggests that the Dreamer has *not* accepted the marriage of the Pearl-Maiden or the success of his rival, the Lamb, who has washed the Pearl-Maiden in "Hys blod" (l. 766), crowned her in virginity, and arrayed her in pearls (ll. 767–68).

The Pearl-Maiden immediately understands the implications of the Dreamer's word choice. She accepts "maskellez" as an appropriate compliment, but rejects "makelez": "Bot 'makelez quene' thenne sade I not" (l. 784). She goes on to explain that her Lord has many brides. She also enters into a lengthy discourse on Christ's crucifixion in Jerusalem.

After this, the Dreamer finally begins to realize he cannot compete with God: "I schulde not tempte thy wyt so wlonc; / To Krytez chambre that art ichose" (ll. 903–4). Yet he still seeks to be near the Pearl-Maiden, from whom he has been kept throughout their conversation by the stream that flows between them. He asks her where she lives (ll. 917–18), and then he asks to "se thy blysful bor" (l. 964). The Pearl-Maiden warns the Dreamer that he "may not enter withinne Hys tor" (l. 966), but says she has obtained permission for him to see her dwelling place. Their conversation ends, and the Dreamer has a vision of the New Jerusalem. As he watches, the Dreamer is filled with delight.

The word "delyt" is used throughout *Pearl*, but it is especially important as the poem nears its conclusion. In section 19 of the poem, the word is repeated in the last line of each stanza. The Dreamer uses the phrase "gret delyt" to express a spiritual admiration for the vision of the New Jerusalem and the procession of the Lord and His 144,000 brides. However, the Dreamer's sentiments do not remain on the level of spiritual admiration. Instead, they increase in an agitated and earthly fashion:

> That sygt me gart to thenk to wade
> For *luf-longyng* in gret *delyt*.
> *Delyt* me drof in yge and ere,
> My manez mynde to maddyng malte;
> Quen I sey my frely, I wolde be there
> Bygonde the water thag ho were walte.
> (ll. 1151–56, my emphases)

"Delyt" in the passage stems from the "manez mynde"—from the Dreamer's corporeal, earthly self, not his heavenly spirit—and as such, the word suggests sensual, not spiritual, longing and desire.[56]

"Delyt" and "luf-longyng" are equated in this passage. "Luf-longyng," the Middle English equivalent of *quia amore langueo*, is a perfect example of love language from the Song of Songs that may have either a spiritual or sensual meaning.[57] Julian of Norwich, a contemporary of the *Pearl*-poet, uses "luf-longyng" in a spiritual sense: "Glad and mery and sweet is the blisfull lovely cher of our lord to our souleis; for he havith us ever lifand in *lovelongeing*, and he will our soule be in glad cher to gevin him his mede" (my emphasis).[58] However, the word was also used to denote sensual love, as in the following lyric, which celebrates a poet's romantic love for Alisoun.

> Ich libbe in *love-longinge*
> For semlokest of alle thinge:
> He may me blisse bringe;
> Ich am in hire baundoun. (ll. 5–8, my emphasis)[59]

The Dreamer's "luf-longyng" seems to participate in both the spiritual and sensual meanings of the word. He longs for a place in the Lord's procession while at the same time longing for reunion and possession of the Pearl-Maiden herself. In the end, however, since crossing the stream is an act the Maiden warned him against, the "luf-longyng" that spurs him to attempt the crossing is more earthly than heavenly. It is a frustrated love that he unsuccessfully tries to resolve by reaching out to a woman who belongs entirely to God.

The Dreamer's attempt to cross the stream can be interpreted as a jealous act motivated by a desire to possess his beloved Pearl-Maiden, an act forestalled by Christ himself. It constitutes the climactic conclusion of the Dreamer's longing to join the Pearl-Maiden after his efforts to woo her have failed. As he plunges into the water, he suddenly wakes to ponder the implication of his dream and explicate what he has learned. Although his admiration for Christ does not reach the heights of the Pearl-Maiden's, it is nevertheless present: "For I haf founden Hym, bothe day and nagte,/A God, a Lorde, a frende ful fyin" (ll. 1203–1204). Only through his dream vision, through an interaction with the woman he loved in life but could not possess in death, is the Dreamer able to overcome the greater part of his grief and discover solace in the friendship of God.

Conclusions

While *Pearl* may depict a father mourning the death of his daughter, the poem may also represent a man grieving over the loss of the woman he loves. The textual evidence supporting the idea that the Dreamer is the Pearl-Maiden's father is sufficiently ambiguous to allow for this possibility. The love language of *Pearl*, which has led some critics to suggest the poem contains implications of incest, may in fact express a lover's desire for his beloved. The influence of the Song of Songs on secular Middle English love lyrics provides a literary context for interpreting the relationship between the protagonists in *Pearl* in just this way.

Yet though the Dreamer may love the Pearl-Maiden, he is compelled through his encounter with her to learn about the love of God. This knowledge transforms him from a suitor to a servant, one who affirms the Lord "gef vus to be His homely hyne, / Ande precious perlez vnto His pay" (ll. 1211–12). He recognizes Christ as his friend, which gives the Dreamer a new identity as the friend of the Bridegroom.[60]

Pearl is an exquisite and beautiful poem, the complexity of which cannot and should not be readily reduced to a single, definitive reading. To answer the question with which this chapter began, it is certainly an elegy. But that is not all that it is.

Notes

1. Richard Morris, "On *The Pearl*, an Excerpt," repr. in *The Middle English Pearl: Critical Essays*, ed. John Conley (South Bend, IN: University of Notre Dame Press, 1970), 3.
2. W.H. Schofield, "Symbolism, Allegory, and Autobiography in *The Pearl*," *Publications of the Modern Language Association* 24 (1909), 658.
3. A major factor in this wide-spread acceptance has been, and continues to be, editions and translations of the poem that assume an elegiac interpretation, and a father-daughter relationship, as a given and the use of these in college and university classrooms. For discussion, see my essay, "The Relationship between the Pearl-Maiden and the Dreamer," in *Approaches to Teaching the Middle English Pearl*, ed. Jane Beal and Mark Bradshaw Busbee (New York, NY: MLA, 2017).
4. See Laurence Eldredge, "The State of *Pearl* Studies Since 1933," *Viator* 6 (1975): 171–94 and A.C. Spearing, "Symbolic and Dramatic Development in *Pearl*," 1–12.
5. See, for example, Herbert Pilch, "The Middle English *Pearl*: Its Relation to the *Roman de la Rose*," *Neuphilologische Mitteilungen* 65 (1964): 427–46 or as translated by Heide Hyprath in *The Middle English Pearl: Critical Essays*, ed. John Conley (South Bend, IN: Notre Dame University Press, 1970), 163–84.
6. Charlotte Gross, "Courtly Language in *Pearl*," *Text and Matter: New Critical Perspectives of the Pearl-Poet*, ed. Robert J. Blanch, Miriam Youngerman Miller, and Julian N. Wasserman (Troy, NY: Whiston, 1991), 77.
7. Gross, "Courtly Language," 83.
8. Jane Gilbert, "Gender and Sexual Transgression," in *A Companion to the Gawain-Poet*, ed. Derek Brewer and Jonathon Gibson (Rochester, NY: D.S. Brewer, 1997), 59.
9. Sarah Stanbury, "Feminist Masterplots: The Gaze on the Body of the *Pearl's* Dead Girl," 109. It's worth noting, however, that here Stanbury is using terms from Freudian and Lacanian psychoanalysis to suggest the Pearl-Maiden,

though a daughter, has assumed a maternal teaching role and that the incest is metaphorically between mother and son.
10. María Bullón-Fernández, "'Beyond the Water': Courtly and Religious Desire in *Pearl*," *Studies in Philology* 91 (1994): 39.
11. Notable examples of allegorical interpretations are Sister Mary Madeleva, *Pearl: A Study in Spiritual Dryness* (New York, NY: D. Appleton and Company, 1925) and Ian Bishop, *Pearl in Its Setting: A Critical Study of the Structure and Meaning of the Middle English Poem* (Oxford: Basil Blackwell, 1968).
12. Mother Angela Carson, "Aspects of Elegy," 17–27. Reviewed in Eldredge, "The State of *Pearl* Studies."
13. All *Pearl* quotations are from *The Poems of the Pearl Manuscript*, 5th ed., ed. Malcolm Andrew and Ronald Waldron (Exeter: Liverpool University Press, 2007).
14. See Malcolm Andrew, "*Pearl*, Line 161," *The Explicator* 40/1 (1981): 4.
15. Andrew, "Pearl, Line 161," 4.
16. Carson, "Aspects of Elegy," 26n.
17. See Matt. 19:13–15, Mark 10:13–16, and Luke 18:15–17.
18. The modifier "oure" is also significant, reinforcing as it does the Dreamer's belief that he shared his country with the Pearl-Maiden.
19. Carson, "Aspects of Elegy," 19.
20. The weight of scholarly opinion in favor of the Pearl-Maiden-as-daughter interpretation has apparently prevented most critics from arguing that the Pearl-Maiden is the Dreamer's sister. Ian Bishop, who accepted the Pearl-Maiden-as-daughter reading but prefers an allegorical interpretation of the poem, did note in passing in *The Pearl in Its Setting* that the Pearl-Maiden "may have been a god-child, a grandchild or even a *younger sister*" (8, my emphasis). This latter possibility is at least as likely as the suggestion that the Pearl-Maiden is the Dreamer's daughter.
21. According to Andrew and Waldron, "Spice is a traditional metaphor for an admired woman, probably as a reminiscence of Song of Songs 4: 12–16" (65n).
22. Norman Davis, "A Note on *Pearl*," *Review of English Studies* 16 (1965): 233–34; repr. in *The Middle English Pearl*, ed. John Conley, 329.
23. Davis, "A Note," 330.
24. Boccaccio, "Olympia," in *Pearl: An English Poem of the XIVth Century, Edited, with Modern Rendering, Together with Boccaccio's Olympia*, ed. Sir. Israel Gollancz (London: Chatto and Windus, 1936), 262–63. Translation by Gollancz.
25. It is also unlikely that the *Pearl*-poet knew of Boccaccio's eclogue. In his introduction to his 1936 translation of *Pearl*, published with the Latin edition and English translation of Boccaccio's "Olympia," Sir Israel Gollancz himself freely admitted, "There is no clear evidence that this most charming of Boccaccio's shorter poems was known to our poet or was one of his sources of inspiration" (xxviii).
26. The illustrations are now available online, in full color, at the Cotton Nero A.x Project medievalpearl.wordpress.com, and Wikimedia Commons, since they are in the public domain; they have been reproduced as black and white plates in Robert Blanch and Julian Wasserman, *From Pearl to Gawain: Forme to Fynisment* (Gainesville, FL: University of Florida Press, 1995), 95–96 as well.
27. See Jennifer Lee, "The Illuminating Critic: The Illustrator of Cotton Nero A.x," *Studies in Iconography* 3 (1977): 17–46.

28. *Pearl*, line 61.
29. The illustrator himself emphasizes the stream, for it appears in three of the four pictures prefacing *Pearl*.
30. "Ichthus" is the Greek word for fish. It is also an acrostic: "Ἰησοῦς Χριστὸς Θεοῦ Υἱὸς Σωτήρ", (Iēsous Christos Theou Hyios Sōtēr), meaning, *Jesus Christ, Son of God, Savior*. The source of this interpretation of the acrostic is Augustine, *De Civitate Dei*, XVIII.23.
31. On the sexual implications of the Dreamer's impasse at the stream, see Bullon-Fernandez, "Beyond the Water," 47–48.
32. Matt. 4:18–19.

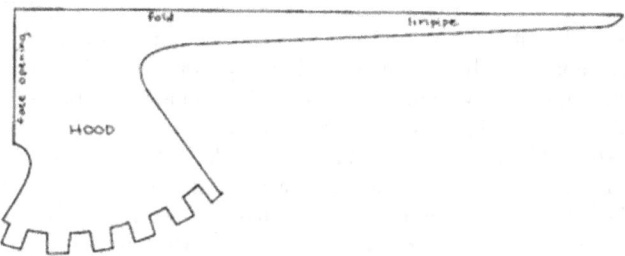

Figure 1.1 Medieval Hood

33. The symbol for pisces is, however, two fish connected to one another and pulling in different directions, which the *Pearl* manuscript illustrator does not depict.
34. Note that the *Pearl*-poet describes the Pearl-Maiden's hair as free-flowing, not braided (ll. 213–14). The fact that she is depicted with braided hair in the illustrations contrasts with Jennifer Lee's claim that the illustrator is consistently faithful to the text of the poems he illustrates. For a discussion of the possible significance of the Pearl-Maiden's hair-style, see Peter J. Lucas, "The Pearl-Maiden's Free-Flowing Hair," *English Language Notes* 15 (1977–78): 94–95.
35. See Paul F. Reichardt, "'Several Illuminations, Coarsely Executed': The Illustrations of the *Pearl* Manuscript." *Studies in Iconography* 18 (1997): 119–42.
36. It can be interesting to contrast the fourteenth-century illustrations from the manuscript with the modern illustration on the front cover of the CD for the Chaucer Studio's recording of the *Pearl* poem. The latter is of a very childlike, young girl with a round face and blonde hair who could easily be two years old.
37. For the image of a lover's outstretched hand in a garden setting, compare the illustrations from the Pearl manuscript with an image of two lovers playing a game in the Luttrell Psalter (folio 76v), reproduced in Janet Backhouse, *Medieval Rural Life in the Luttrell Psalter* (Toronto: University of Toronto Press, 1989), 47.
38. Gross, "Courtly Language," 83.
39. E. Ann Matter, *The Voice of My Beloved* (Philadelphia: University of Pennsylvania Press, 1990) and Ann Astell, *The Song of Songs in the Middle Ages* (Ithaca: Cornell University Press, 1990).
40. Astell, *The Song of Songs in the Middle Ages*, 1.
41. *Origène: Commentaire sur le Cantique des Cantiques*, ed. Luc Brésard (Paris: Editions du Cerf, 1991).
42. *Origin: The Song of Songs: Commentary and Homilies*, ed. R.P. Lawson (Westminster, MD: Newman Press, 1957), 21.

43. Matter, *The Voice of my Beloved*, 6.
44. Astell, *The Song of Songs in the Middle Ages*, 9.
45. See Jaufré Rudel, "Lanquan li jorn son lonc en may," 4 June 2002 (//perso.wanadoo.fr/moulin.veste/rudel.htm) or *The Songs of Jaufré Rudel*, ed. Rupert T. Pickins (Toronto: Pontifical Institute of Mediaeval Studies, 1978).
46. See *Canticum Canticorum* in B. Fischer et al., ed., *Biblia Sacra Iuxta Vulgata Versionem* (Stuttgart: Deutsche Bibelgeseschaft, 1994). The translations given here are my own.
47. "Quia amore langueo" is found in MS Bodleian 21896 and edited from this manuscript in Maxwell S. Luria and Richard L. Hoffman, eds., *Middle English Lyrics* (New York, NY: W.W. Norton, 1974), 187. It is also found in MS Douce 322 and printed in Carleton Brown, ed., *Religious Lyrics of the XIVth Century* (Oxford: Clarendon Press, 1952), 234–37. My citations are from "Quia amore langueo" and from the Hoffman and Luria edition.
48. "O excellent sovereigne, most semely to see" is found in MS Bodleian 12653 and printed in Luria and Hoffman, 42. See also R.H. Robbins, ed., *Secular Lyrics of the XIVth and XVth Centuries*, 2nd ed. (Oxford: Clarendon Press, 1955), 126–28.
49. For a discussion of the influence of the Song of Songs on medieval lyrics, see Peter Dronke, "The Song of Songs and Medieval Love-Lyric," in *The Bible and Medieval Culture*, ed. W. Lourdaux and D. Verhelst (Leuven: Leuven University Press, 1979), 236–62 and *The Medieval Lyric* (London: Hutchinson University Library, 1968), 80–81, 101, 175–76.
50. "Upon a lady my love is lente" is found in MS B.M. Cotton Cleopatra D.vii and printed in Luria and Hoffman, 177.
51. Andrew and Waldron, 11n.
52. *Ovid: Metamorphoses*, ed. and trans., Frank Justus Miller (Cambridge, MA: Harvard University Press, 1964), Book 10, ll. 247–54.
53. *Ovid's Metamorphoses*, trans. Rolfe Humphries (Bloomington, IN: University of Indiana Press, 1983), Book 10, ll. 247–54.
54. Robert J. Blanch and Julian N. Wasserman, *From Pearl to Gawain: Forme to Fynisment* (Gainesville, FL: University of Florida Press, 1995), 56.
55. The Middle English word "make" can mean mate, wife, spouse or equal.
56. "Delyt" can denote both joy and sensual pleasure. Chaucer's remarks in the consummation scene in *Troilus and Criseyde* suggest an instance when the word "delyt" conveys both sentiments: "Of hire *delit* or joies oon the leeste / Were impossible to my wit to seye; / But juggeth ye that han ben at the feste" (Book III, ll. 1310–13, my emphasis). See *The Riverside Chaucer*, ed. Larry D. Benson (Boston, MA: Houghton Mifflin Company, 1987).
57. Andrew and Waldron note, "Implicit in this passage is the familiar metaphor drawn from secular love, of passion overcoming reason and the lover being smitten by beauty through the eyes" (108n).
58. *Julian of Norwich: A Revelation of Love*, ed. Marion C. Glasscoe (Exeter: University of Exeter Press, 1993), 114.
59. "Bitwene Marsh and Averil" is found in B.M. Harley 2253 and printed in Luria and Hoffman, 23.
60. Consider line 1204 in terms of John 3:29.

2 Allegorical Meaning
Rejoicing in Salvation

The exquisitely beautiful, fourteenth-century, Middle English dream vision *Pearl* can be interpreted as an allegory. Several literary scholars certainly have seen the Pearl-Maiden as an allegorical figure, interpreting her variously as a representation of maidenhood or virginity,[1] the Dreamer's own soul,[2] the Dreamer's own soul in mystical union with Christ (qua *sponsa Christi*),[3] the Dreamer's regenerate soul, eternal life, and/or beatitude,[4] the Dreamer's lost innocence,[5] the perfectly innocent (that is, the members of the Church to be included in the celestial process of the 144,000),[6] an angel,[7] and "the image of Heaven, instructing him [the Dreamer] in Christian doctrine. His yearning for her is at once a human inclination and a manifestation of the divine within him."[8] J.R.R. Tolkien, who firmly believed the poem to be an elegy that emerged from the life experience of the poet,[9] still acknowledged the existence of allegorical aspects to *Pearl*. He saw the Pearl-Maiden as the "spirit of celestial charity."[10] He also noted that while the poem is not a complete allegory, like the *Romance of the Rose* or the *Vision of Piers Plowman*, nevertheless there are "minor allegories within *Pearl*,"[11] such as the Parable of the Laborer in the Vineyard and the opening stanza itself, in which the pearl, slipping from the Dreamer's hand and into the grass, represents the death and burial of the beloved Pearl-Maiden.

Like J.R.R. Tolkien, we can read *Pearl* as an elegy with allegorical elements—or even an elegy on one level of meaning and an allegory on another level of meaning. The two understandings need not oppose one another, but can instead mutually inform one another. Allegory is not simply a generic form that presents allegorical figures with a one-to-one correspondence to a particular vice or virtue. *Allegoresis* is a creative process, a complex sign system used by medieval poets not only for interpretation of scripture, but also for the composition of poetry. As Ann Meyer insightfully observes:

> Some readers may be inclined to associate allegory with representation of abstract thought through personification. This is wholly inaccurate in complex medieval allegory. A character's name called "Avarice," or "Greed," does not require interpretation. Personification of an idea requires little reflection on the meaning to be conveyed. Complex

allegory, however, like that which we see in *Pearl*, requires the reader to participate as pilgrim, as dreamer in constant movement toward beatitude.[12]

Indeed, the poem invites readers into a complex and creative process of interpretation in many ways. It is the purpose of this chapter to explore three of those ways: the allegorical use of spiritual language, allusions to Ovidian love stories, and the implications of liturgical time in the structure and narrative of *Pearl*.

Subtly but surely, the language of *Pearl*, which so often has a double sense, invites allegorical interpretation. The *Pearl*-poet's memory of two classical myths, that of Orpheus and Eurydice (implied) and that of Pygmalion and Galatea (overt), invokes not only the Virgilian and Ovidian sources but also the tradition of allegorical interpretation associated with them. For the strategies used in scriptural interpretation were also used to "moralize" these classical myths and relate them to Christian faith in the *Pearl*-poet's day. Furthermore, the poem invokes the larger spiritual (*sic* allegorical) universe because it is structured in relation to liturgical time.

Liturgical readings, with their typological pairing of Old and New Testament texts, were selected to honor seasons and feasts throughout the year that recurred cyclically and highlighted not simply a literal, chronological unfolding of earthly history but also a spiritual, eternal unfolding of heavenly reality.[13] In *Pearl*, these two ways of understanding time intersect when heaven and earth meet in a dream: the Dreamer falls asleep in a garden in August remembering the loss of his beloved Pearl-Maiden and then sees a vision of her in Paradise before witnessing a Paschal vision of the New Jerusalem complete with the bleeding Lamb in procession; he finally awakens once more with the image of the Eucharistic bread and wine from the Mass in mind. The poem's triptych structure, with the central drama (the journey toward the resurrection hope of Easter) set in one time and the two "outside panels" (both set in Ordinary Time) framing it, corresponds to one of the major ways medieval interpreters of scripture sought to represent in art eternal truths unfolding for time-bound human beings. Understanding the liturgical contexts of *Pearl*—seasons, two important dates, and the lessons read during the Mass on those dates—can broaden our understanding of the potential allegorical significance of the Pearl-Maiden herself.

Before examining the use of spiritual language, Ovidian love stories, and liturgical time in the poem, this chapter will consider the larger world of medieval allegorical tradition that provides the context for the *Pearl*-poet's creativity.

The World of Medieval Allegory

During the Middle Ages, commentators often interpreted the Bible either literally or allegorically. The Bible itself provided the impetus for allegorical reading in the epistle to the Galatians, in which the apostle Paul considered

Hagar and Sarah to represent two covenants, with Hagar corresponding conceptually to slavery and the Mosaic law given at Mount Sinai (which Paul further equates with first-century Jerusalem) while Sarah stands for freedom and life through the Spirit in the heavenly Jerusalem.[14] Following Paul's exegetical example, medieval biblical commentators began to interpret the whole Bible in allegorical terms. While there was a general distinction between the literal (historical) and the allegorical (spiritual) senses of scripture, the understanding of allegory gradually developed to include the allegorical, moral, and anagogical senses.[15] A saying developed to explain the four senses of scripture: *littera gesta docet, quod credas allorgia, moralia quod agas, quo tendas anagogia* ("the literal teaches deeds, the allegorical what you believe, the moral what you do, and the anagogical where you are going.") Thus, the allegorical sense could include or be distinguished from the moral and anagogical senses.

The typological understanding of scripture developed as another form of allegorical interpretation in which specific places, persons, and events ("types") in the Old Testament were linked to specific people, places, and events in the New Testament that somehow corresponded to or fulfilled their antecedents ("antitypes"). In John's gospel, Jesus himself makes this kind of connection when he foretells his own crucifixion by saying:

> Et sicut Moses exaltavit serpentem in deserto, ita exaltari oportet Filium hominis ut omnis qui credit in ipso non pereat sed habeat vitam aeternam.
>
> (John 3:14)
>
> ("For just as Moses lifted up the serpent in the desert, so must the Son of Man be lifted up in order that all who believe in him may not perish but have eternal life.")[16]

From this origin, typological exegesis proliferated; the apotheosis of medieval typology is, perhaps, the fifteenth-century block-book known as *Biblia pauperum* with its elaborate triptych-structured pages featuring 40 scenes from the life of Christ in the center with two side panels depicting corresponding events from the Hebrew Bible.[17]

Ann Meyer's detailed exposition of the word "allegory" reflects how allegoresis further developed through Augustine's study of scripture:

> The word "allegory" combines the Greek *allos* (other) and *agoreuein* (to speak). The meaning conveyed by the Greek, *allegoria*, then, is "to speak otherwise," "to say other things." The single use of the word (as a participle), *allêgoroumena* in the New Testament appears in Paul's Letter to the Galatians (4.24) to designate the relation between Old and New Covenants. Other uses of the word and its related forms appear in writings of major theologians in the medieval west. Augustine, for example, cites Paul's Letter to Galatians and glosses it with the

phrase, *quae sunt aliud ex alio significantia* ("which things signify one thing by another") [*De Trinitate* XV 9; see *also civ. Dei* XV 18–19]. Ancient and medieval writers used "allegory" and its related verbal and adjectival forms in conjunction with, and often as a substitution for, a whole range of terms to designate identical or closely related meanings. These terms include *symbolon* (symbol), *figura* (figure), *signum* (sign), *imago* (image), *eikon* (icon), and *aenigma* (enigma). To cite the influential example of Augustine once again, he shows great flexibility in his use of *allegoria* and *figura* in biblical exegesis, not wishing to distinguish these terms from the Pauline *typos* (Lat. figura in I Corinthians 10.6) and *typikôs* (Lat. figura in I Corinthians 10.11) or from *similitude*, *umbra*, *sacramentum*, *mysteria*, and *imago*.[18]

Augustinian thought in turn influenced the whole of scriptural and literary interpretation in the Middle Ages.

In universities and monasteries, educated medieval readers familiar with the tradition of allegorical and typological exegesis of the Bible began to apply their interpretive skills not only to the scriptures but to classical literature as well. While, as Charles Singleton first pointed out years ago writing about Dante's *Convivio*, the "allegory of the theologians" commenting on the Bible was recognized for its correspondence to divine truth, the "allegory of the poets" commenting on Greco-Roman mythology was typically regarded as delightful fiction.[19] In practice, the process of discovering Christian allegorical possibilities in classical literature essentially redeemed Greco-Roman mythology for medieval readers, making it possible to integrate it into the university curricula and intellectual culture of the late Middle Ages.[20] This can be seen in three examples: Boethius's *Consolation of Philosophy*, Guillaume de Lorris's *Romance of the Rose,* and Dante's *Divine Comedy*, each of which develops an allegorical sense from an elegiac moment, integrates classical and Christian love stories, and, in Dante's case, specifically uses liturgical time to shape the narrative of his journey through the spiritual realms of hell, purgatory, and heaven.

For Boethius, the elegiac moment occurs with his loss of freedom, for he most likely wrote the *Consolation of Philosophy* either while in exile under house arrest or in prison awaiting execution. His dialogue represents his speaking to Philosophy, who is personified as a woman, an allegorical figure. Boethius was a devout Christian, but the Christianity he expresses in the *Consolation* is limited, and instead he adapts a great deal of classical knowledge (including the love story of Orpheus and Eurydice) in order to make his point that there is a God and everything is secondary to that divine providence.[21] For Lorris, the elegiac moment is bound to his experience of *fin amour*, which may or may not be unrequited but is certainly unfulfilled.[22] This inspires him to write a complete and elaborate allegory about the Lover pursuing the Rose, who proves unattainable because of multiple allegorical obstacles and despite multiple allegorical helpers. The medieval French text is dense with allusion to both classical and Christian material. For Dante, the elegiac moment is the death of his beloved Beatrice.[23] Throughout his *Divine Comedy*, he interweaves classical and Christian stories as he encounters countless souls on his journey through the other world. Famously, his journey takes place during Holy Week of the year 1300, so that like Christ and medieval Christians celebrating in memorial, he goes through hell during Good Friday, Purgatory during Holy Saturday, and heaven during Resurrection Sunday.

Many scholars have drawn comparisons between the *Pearl* and all three of these great works.[24] Although it cannot be proved that the *Pearl*-poet knew these works or their authors directly, nevertheless he was an educated medieval Christian in a cultural milieu that would empower him to use the same strategies as Boethius, Lorris, and Dante: to experience a literal, elegiac moment of loss as an opportunity for meditation that would lead him to compose in an allegorical manner, to interweave classical and Christian knowledge to make a moral point, and to set the narrative of his journey in the context of a liturgical (that is, spiritual and cyclical rather than calendric and chronological) time-frame. As this study shows, the *Pearl*-poet carefully crafted his poem using each of these strategies, and he begins with language that can be dually interpreted on a literal and allegorical level—using this as an invitation to the readers who can then ponder his Christian use of classical love stories as well as of liturgical time.

The Spiritual Language of *Pearl*

As readers of *Pearl* have recognized for decades, the poem is one that defies a strictly literal interpretation. It does possess a literal sense, which is certainly the foundation and inspiration of *Pearl*. But *Pearl* is no prose memoir in which a man patiently remembers his grief over the death of his beloved. The poem is far more complicated than that. The *Pearl*-poet invites allegorical interpretation of his poem by purposefully ambiguating the literal or historical sense, by direct allusion and paraphrasing of biblical matter that has an allegorical or spiritual meaning and by word-play and *double-entendre*.[25]

Consider just two of the most obvious examples from the beginning of the poem. First, the lost pearl is clearly not just a literal pearl that was fished out of an oyster, but rather a rich symbol, the vehicle of a metaphor with more than one tenor. Second, the landscape of the Dreamer's vision—with sands of orient pearls, cliffs of crystal, and trees of blue and silver—is clearly not meant to recall any specific earthly geography but is instead an allegorical landscape with closest connections to the mysteries of the east, India, and Paradise. The poet is constantly at play with his pearl and his increasingly fabulous geography. He refuses to reduce either his central symbol, the pearl, or his exquisitely bejeweled landscape to one tenor, to one literal or historical sense. This is part of the power of his poetry, one of the strategies for inviting readers to understand his poem allegorically.

A second invitation is evident in his allusions and paraphrases of biblical material that have an allegorical or spiritual sense. Again, the two most obvious examples from the poem include the Pearl-Maiden's re-telling of the Parable of the Laborers in the Vineyard and the Dreamer's vision of the New Jerusalem.[26] Readers familiar with the biblical sources of these passages know that the penny in question in the parable represents salvation, and the New Jerusalem, from John's Apocalypse, is a picture of God's heavenly kingdom.[27] The penny and Jerusalem, though they have a literal sense and historical incarnation, simultaneously have a spiritual meaning. In *Pearl*, they act as "vehicles" of the metaphor, the allegory, with a "tenor" hidden precisely so it can be revealed. These biblical precedents and their re-tellings in *Pearl* act as a second invitation to the reader to search for the allegorical meaning of the poem.

A third invitation is issued repeatedly throughout the poem in the form of word-play and *double-entendre*. It is interesting, for example, to consider how the reality of what the Dreamer is seeing in his vision is undermined by the Pearl-Maiden when she says:

> *Þou says þou trawez me in this dene*
> *Bycawse þou may with eʒen me se;*
> Another, þou says in þys countré
> Þyself schal won with me ryʒt here;
> Þe þrydde, to passe þys water fre:
> Þat may no joyful jueler. (ll.295–300, my emphases)[28]

When the Pearl-Maiden says, "You say that you believe me to be here in this valley / Because you see me with your eyes," her statement implies that the Dreamer's vision of the Pearl-Maiden does not correspond to her corporeal or real presence.[29] This idea is further intensified in the poet's description of the Pearl-Maiden as one type of *figura*, a figure representing not what is seen but something that is unseen.

When the Dreamer first sees the Pearl-Maiden, after his spirit has sprung from the garden spot into the space of his dream, he studies her face:

> The more I frayste hyr fayre face,
> Her *fygure* fyn quen I had fonte,
> Suche gladande glory con to me glace
> As lyttel byfore þerto watz wonte. (ll. 169–72)

Here, the Dreamer studies the Pearl-Maiden's face and "figure," and her figure seems at first to correspond literally to her body. In fact, the Middle English Dictionary glosses the word "fygure" as "appearance" or "representation." But the Middle English "fygure" is a loanword from the Latin *figura* that appears to include its original denotation. Meditation on the medieval understanding of the Latin *figura* suggests a broader range of possible meaning.

Erich Auerbach has written meaningfully about *figura* in his seminal work, *Scenes from the Drama of European Literature*:

> Figural interpretation establishes a connection between two events or persons, the first of which signifies not only itself but also the second, while the second encompasses or fulfills the first. The two poles of the figure are separate in time, but both, being real events or figures, are within time, within a stream of historical life. Only the understanding of the two persons or events is a spiritual act, but the spiritual act deals with concrete events whether past, present, or future, and not with concepts or abstractions; these are quite secondary, since promise and fulfillment are real historical events, which would have either happened in the incarnation of the Word or will happen in the second coming.[30]

Hence medieval theological understandings of relationships between the Old Testament and the New Testament—wherein, for example, the Tree of the Knowledge of Good and Evil is related to the Cross, the first Adam is related to the second Adam, that is Christ; and Eve is related to Mary and so on—become the basis for typological interpretation not only of scripture, but of the classical mythology and history that medieval readers inherited. In *Pearl*, and other medieval literature, figural interpretation also became a mode of generating poetry and meaning within that poetry. Within the framework of the poem, the Pearl-Maiden herself can be seen as a figure that corresponds allegorically to something else.

Of course, the Pearl-Maiden might not be only a strictly allegorical figure, but an anagogical one—possessed, in fact and by the poet's intention, of a future sense. As Henri de Lubac writes, definitions of allegory by Quintilian and St. Ambrose were both popular in the Middle Ages: Quintilian said allegory "points to something in words but something else in sense," while Ambrose asserted "there is allegory when one thing is being done, another is being figured."[31] In Christian allegory, that "something else," as Quintilian named it, often concerns what is to come, especially the person of Jesus. Thus, allegorical figures are *futura mysteria*.[32] At the simple level of comparison, just as a woman in the Proverbs represents wisdom; a lady in Boethius's *Consolatio* represents philosophy; and Beatrice in Dante's *Divine Comedy* represents Christ, divine love, and blessedness, so the Pearl-Maiden represents some essential quality of the divine being revealed in this poem. What might that be?

The Dreamer considers the Pearl-Maiden as a figure a second time in the poem, after her lengthy homily on the Parable of the Laborers in the Vineyard.

> O maskelez perle in perlez pure,
> Þat berez, quoþ I, þe perle of prys,
> Quo formed þe þy fayre *fygure*? (ll. 745–47, my emphasis)

This question is followed by allusions to Pygmalion, who shaped Galatea from ivory and then fell in love with her, as well as to Aristotle. It appears that the Dreamer has been gazing at the Pearl-Maiden's body while she has been preaching to him about his soul. And it may be literally true that the Dreamer's gaze is focused on the Pearl-Maiden's embodied person. But typologically and allegorically, there are deeper implications.

The question, "Who formed thy fair figure?," deserves consideration. It is an invitation to interpret the Pearl-Maiden as an allegorical figure. The question prompts multiple answers. On one level, in the world of medieval England, it is certainly the poet who formed this figure of the Pearl-Maiden for consideration. On another level, however, in the world imagined in the poem and according to the world-view of the poet's anticipated audience, it is clearly God, the "Fasor"—the Creator—who made her. How might the poet in England, or God in the poem, intend this figure to be understood? The meaning is hidden, as allegorical meaning often is, at a deeper, allusive level: in the *Pearl*-poet's understanding of the love stories of Orpheus and Eurydice and Pygmalion and Galatea that undergird the poem called *Pearl*.

The Memory of Ovidian Love Stories in *Pearl*

The Bible was not the only medieval text interpreted at four levels of meaning in the Middle Ages. Secular literature and legends, particularly the Greco-Roman classics, were also searched by medieval readers to discover both a literal and an allegorical sense. In this period, Christian allegorical commentaries on classical stories began to circulate among the learned, and, as is the case with Boethius, Lorris, Dante, and the *Pearl*-poet, began to be used not only to interpret Latin texts but also to compose poetry.

This is particularly true of the Orpheus legend. As Sarah Stanbury has noted, "Like Orpheus, a bereaved lover who sings stories of lovers, the *Pearl* narrator comes to his garden to mourn the death of a girl and there attempts to resolve his loss through repeated encounters with her transformed body."[33] Yet the connections between the Orpheus legend and *Pearl* go beyond the elegiac connections of mourning, a man's meditation on a woman's body, and the feminist master plots that Stanbury analyzes from the viewpoint of modern psychoanalytic and cinematic theory; they concern the fundamental literary context of allegorical interpretation in the medieval period. Understanding this requires readers to remember the story of Orpheus and learn about medieval allegorical interpretations of it in order to see the relation to *Pearl*.

Orpheus was born in Thrace, the son of a muse, and he had the gift of music. When he played the lyre, all of nature responded by listening, as if captivated by a spell. Animals that were usually enemies, like predatory lions who seized upon lambs for prey, would make peace with one another at the sound of Orpheus' lyre. It so happened that this Orpheus fell in love and sought to marry his beloved Eurydice. On the day of their wedding, however, she stepped on an adder that bit her ankle, and from the poison of the snakebite, she died. Orpheus, grieving from this loss, went nearly mad. He went throughout the world until he found an entrance into Hades. He descended to the underworld, and there, playing his lyre, he made his way—a living being—into the realms of the dead. He won an audience with Hades himself and his dark queen, Persephone, whose hearts were somehow softened by his music. They agreed to give Eurydice back to Orpheus on the condition that he not look back at her until both of them had emerged from hell. But when they had almost reached the exit that would have brought them back above the earth, Orpheus did look back, and he lost his love a second time.

Thereafter, Orpheus did not love women, but boys, and wandered the world unhappy. Some legends say he was one of the Argonauts who sailed with Jason in search of the Golden Fleece; others say that he had a son, Museaus, who was gifted as he was. But Orpheus's life ended when Maenads, ecstatic worshippers of Bacchus, tore his body apart in one of their fits of religious madness. The head of Orpheus drifted in the Mediterranean until it came to Lesbos, where it was enshrined. But the soul of Orpheus descended into Hades and was reunited with Eurydice in Elyseum.

This, at least, is the legend as Ovid recollects it in the *Metamorphoses* (X.1–111 and XI.1–84).[34] Virgil also recalls the story in the fourth book of the *Georgics*. The Virgilian tale is slightly different, however, as it includes the shepherd Aristeas, a man who is rapaciously chasing Eurydice on the day of her wedding. It is because of Aristeas that she runs, treads on the snake, and is consequently bitten and poisoned to death. The motivations for Orpheus's backward glance are different in Ovid and Virgil as well. In Ovid, Orpheus looks back because of his love for Eurydice and his concern that she may stumble. In contrast, in Virgil, the *incautum amantem* ("incautious lover") Orpheus looks back because a sudden madness (*dementia*) seizes him.[35] Furthermore, in Ovid, Eurydice's response to Orpheus is a barely audible farewell, given with the suggestion that she knows he loves her. In Virgil, Eurydice verbally chastises Orpheus for his moral failure before her spirit returns to Hades. These differences reflect Ovid's emphasis on passionate love and Virgil's on Stoic morality.

A third version of the Orpheus story can be found in Boethius's *Consolation of Philosophy*. In it, Boethius presents the first allegorical reading of the story. Commenting on Orpheus's backward glance toward Eurydice, he writes:

> Nam qui Tartareum in specus
> Victus lumina flexerit,
> Quidquid praecipuum trahit
> Perdit dum videt inferos.
>
> (The conquered one who has turned
> the light of his eyes toward the cave of Tartarus
> loses the precious things he brought forth
> when he sees the things below.)[36]

52 Allegorical Meaning

The Ovidian, Virgilian, and Boethian versions of the Orpheus story were transmitted to medieval readers as school texts that were read, paraphrased, and commented upon in Latin. They were also translated into the vernacular languages of Western Europe. The significant body of commentary on the Orpheus story has been considered by John Block Friedman in his book, *Orpheus in the Middle Ages*.[37]

It is clear that allegorical commentary on Orpheus divided into two basic schools. The first, in the field of morality, viewed Orpheus as an allegorical figure of "reason" and Eurydice as a figure of "sensuality." This reading begins with Remigius of Auxerre (ca. 904) in his commentary on Boethius and is evident in the late-thirteenth or early-fourteenth century French commentary *Ovide moralisee*.[38] The other, in the field of music or rhetoric, viewed Orpheus as a representative of the "best voice" and Eurydice as that of "profound judgment." This reading also originates with Remigius of Auxerre in his commentary on the *De Nuptiis* of Martianus Capella and is evident in Dante's *Convivio*.[39] By the eleventh century, as C. Stephen Jaeger has shown, the authors of "The Marriage of Mercury and Philology," "Quid suum virtutis," and the Liège Songs were all using the Orpheus story as an allegory for the individual's educational progress: "Orphic poetry has a civilizing mission like that of rhetoric as the educator of warriors and temperer of royal judgment ... Orpheus and Eurydice becomes a defining myth for the mission of the educated man."[40] This theme that Jaeger identifies in the commentaries adds a third dimension to understanding the treatment of Orpheus in the commentaries and thus in *Pearl*.

While many medieval Christian commentaries on the legend of Orpheus echo the stoicism of Virgil or the moralizing of Boethius, some pay particular attention to the Ovidian emphasis on love between Orpheus and Eurydice in the *Metamorphoses*. Because of the wide-spread Christian belief in the miracle of resurrection, the translations, paraphrases, and commentaries on the Orpheus story began to imagine that Orpheus's love had the power to bring Eurydice back from the dead. In Middle English vernacular literature, the notable example is, of course, the romance *Sir Orfeo*.[41] In these retellings, Eurydice no longer languishes in hell but is instead set free from the bonds of death (or, in the case of *Sir Orfeo*, the nether-world of the King of Faery) and then restored to her husband. This new ending to the legend seems to have been made possible because of allegorical interpretations of the story that viewed Orpheus as a type of Christ and Eurydice a type of the human soul.[42]

Perhaps the most apt allegorical interpretation of Orpheus in this vein, insofar as it relates to *Pearl*, comes from Pierre Bersuire in the fourteenth century:

> Dic allegorice quod Orpheus, filius solius, est Christus, filius dei patris, qui a principio Euridicem .i. animam humanam per caritatem & amorem duxit ipsamque per specialem prerogativam a principio sibi coniunxit. Verumtamen serpens, diabolus, ipsam novam nuptam .i. de novo creatam, dum flores colligeret .i. de pomo vetito appeteret, per

temptationem momordit, & per peccatum occidit, & finaliter ad infernum transmisit. Quod videns Orpheus Christus in infernum personaliter voluit descendere & sic uxorem suam .i. humanam naturam rehabuit, ipsamque de regno tenebrarum ereptam ad superos secum duxit, dicens illud Canticorum .ii. "Surge, propera amica mea & veni."

(Let us speak allegorically and say that Orpheus, the child of the sun, is *Christ the son of God the Father*, who from the beginning led Eurydice, that is, *the human soul*, to himself. And from the beginning, Christ joined her to himself through his special prerogative. But the devil, a serpent, drew near *the new bride*, that is, created *de novo*, while she collected flowers, that is, while she seized the forbidden apple, an bit by her temptation and killed by her sin, and finally she went to the world below. Seeing this, *Christ-Orpheus wished to descend to the lower world and thus he retook his wife*, that is, human nature, ripping her from the hands of the ruler of Hell himself; and he led her with him to the upper world, saying this verse from Canticles 2:10: "Rise up, my love, my fair one, and come away.")[43]

Here, Orpheus appears as a figure of Christ, and Eurydice is a figure of the human soul, the bride of Christ. The serpent Eurydice stepped on is the devil, and Orpheus's descent into hell is Christ's harrowing of hell.[44] In Bersuire's commentary, no longer is Orpheus's backward glance a moral failing; now it is a moral imperative because it represents Christ's desire to seek and save the lost.

The *Pearl*-poet was apparently well aware of the medieval commentary tradition on scripture and secular literature that interpreted texts in terms of their literal, allegorical, moral, and anagogical senses. He was familiar with Ovid's *Metamorphoses*, and there are intriguing literal parallels between the elegiac plot of *Pearl* and the legend of Orpheus and Eurydice: the love of a man for a woman who dies before that love can be consummated in marriage, the man's grief over her loss, and the man's pursuit of her in the other-world.[45] The Dreamer appears in the poem as an Ovidian Orphic figure, looking back in love and fear. He seems to view himself as reasonable and the Pearl-Maiden as sensual, along the Remigian allegorical interpretive lines laid down in the *Ovide moralisé*, but the Pearl-Maiden seems to view his voice and hers in Dantesque terms: a "best voice" whose questions evoke her "profound judgment." Yet there is another Orphic figure in the poem, one who corresponds not to the literal one in Ovid's *Metamorphoses* but who rather corresponds to the allegorical one exemplified in Bersuire's commentary: Christ.

When the Dreamer asks, "Who formed your fair figure?," the Pearl-Maiden's answer takes the reader farther away from the literal sense and deeper into the allegorical meaning, for it emphasizes the Pearl-Maiden's marriage to her matchless Lamb.

'My makelez Lambe þat al may bete,
Quoþ scho, 'my dere Destyné,

> Me ches to Hys make, althaʒ vnmete
> Sumtyme semed that assemblé.
> When I wente fro yor worlde wete
> He calde me to Hys bonerté:
> "Cum hyder to Me, My lemman swete,
> For mote ne spot is non is þee."' (ll. 757–64)

The answer itself is allegorical, a spiritual picture, because no literal girl dressed in pearls ever married a white lamb, of course, but the soul of a virgin girl who died young and entered into heaven could certainly be understood by medieval Christians as married to Christ Jesus, who is called the Lamb because He was sacrificed.[46] It is Christ in the poem who draws near "the new bride," who descends to the "lower world" to retake his wife, and who says, "Come hither to me" and "Rise up, my love, my fair one, and come away." So there are clearly parallels between the Ovidian Orpheus story and the literal, elegiac experience of the Dreamer in *Pearl*, and at the same time, there is a parallel between Bersuire's Orpheus and the spiritual, allegorical sense of Christ's actions in *Pearl*. Thus, both the Dreamer in the first case and Christ in the second case can be Orphic figures.

Clear parallels to the love story of Orpheus and Eurydice emerge in *Pearl* when examined in the light of the commentary tradition on Ovid's *Metamorphoses*. Yet the two mythological figures are not mentioned directly in the poem. Instead, their presence in the poet's memory, creating parallels in his poem, remains implied rather than overt.[47]

The poet does name Pygmalion and alludes to Galatea, two figures from another Ovidian love story. These two lovers had a rich tradition of allegorical interpretation associated with them in the Middle Ages as well. The reference to Pygmalion comes immediately after the Dreamer's question, "Who formed your fair figure?":

> 'O maskelez perle in perlez pure,
> Þat berez,' quoth I, 'þe perle of prys,
> Quo formed þe þy fayre fygure?
> Þat wrogt þy wede he watz ful wys;
> Þy beauté com neuer of nature—
> Pymalyon paynted neuer þy vys,
> Ne Arystotel nawþer by hys lettrure
> Of carped þe kynde þese propertéz;
> Þy colour passez þe flour-de-lys,
> Þyn angel-hauyng so clene cortez.' (ll. 745–54)

In this passage, the poet's reference to Pygmalion in the Dreamer's voice invokes a complex array of interpretive possibilities. Because Pygmalion and Galatea were lovers, at one level, this moment invokes romantic love, associating Pygmalion with the Dreamer and Galatea with the Pearl-Maiden.

At another level, Pygmalion corresponds to the poet himself. In the context of these lines, his allusion is not only to the Ovidian lover but to the Ovidian sculptor-artist who had the power to imitate and create life. For that is what Pygmalion did when he formed Galatea from ivory (artistic imitation), prayed for Venus to breathe life into her, and once she awakened to his kisses made love to her so that she gave birth to their daughter, Paphos (natural pro-creation).[48]

The poet even dares to venture into the debate over which force had the greater power, art or nature, when he makes the Dreamer assert: "Your beauty never came from nature—Pygmalion never painted your face!"[49] An odd claim, since, if her beauty comes neither from the Pearl-Maiden's earthly nature nor from the poet's art, readers are left to wonder where it does come from. Does the poet seek to imply, through the Dreamer's astonishment, that heavenly grace is the source of the Pearl-Maiden's beauty? An answer, once again, can be found in the commentary tradition.

Like Orpheus and Eurydice, Pygmalion and Galatea appear in the *Metamorphoses* but take on a larger life in the medieval commentary traditions. On the one hand, Pygmalion stood for the literary debate over the value of art versus nature, as exemplified in Jean de Meun's *Roman de la Rose* in the twelfth century,[50] Chaucer's "Physician's Tale" in the fourteenth century, and the Jean Molinet's *Roman de la Rose Moralisé* in the fifteenth century. It is interesting to consider a Chaucerian view as he, the *Pearl*-poet's contemporary, allows Nature to assert to her pride of place over Art—in a way that specifies why and gives insight about the origin of the Pearl-Maiden's beauty:

> ... Lo, I, Nature,
> Thus kan I forme and peynte a creature,
> Whan that me liste: who kan me contrefete?
> Pigmalion noght, though he ay forge and bête,
> Or grave or peynte ...
> For He that is the formere principal
> Hath maked me his vicaire general,
> To forme and peynten erthely creaturis
> Right as me list ...
> My lord and I been ful of oon accord.
> I made hire to the worshipe of my lord;
> So do I alle myne other creatures,
> What colour that they han or what figures. (PhysT, ll. 11–15, 19–22, 25–28)[51]

In this case, Nature is supreme over Art and especially Art as represented by Pygmalion, specifically because she is the vicar of the "formere principal," the first shaper, God. By comparing the Pygmalion reference here in Chaucer's *Canterbury Tales* to the one in the *Pearl*-poet's poem, we see the clear implication that the Pearl-Maiden's beauty does ultimately come not from Art (Pygmalion) or Nature, but from God.

But the correspondence between Pygmalion and Art is not always consistent. In addition to his allegorical meaning, he also has a typological significance. In the *Ovide moralisé* and Molinet's *Roman de la Rose Moralisé*, he comes to stand for the divine. Claire M. Croft has aptly stated how in her comparison of the treatment of Pygmalion in both works:

> The author [of the *Ovide moralisee*] first claims that Pygmalion and his statue represents a great lord taking in a poor girl, who is beautiful, but knows nothing of the world around her. After educating her, the Lord falls in love with her and takes her as his wife. The author of the *Ovide moralisee* continues that "autre sentence i puet avoir" (X, v. 3586) and presents a second interpretation of the account. It is the second interpretation of the Pygmalion account which is a specifically Christian one, equating Pygmalion with God, and the statue with God's creation, mankind. This is analogous to Molinet's interpretation, reading into the Pygmalion myth the story of the Creator and his chosen people. However, where Molinet chooses to see Pygmalion as representing Christ, the author of the *Ovide moralisee* interprets him as God. Molinet equates the statue with the Church, whereas in the *Ovide moralisee* the statue is interpreted as the less specific notion of mankind.[52]

Thus, Pygmalion can stand for Art in opposition to God and his vicar, Nature, or in a startling reversal made possible by the complex nature of medieval allegory he can stand for God the Father rescuing humanity from sin or Christ the Son wedding the Church, His bride.[53]

When *Pearl* is read in light of the medieval commentary tradition on Pygmalion and Galatea, the Pearl-Maiden is confirmed in her typological role as the Bride of Christ,[54] and Christ emerges as not only the true Orpheus but the true Pygmalion as well. As we have already seen in the cases of Orpheus and Pygmalion, however, *figura* often correspond to more than one meaning, and this is true of the Pearl-Maiden, too.

Implications of the Use of Liturgical Time in Pearl

The Pearl-Maiden's marriage to the Lamb, like the Parable of the Laborers in the Vineyard and the Parable of the Merchant retold in the poem—like the penny and the pearl and the New Jerusalem—are all allegorical pictures signifying salvation. Yet it appears to be the salvation of the Dreamer's soul that is at issue in the poem, for the Pearl-Maiden clearly counsels him to forsake the world and purchase the pearl that is matchless (ll.743–44). This poem, whatever else it may be about, is certainly about salvation.[55] The pearl on the Pearl-Maiden's breast, drawn from the Parable of the Pearl

Allegorical Meaning 57

of Great Price by the poet into the allegorical world of the poem, symbolizes the possibility of winning the kingdom of heaven—that is, salvation—through the miraculous grace of an unexpected discovery; allegorically, the Pearl-Maiden herself may stand for joy in that salvation.[56]

Because, for medieval Christians, the drama of salvation was built into structures of remembrance—specifically the sacraments and the holy days of the liturgical year—it is no surprise that the *Pearl*-poet uses these structures to shape his poem. In exploring the use of liturgical time in *Pearl*, readers can venture to interpret another dimension of the Pearl-Maiden's allegorical significance: the relationship of joy to salvation.

The poet is vividly aware of the importance of liturgical time and the way that it communicates heavenly reality—eternity—to people living in earthly realms bound by time. To emphasize how heaven and earth meet in the garden of the Dreamer's mind, he uses key dates and parables from the Church's liturgy to structure his poem.[57] The poem is structured like a triptych, one that begins with the image of a garden in August and ends with the image of the bread and the wine of the Eucharist from the Mass (the outer panels) but focuses the reader's attention inward toward the dream and the Dreamer's spiritual progress on his Orphic journey toward the resurrection hope of Easter (the central panel).[58]

Although some scholars have previously associated *Pearl* with the feast of the Holy Innocents that takes place during the Christmas season,[59] closer examination suggests that two key liturgical dates are more relevant to the poem. They are the feast of Mary's Assumption that takes place on August 15th and celebration of the eve of Septuagesima Sunday that takes place three weeks before Lent. Once these liturgical contexts are noted, deeper understanding of the Pearl-Maiden's signifying power becomes possible.

The first liturgical season in the poem is worth examining more closely because this is when the Dreamer is grieving and remembering the losses he experienced in earlier seasons of the year. In August (Ordinary Time), in the first panel of the triptych as it were, he looks back and remembers his Lenten and Paschal experiences.

> To þat spot that I in speche expoun
> I entred in þat erber grene,
> *In Auguste in a hyȝ seysoun,*
> *Quen corne is coruen wyth crokez kene.* (ll. 37–40, my emphasis)

Scholars have suggested three ecclesiastical holidays might be meant by this reference to a "high season": Lammas on August 1st, the Transfiguration of Christ on August 6th, and the Assumption of the Virgin Mary on August 15th. Andrew and Waldron find Lammas to be the more probable date alluded to because it is the festival of the first wheat harvest of the year, and the very next line of the poem concerns harvest.[60] Harvesting imagery, in Christian tradition, is clearly associated with resurrection. Yet August 15th may be the more likely date because the line about the sickle being taken to the corn is a direct paraphrase of the Parable of the Growing Seed that is read as the gospel lesson in the liturgy of August 15th, Mary's Assumption Day.

> Sic est regnum Dei quemadmodum si homo iaciat sementem in terram et dormiat et exsurgat nocte ac die et semen germinet et increscat dum nescit ille ultro enim terra fructificat primum herbam deinde spicam deinde plenum frumentum in spica et cum se produxerit fructus statim mittit falcem quoniam adest messis.
>
> (So the kingdom of God is like a man who scatters seed on the ground. He sleeps and rises night and day, and the seed sprouts and grows, but he does not know how. Moreover, the earth produces first the blade, then the ear, then the full grain in the ear. But when the grain is ripe, at once he puts in the sickle because the harvest has come.)[61]

Within the poem, it seems that this is the day when the Dreamer remembers the loss of his beloved that occurred earlier in the year. Furthermore, it is more likely that the poet is alluding to Mary's Assumption Day than to the feast of Lammas, given the importance of Mary to the poet, who recognizes her as the Queen of Heaven and then closely associates the Pearl-Maiden with her in his poem.[62] This also fits better with the poet's tendency to create biblical paraphrases, especially of parables, from the lessons of the Mass in his poem.[63] He uses parables in this way in order to place events in his poem in the context of liturgical time.

The central parable of *Pearl* is, of course, the Parable of the Laborers in the Vineyard, which the Pearl-Maiden discourses upon in her sermon to the Dreamer as they stand separated from one another by the stream. In the Sarum Rite that was used in England in the fourteenth century (though not in the Roman one that is used today), that parable was read on Septuagesima Sunday three weeks before Lent began. Thus, the Parable of the Laborers in the Vineyard was usually read in January or February, as Lent is 40 days before Easter, and Easter is a movable feast. The repetition of the word "date," the concatenation word in the section of *Pearl* that retells the Parable of the Laborers, draws attention to the idea—as earlier with August 15th—that Septuagesima Sunday is the liturgical date on which the parable is read.

This prompts a reconsideration of the implications of liturgical time in the poem. Such reconsideration can lead to the conclusion that the Dreamer's vision unfolds, in a spiritual sense, between Septuagesima Sunday (when the Parable of the Laborers in the Vineyard is read) and three weeks after Easter (when Revelation is read). The possibility that Septuagesima Sunday is the day that the Pearl-Maiden died is suggested by the Pearl-Maiden herself, who speaks of her death in metaphorical terms in this section of the poem[64] and by an investigation of what happened on Septuagesima Sunday in medieval churches: the burial of the alleluia.

Allegorical Meaning 59

In the Sarum Rite, three weeks before Lent begins and throughout the season of Lent itself, the alleluia is neither said nor sung. To recognize this significant change in the liturgy—the silencing of the alleluia—on the Saturday evening before Septuagesima Sunday, a procession, including the priest and the choirboys of the congregation, buries the alleluia, written on parchment, underground. A description of this can be found in the fifteenth-century statute book of the Church of Toul in France:

> On Saturday before Septuagesima Sunday, all the choir-boys gather in the sacristy during the prayer of the None to prepare for the burial of the Alleluia. After the last Benedicamus, they march in procession, with crosses, tapers, holy water, and censers, and they carry a coffin, as in a funeral. Thus they proceed through the aisle, moaning and mourning, until they reach the cloister. There they bury the coffin; they sprinkle it with holy water and incense it; whereupon, they return to the sacristy by the same way.[65]

The farewell to the alleluia is thus ceremonialized as if it were the burial of a beloved person.

The fact that the Dreamer bewails his pearl that has been closed in a "forser" (l. 263)—a casket—together with the emphasis on the word "date" in the section dealing with the Parable of the Laborers in the Vineyard, which is read on Septuagesima Sunday, prompts two questions: is the poet trying to tell us, literally and historically, that the Pearl-Maiden died on the evening before Septuagesima Sunday? Is the Pearl-Maiden, allegorically, a figure who stands for the alleluia?

In keeping with this latter possibility, it is noteworthy that the word *alleluia* never occurs in *Pearl*, but the Dreamer directly addresses the Pearl-Maiden as if she stands for a single word when he says:

> 'O perle,' quoþ I, 'of rych renoun
> So watz hit me dere þat þou con deme
> In þys veray avysyoun!
> *If hit be ueray and soth sermoun*
> *Þat þou so strykez in garlande gay,*
> So wel is me in þys doel-doungeoun
> Þat þou art to þat Prynsez paye. (1182–88, emphasis added)

The word "sermoun" is glossed by Andrew and Waldron to mean "speech" or "account" in this line, but like "fygure" (*figura*), it is a Middle English rendering of a Latin word, in this case, *sermo/sermonis*, which can mean "talk, conversation, discourse" or more simply "a word."[66] Marie Borroff, in her elegant modern English version of the poem, translates "sermoun" as "word" in this line.[67] The fact the Pearl-Maiden "strykez" ("strikes, pierces," or by connotative extension, "stands for, represents") this "sermoun" is evocative diction indeed.[68] It suggests that, allegorically interpreted, the Pearl-Maiden could be a figure of the Dreamer's *alleluia*: the "sermoun" (l. 1185), the one word, that represents his joy: "my blysse" (l. 372).[69]

Conclusions

The spiritual language, Ovidian love stories, and use of liturgical time in *Pearl* all invite allegorical interpretations of the poem. While there is clearly a literal, elegiac sense to the poem, there are also allegorical meanings. This makes perfect sense in light of the tradition of four-fold scriptural and literary interpretation in the Middle Ages, which the *Pearl*-poet clearly used to understand biblical parables and compose his poetic masterpiece. The poet's use of metaphoric language, memory of the legends of Orpheus and Eurydice and Pygmalion and Galatea, and astute interweaving of parables from the church liturgy alongside invocations of the Lenten and Paschal liturgical seasons within his dream vision all invite readers into a deeper understanding of the allegorical sense of *Pearl*. If we accept the invitation, we pass through an open door that, afterwards, no one can shut.[70] For once the possibilities of allegorical interpretation are re-captured, readers gain a richer sense not only of the elegiac meaning of the poem but also of the greater signifying power of *Pearl*.

Notes

1. Schofield, "Symbolism, Allegory, and Autobiography," 585–675.
2. Madeleva, *Pearl: A Study in Spiritual Dryness*.
3. Sister Mary Vincent Hillmann, "Interpretation," in *The Pearl: A New Translation and Interpretation*, trans. Hillmann (South Bend, IN: University of Notre Dame Press, 1961, 1967), xx.
4. M.P. Hamilton, "The Meaning of the Middle English *Pearl*," PMLA 70 (1955): 805–24.
5. A.C. Cawley and J.J. Anderson, "Introduction," in *Pearl, Cleanness, Patience, Sir Gawain and the Green Knight* (London: Dent, 1962, 1967), xi.
6. D.W. Robertson, "The Pearl as Symbol," 161.
7. Jane Chance, "Allegory and Structure in *Pearl*," 85.
8. Ann Meyer, *Medieval Allegory and the Building of the New Jerusalem*, 150.
9. J.R.R. Tolkien wrote, "It is overwhelmingly more probable that it [*Pearl*] too was founded on a real sorrow and drew its sweetness from a real bitterness." See "Introduction III: *Pearl*," in *Sir Gawain and the Green Knight, Pearl, and Sir Orfeo* (New York: Ballantine Books, 1975), 16.
10. Tolkien, "Introduction III: *Pearl*," 18.
11. Tolkien, "Introduction III: *Pearl*," 11.
12. Beal and Meyer, "Symbolism and Allegory in *Pearl*," (forthcoming).
13. The liturgical seasons of the Church were and are, of course, Advent, Christmas/Epiphany, Lent, Easter, Pentecost, and Ordinary Time.
14. See Gal. 4:21–31.
15. See Henri de Lubac, *Medieval Exegesis: The Four Senses of Scripture*, Vol. I, trans. Mark Sebanc (Grand Rapids, MI: Eerdmans, 1998) and Vol. II, trans.

E.M. Macierowski (Grand Rapids, MI: Eerdmans, 2000) and Vol. III, trans. E.M. Macierowski (Grand Rapids, MI: Eerdmans, 2009).
16. The verse here is quoted and translated from the *Biblia Sacra Vulgata* (Stuttgart, 1969, repr. 1994). See also Matt. 12:40, in which Jesus compares his death and burial to the three days Jonah spent in the belly of the whale, and 1 Cor. 15:45, in which Paul compares Adam and Christ, the new Adam.
17. For Paul's typological view of Adam and Christ, see 1 Cor. 15:45; for an edition of the *Biblia pauperum*, see Albert C. Labriola and John W. Smeltz, eds., *The Bible of the Poor: A Facsimile and Edition of BL Blockbook C.9 d.2* (Pittsburgh, PA: Dusquesne University Press, 1990). For discussion, see Jane Beal, "*Mens tua hortus meus est:* Christ and the Canticle Bride in the *Biblia pauperum*," *Integrité: A Journal of Faith and Learning* 14 (Fall 2015): 3–19.
18. Beal and Meyer, "Symbolism and Allegory," (forthcoming).
19. Charles Singleton, "Appendix: Two Kinds of Allegory," in *Commedia: Dante Studies I* (Cambridge: Harvard University Press, 1965) and further discussed in *Commedia: Elements of Structure* (Baltimore, MD: Johns Hopkins University Press, 1977).
20. See Jane Chance, *Medieval Mythography: From Roman North Africa to the School of Chartres, A.D. 433–1177* (Gainesville, FL: University of Florida Press, 1994).
21. Boethius's retelling of the Orpheus and Eurydice legend occurs in Book III, Meter 12 of his *Consolation of Philosophy.*
22. This contrasts with Jean de Meun's later, lengthy addition to the *Romance of the Rose*, which includes the rape of the rose near the end of the poem.
23. Dante's grief over Beatrice is made very clear in his *Vita Nuova*, a prelude to the *Divine Comedy.*
24. For a brief overview, see Marie Borroff's comments on "The Literary Background" in her introduction to her translation of the poem in *The Gawain Poet: Complete Works* (New York, NY: W.W. Norton, 2011), 118–19. For more specific detail, see Michael Cherniss, *Boethian Apocalypse: Studies in Middle English Vision Poetry* (Norman, OK: Pilgrim Books, 1987), 151–68; Herbert Pilch, "The Middle English *Pearl*: Its Relation to the *Roman de la Rose*," trans. Hyprath, 163–84; Warren Ginsberg, "Place and Dialectic in *Pearl* and Dante's *Paradiso*," *ELH* 55 (1988): 731–53.
25. Concatenation, which the poet uses to structure the entire poem, is important to recall when considering the multi-layered meaning of language of the poem. The same word that occurs at the beginning and end of each stanza in a section of the poem changes meaning throughout the section—and meaning may change depending on whether the Dreamer, the Pearl-Maiden, or the narrator is articulating the specific key word. For a discussion of *Pearl* that pays close attention to the poet's language, see the first chapter on *Pearl* in J.J. Anderson, *Language and Imagination in the Gawain-Poems* (Manchester: Manchester University Press, 2005), 17–81.
26. On the representation of the New Jerusalem in *Pearl*, see Rosalind Field, "The Heavenly Jerusalem in *Pearl*," *Modern Language Review* 81 (1986): 7–17, Stanbury, "The Body and the City in *Pearl*," 271–85, and Meyer, *Medieval Allegory and the Building of the New Jerusalem.*
27. For the parable of the vineyard, see Matt. 20:1–16. For the vision of the heavenly Jerusalem, see Rev. 21: 9–27, 22:1–5.
28. As previously mentioned, all quotations from the *Pearl* are taken from *The Poems of the Pearl Manuscript*, 5th ed. Malcolm Andrew and Ronald Waldron. Translations are my own.

62 *Allegorical Meaning*

29. I use the phrase "real presence" as an allusion to Christ's presence in the Eucharist. According to Catholic theology, Christ is really present in the sacrifice of the Eucharist upon the altar by a priest. Yet here, the Pearl-Maiden implies she is not really present in that way nor is she really present corporally. Everything is being shown to the Dreamer in a way he can understand *figuratively* (the vehicle) but not as it really is *spiritually* (the tenor) because he cannot grasp spiritual reality with his five senses—no time-bound, earth-bound person can—even in a dream. The Pearl-Maiden's presence in the dream is perhaps "more real" than the things of earth—but still not as fully real as she is in heaven. Thus we see the ineffable reality of heaven comes down to the Dreamer in his vision, but his experience of it is still only partial, an intimation of what will be, which fills his heart with longing and anticipation. For further thoughts in this vein, see J. Allan Mitchell, "The Middle English *Pearl*: Figuring the Unfigurable," *Chaucer Review* 35 (2000): 86–111.
30. Erich Auerbach, *Scenes from the Drama of European Literature*, trans. Ralph Manheim (Minneapolis: University of Minneapolis Press, 1984), 53. For discussion of Auerbach's ideas in relationship to interpreting *Pearl*, see Mitchell, "The Middle English *Pearl*: Figuring the Unfigurable," 87.
31. Henri de Lubac, *Medieval Exegesis, Volume 2: The Four Senses of Scripture*, trans. E.M. Macierowski (Grand Rapids, MI: Eerdmans, 2000), 89–90.
32. Ibid, 94.
33. Sarah Stanbury, "Feminist Masterplots: The Gaze on the Body of the *Pearl's* Dead Girl," 99. Note that Christopher Tolkien made comparison inevitable when he published his father J.R.R. Tolkien's modernized English versions of *Pearl* and *Sir Orfeo* in *Sir Gawain and the Green Knight, Pearl, Sir Orfeo* (New York, NY: Random House, 1979). J.R.R. Tolkien wrote in the essay prefacing his translation of *Pearl* that if the Dreamer had not been consoled at the poem's end, "he would have awakened by the mound again, not in the gentle and serene resignation of the last stanza, but still as he is first seen, *looking only backwards*, his mind filled with the horror of decay ..." (19, emphasis added). This phrase may suggest that Orpheus's backward glance was in Tolkien's mind when he wrote this essay. That the Dreamer is consoled shows how his Christian faith redeems his Orphic journey.
34. For a facing-page edition of the Latin and translation into English, see Ovid, *Metamorphoses*, trans. Frank Justus Miller, Loeb Classical Library Vol. II (Cambridge, MA: Harvard University Press, 1916, repr. 1939) or for a fine English translation, see Ovid, *Metamorphoses*, translated by Rolfe Humphries (Bloomington, IN: Indiana University Press, 1955, 1983).
35. Virgil, *Georgics*, trans. H. Rushton Fairclough, Loeb Classical Library Vol. 63 (Cambridge, MA: Harvard University Press, 1999), 252.
36. Boethius, *Theological Tractates and the Consolation of Philosophy*, ed. Jeffrey Henderson, Loeb Classical Library Vol. 74 (Cambridge, MA: Harvard University Press, 1973). The translation given here is my own.
37. John Block Friedman, *Orpheus in the Middle Ages* (Cambridge, MA: Harvard University Press, 1970; repr. Syracuse, NY: Syracuse University Press, 2000). See also a collection of essays on the subject, *Boethius in the Middle Ages: Latin and Vernacular Traditions of the Consolatio Philosophiae*, ed. Maarten J.F.M. Hoenen and Lodi Nauta (Leiden: Brill, 1997) and Gerard O'Daly, *The Poetry of Boethius* (Chapel Hill, NC: University of North Carolina Press, 1991).

38. Friedman, 98 and 124.
39. Ibid, 87–88.
40. C. Stephen Jaeger, "Orpheus in the Eleventh Century," *Mittellateinisches Jahrbuch* 27 (1992), 148.
41. Henryson's fifteenth-century Scottish version of the Orpheus and Eurydice legend is Boethian in character and reads the backward glance negatively, not allowing Eurydice to come back to life from death. However, in Walter Map's twelfth-century Latin *De Nugis Curialium*, there is a Celtic story with an Orphic plot, wherein a knight rescues his dead lady from a band of faery dancers, and the original folktale may have influenced *Sir Orfeo*. See Walter Map, *De Nugis Curialum*, ed. and trans. M.R. James, rev. by C.N.L. Brooke, and R.A.B. Mynors (Oxford: Clarendon Press, 1983).
42. C. Stephen Jaeger, "Orpheus in the Eleventh Century," 141–68.
43. Quoted in Friedman, 127 (my emphases).
44. Interestingly, Eurydice is also identified here with Persephone from Greco-Roman mythology, when she was gathering flowers before she was kidnapped by Hades, and with the beloved from the Song of Solomon.
45. Beal, "The Pearl-Maiden's Two Lovers," 1–21 or chapter 1 of this book.
46. See Santha Bhattacharji, "*Pearl* and the Liturgical 'Commons of Virgins,'" *Medium Aevum* 64 (1995): 37–51. Also note that as lambs were sacrificed in Jewish atonement practices, so Jesus was sacrificed on the Cross and thus, in medieval Christian belief, he was the Lamb who made possible the salvation of human souls. For evocative discussion of this and its influence on western culture, see René Girard, *Violence and the Sacred*, trans. Patrick Gregory (Baltimore: Johns Hopkins University Press, 1977).
47. There can be no doubt that the *Pearl*-poet was familiar with Ovid's *Metamorphoses*, which includes the love stories of both Orpheus and Eurydice and Pygmalion and Galatea. While the poet names Pygmalion directly, thus making a connection to Pygmalion that is critically indisputable, the Orphic connection is perhaps even more essential to the poem in the parallels in supplies and the deeper meanings it implies—hence the consideration given to it in this study.
48. Ovid, *Metamorphoses*, trans. Rolfe Humphries (Bloomington: Indiana University Press, 1983), 241–43.
49. Lines 749–50.
50. E.V. Gordon thought it likely that the poet echoes the *Romance of the Rose* when that French allegory argues that neither Plato nor Aristotle "nor the artist, not even Pygmalion, can imitate successfully the works of Nature" (ed. Langlois 16013f). In contrast to Gordon, Herbert Pilch argued that Jean de Meun's point was that both Nature and Art are inferior to God. See Pilch, "The Middle English *Pearl*: Its Relation to the *Roman de la Rose*," trans. Hyprath, 163–84. Pygmalion's story was also used to warn against the seductions of art and the dangers of idolatry. See Michael Camille, *The Gothic Idol: Ideology and Image-Making in Medieval Art* (Cambridge: Cambridge University Press, 1991), 316–38 and D.W. Robertson, Jr., *A Preface to Chaucer: Studies in Medieval Perspectives* (Princeton, NJ: Princeton University Press, 1969), 99–103, 157–58.
51. *The Riverside Chaucer*, ed. by Larry Benson (Geneva, IL: Houghton Mifflin Company, 1987), 190. For discussion of Chaucer's deployment of Pygmalion, see the final chapter of Jane Chance, *The Mythographic Chaucer: The Fabulation of Sexual Politics* (Minneapolis, MN: University of Minnesota Press, 1995).

64   Allegorical Meaning

She also notes that Bersuire, commenting on Pygmalion as well as Orpheus, sees him as representative of preachers since they "know how to sculpt and paint a soul with corrections and virtues" (quoted in Chance, 268).

52. Claire M. Croft, "Pygmalion and the Metamorphosis of Meaning in Jean Molinet's *Roman de la Rose Moralisé*," *French Studies* 59:4 (2005): 453–66. There is no modern edition of Molinet's work, though there is one from the early-sixteenth century: Jean Molinet, *La Roman de la Rose Moralisé* (Lyons: Guillaume Balsarin, 1503).
53. It is worth noting here that the entire story of Pygmalion in the *Ovide moralisé* is narrated by none other than Orpheus. See Book X in *Ovide moralisé: poème du commencement du quatorième siècle*, ed. C. de Boer, 5 vols. (Amsterdam: Johannes Müller, 1915–38).
54. Similarly, Hamilton sees the Pearl-Maiden as an allegorical representation of the human soul. See Marie Padgett Hamilton, "The Meaning of the Middle English *Pearl*," in *Middle English Survey: Critical Essays*, ed. Edward Vasta (South Bend: University of Notre Dame Press, 1965), 117–45. For further insight on the Pearl-Maiden's allegorical signification, see James Wimsatt, *Allegory and Mirror: Tradition and Structure in Middle English Literature* (New York, NY: Pegasus, 1970) and James Earl, "Saint Margaret and the Pearl-Maiden," *Modern Philology* 70 (1972): 1–8.
55. For a relevant discussion, see Nicholas Watson, "The *Gawain*-Poet as Vernacular Theologian," in *A Companion to the Gawain-Poet*, ed. Derek Brewer and Jonathan Gibson (Woodbridge: D.S. Brewer, 1997), 293–313.
56. See Matt. 13:45–46. The Parable of the Hidden Treasure, which directly precedes the Parable of the Pearl of Great Price and is obviously related to it in *Pearl*, specifies that the man who obtained the treasure experienced great "joy" upon discovering the treasure and, as a result, sells all he has to buy the field in which the treasure resides.
57. For another view of the poet's use of time, grounded in the calendrical year rather than the liturgical one, see Lynn Staley Johnson, "The Pearl Dreamer and the Eleventh Hour," in *Text and Matter: New Critical Perspectives of the Pearl-Poet*, ed. Robert Blanch, Miriam Youngerman Miller, and Julian Wasserman (Troy, NY: The Whitston Publishing Company, 1991), 3–15.
58. For another interpretation of the poem's structure, see Britton J. Harwood, "Pearl as Diptych," in *Text and Matter: New Critical Perspectives of the Pearl-Poet*, ed. Robert J. Blanch, Miriam Youngerman Miller, and Julian N. Wasserman (Troy, NY: Whitston, 1991), 61–78.
59. Ian Bishop made the case for a Christmas liturgical context for *Pearl* more than 45 years ago in *The Pearl in Its Setting* (Oxford: Blackwell, 1968) when he noted the Mass of the Holy Innocents contains a passage from Revelation that is paraphrased in *Pearl*. However, the same passage from Revelation is read as part of the Divine Office in the three weeks following Easter as well. In fact, all the paraphrased passages from Revelation in *Pearl* are read three weeks after Easter because the entire last book of the Bible is read at this time. Furthermore, unlike the companion poem *Sir Gawain and the Green Knight* in the Cotton Nero A.x manuscript, it is clearly Paschal, not Christmas, imagery that predominates in *Pearl*.
60. Andrew and Waldron, eds., *The Poems of the Pearl Manuscript*, 56n.
61. Mark 4:26–29.

Allegorical Meaning 65

62. For a detailed exploration of correspondences, see Teresa Reed, "Mary, the Maiden, and Metonymy in *Pearl*," *South Atlantic Review* 65:2 (2000): 134–62. However, since the poet refers to the "high season," perhaps he refers to the two-week period beginning with Lammas and ending with the feast of the Assumption of Mary.
63. For analysis of parables in *Pearl*, see Sandra Pierson Prior, *The Fayre Formez of the Pearl-Poet* (East Lansing, MI: Michigan State University Press, 1996) and Douglas Thorpe, *A New Earth: The Labor of Language in Pearl, Herbert's Temple, and Blake's Jerusalem* (Washington, DC: Catholic University Press, 1991).
64. How the Pearl-Maiden actually died is never actually specified in the poem, though Jean-Paul Freidl and Ian J. Kirby have argued that the Pearl-Maiden died as a result of one of the fourteenth-century outbreaks of the plague. See "The Life, Death, and Life of the *Pearl-Maiden*," *Neuphilologische Mitteilungen* 103 (2002): 395–98.
65. Cited in Francis Weiser, *Easter Book* (New York, NY: Harcourt, Brace, and Company, 1954) and online at http://www.fisheaters.com/septuagesima.html (accessed 24 February 2016).
66. "Sermo" and "verbum" could be used interchangeably. Years after *Pearl* was written, Erasmus rendered the opening of John's Gospel "in principio erat sermo," instead of giving Jerome's traditional translation "erat verbum," and he created a defense of his choice by arguing quite correctly that the Church Fathers often used "sermo" and "verbum" interchangeably. See C.A.L. Jarrott, "Erasmus' 'In Principio Erat Sermo': A Controversial Translation," *Studies in Philology* 61:1 (1964): 35–40.
67. Marie Borroff, trans., *Pearl: A New Verse Translation* (New York, NY: W.W. Norton, 1977).
68. Reading the lines this way eliminates the need to emend "strykez" to "stykez" ("go") as Sir Israel Gollancz (1921) did in his edition of the poem, and which first E.V. Gordon (1953) and then Sister Mary Hillman (1961, repr. 1967) retained in theirs, or to suppose that "garlande gaye" stands metaphorically for the heavenly procession when it simply refers to the crown of pearls the Pearl-Maiden is wearing as she speaks to the Dreamer just as Andrew and Waldron agree (see their note on lines 1185–87 in their 1978 edition).
69. The Dreamer repeatedly refers to the Pearl-Maiden as his joy, calling her "my blysfol beste" (l. 279), "my blysse" (l. 372), "Blysfol" (l. 421), and so on.
70. See Rev. 3:8. As the Pearl-Maiden herself remarks, "Rygtwysly quo con rede / He loke on bok and be awayed" (ll. 709–10).

3 Moral Purpose
Consoling the Heart

The exquisitely beautiful, fourteenth-century, Middle English dream vision *Pearl* can be interpreted as a consolation. In early scholarship on the poem, literary critics engaged in a vigorous debate over whether the poem was an elegy or an allegory,[1] and in response, John Conley proposed that the poem might belong to a third genre, *consolatio*. Ian Bishop and others subsequently agreed with him.[2] But the idea that the Dreamer of *Pearl* is consoled, or that *Pearl* has a consolatory effect on readers, came under suspicion—even attack. Davenport has argued, for example, that the poem is actually a *contra-consolatio*.[3] Nicholas Watson has made a related case in his essay, "The Gawain-Poet as Vernacular Theologian," asserting of the poem's conclusion (lines 1201–12) that it "is not immediately obvious how the jeweler can derive so comforting a lesson from his bruising encounter with eternity nor how the poet can reconcile this picture of the 'eþe' ["ease"] of Christian living with his analysis of the profound gap between earth and heaven. ..."[4] Using the theoretical paradigms of psychoanalysis for interpretation, which might be characterized as Freudian and feminist respectively, David Aers and Sarah Stanbury have closely considered the emotional progress of the Dreamer of *Pearl* as well.[5] Aers affirms his filiation with *Pearl* scholarship that "focuses on the narrator's 'inability to relinquish old ties' and sees the poem's conclusion as an achievement of 'practical consolation,' of 'acceptance' of death in which the narrator shows 'selflessness and fatherly affection,'"[6] while Stanbury takes an equally nuanced but nevertheless opposing position:

> The final stanza group, in which the narrator recounts his reluctant acceptance of the terms of loss once he has awakened from the dream, resonates with a sense of 'if only' ... But this articulation of words beyond consolation, 'if only, then ...' reminds us finally that the narrative, however formally shaped by religious allegory, returns to human losses and to the melancholic recapitulations of grief ... in *Pearl*, the girl is never forgotten nor are her losses every fully put to rest.[7]

This variety of respected opinions highlights an interpretive crux worthy of further consideration.

In the course of the critical conversation, scholars have interpreted different kinds of literary evidence from *Pearl*, especially the contrast between the Dreamer's emotional devastation in the beginning with his expression of emotional consolation at the end. At least one significant strand of evidence, however, has been neglected: the role of avian imagery and symbolism in the poem. An exploration of this imagery may persuade more readers that the poet intended *Pearl* to be read as a true consolation.

In *Pearl*, birds appear to play a small but beautiful part in the imagery and symbolism for which the poem is justly famous.[8] Yet like the gradually transforming central symbol of the pearl itself, though birds are first represented realistically they slowly take on metaphoric and symbolic qualities, and they function so as to reveal greater depth of meaning in each instance in which they appear.[9] Specifically, in conjunction with other aspects of *Pearl*, they gradually reveal the emotions, and emotional changes, that the Dreamer undergoes as he first mourns, then experiences relief from sorrow, and, after struggling through an intellectual process of trying to understand his loss, finally laughs aloud for joy when he sees the Lamb in the midst of the magnitude of the New Jerusalem. Following the birds of paradise in *Pearl* helps readers to follow the Dreamer's emotional progress: it leads the Dreamer to the Lamb, whose iconic image and what it signifies offer consolation, which the Dreamer accepts, providing an example for readers to follow if they so desire.

To better understand the *Pearl*-poet's artistry in presenting his theme, it is useful to briefly consider instances of avian consolation presented in scripture as well as in key literary antecedents and analogues relevant to the poet's purpose. With this context in mind, it is possible to analyze the realistic representation of birds in the Dreamer's dream, then the metaphoric comparisons of the Dreamer, the Pearl-Maiden, and Mary to different kinds of birds, and finally the significance in the poem of repeated references to John, who among the four evangelists is traditionally represented as an eagle.[10] Following this dramatic development—the flight of the birds through *Pearl*—leads to the Lamb, whose bleeding side the poet contrasts with the Lamb's joyous expression, in order to offer the Dreamer an iconic image on which to meditate and through which to experience true consolation.

Avian Consolation in Scripture and Medieval Literature

The *Pearl*-poet was well versed in scripture.[11] As mentioned earlier, he may have been influenced by Boethius's *Consolation of Philosophy*, the *Romance of the Rose*, and Dante's *Divine Comedy* as well. Whether the poet knew these three key literary antecedents directly is less important than that he was probably aware of them and influenced by some of the same medieval sacred and secular texts that shaped them. The uses these poetic works make of avian consolation are worth noting. For while avian imagery and bird symbolism could be used in other ways in these literary masterpieces—negatively, for example[12]—it is worthwhile to focus on the poetic use of avian consolation by Boethius, Guillaume de Lorris and Jean de Meun, and Dante, as the consolatory tradition was the one that the poet followed in *Pearl*. As we shall see, scripture uses ravens and doves as sources of comfort to humanity in times of distress while songbirds in general bring comfort in the *Consolation*, the *Romance*, and the *Comedy*. In Dante's epic dream vision, the eagle and the griffin play significant symbolic roles in bringing consolation as well.

After their creation on the fifth day in the creation story of Genesis, birds are portrayed in scripture as bringing solace to distressed humanity in several instances: the narrative of the raven and the dove sent out by Noah (whose name means "comfort" in Hebrew) after the Flood (Genesis 9), the feeding of Elijah by the ravens after his persecution by Jezebel (1 Kings 17), the singing of the turtledove after winter has passed (Song of Songs 2), the appearance of the Holy Spirit in the form of a dove at Christ's baptism (the synoptic Gospels), and references to birds in general in the parables and teachings of Jesus, as in Christ's command: "Do not worry about your life ... Consider the birds of the air!"[13] The Church Fathers often interpreted these avian narratives allegorically, linking the Flood narrative typologically to Christ's baptism and likewise Noah's dove to the Holy Spirit, bequeathing a rich symbolic legacy to medieval people that was represented in art and literature.[14] The dove came to stand for both the columbine Church and the Holy Spirit.[15] The Holy Spirit himself was called the Paraclete ("the one who walks beside," the Advocate or Comforter). This association of the third Person of the Trinity with the dove may well have drawn on, at least in part, the Psalmist's use of the idea that those in distress could take refuge in the shadow of God's wings.[16]

Although often used to describe God, avian metaphors in the Bible also were used to imagine the beloved, whose love comforts and consoles as well. The repeated references to the beloved in the Song of Songs as "my dove" (Song of Songs 2:14, 5:2, and 6:9) bespeak an ancient tradition in which the lover compares his beloved to a bird. While the Song of Songs itself is interpreted consistently in the Middle Ages in allegorical terms, as representing the relationship between God and Israel, Christ and the Church, and Christ and the individual soul, still the language of the Song is often incorporated into secular love lyrics, including Middle English ones, and it provides another context for understanding the love language and consolation in *Pearl*.[17]

Like the Bible, Boethius's *Consolation of Philosophy* is an important antecedent for *Pearl*, not only because of similar arguments in the two works and the possible influence of Lady Philosophy on the poet's creation the Pearl-Maiden as a female wisdom figure, but also because of the similar connection made in both works between birds and consolation. In Boethius's work, birds are occasionally presented as part of negative *exempla*, but in at least one significant case birds are connected with the search for freedom from imprisonment (a reality Boethius well understood from personal experience) and the consolation of singing in flight through the woods:

> If the bird who sings so lustily upon the high tree-top, be caught and caged, men may minister to him with dainty care, may give him cups of liquid honey and feed him with all gentleness on plenteous food; yet if he fly to the roof of his cage and see the shady trees he loves, he spurns with his foot the food they have put before him; the woods are all his sorrow calls for; for the woods he sings with his sweet tones.[18]

This image of birds singing in flight through the woods or in a garden is a *topos* in medieval poetry, which appears in another antecedent relevant to *Pearl*, the *Romance of the Rose*.

Literary scholars have agreed that the *Romance of the Rose* is an important precursor text, and likely source, for *Pearl*.[19] In the famous, thirteenth-century, allegorical French dream-vision by Guillaume de Lorris and Jean de Meun, which so elaborately embodies the traditions of *amour courtois*, enchanting bird-song reaches Amans' ears at key points in his quest to obtain his beloved Rose, but especially when he first enters the Garden of Love (cf. lines 45–86, 629–80, 681–717). The *Pearl*-poet's knowledge of medieval romance conventions, especially as seen in the *Romance of the Rose*, may have influenced his decision to use bird-song to affect the Dreamer's emotional state when he enters the new, paradisial landscape of his dream-vision.

Dante's *Divine Comedy* makes much more complex use of avian imagery and symbolism than *Pearl*, but the epic Italian dream vision has at least three significant avian moments relevant to the understanding of avian consolation in *Pearl*. These occur in *Purgatorio*. In Canto IX, Dante the pilgrim dreams that Saint Lucy, in the form of an eagle, seizes him and takes him into a sphere of fire; when he awakens, in fear, he finds that he has been transported to the gate of purgatory.[20] Later, once he has passed through a wall of fire, Dante will enter the terrestrial paradise. In Canto XXVIII, he hears birds singing at the top of the purgatorial mountain and, across a stream, beholds Matilda in the flower-filled terrestrial paradise; this may remind readers of Amans in the *Romance of the Rose* as well as the Dreamer when he first sees the Pearl-Maiden in *Pearl*. Later, in Cantos XXIX–XXXII, Dante will see a magnificent griffin, whose two natures—lion and eagle—correspond symbolically to Christ's human and divine nature.[21] In a sense, the eagle, with her illuminating power, brought Dante toward the Griffin, Christ, who descended from heaven to meet him. A similar pattern will emerge in *Pearl*, but whereas Dante is brought by the eagle to Christ forcibly, the Dreamer of *Pearl* will follow the birds to the Lamb of his own free-will.

As this necessarily brief overview of realistic and metaphoric avian representation in the Bible and three key examples from medieval literature shows, there was an association between birds and consolation, both divine and earthly, in medieval art and poetry. The *Pearl*-poet's extensive knowledge of scripture and well-known use of it in his biblical poetics, taken together with the likelihood of his awareness of the *Consolation of Philosophy*, the *Romance of the Rose*, and the *Divine Comedy*, affirm his awareness of this association. Analysis of *Pearl* reveals how he made use of it.

Bird-Watching in Paradise

The initial, realistic references to birds in *Pearl* in the narrator's dream reveal that birds and their song have a consoling emotional effect on the Dreamer in his distress. These references occur in the narrative transition between the enclosed garden (*hortus conclusus*), where the Dreamer mourns the loss of his pearl, to the dream landscape where he curiously explores a previously unknown territory: the territory, did he but know it, of his own heart as he perceives visions from heaven. The joyful song and colorful flight of the birds awaken the Dreamer's heart to the possibility of gladness in the midst of his sorrow. The narrator declares:

> 3et þo3t me neuer so swete a sange
> As stylle stounde let to me stele.
> Forsoþe þer fleten to me fele. (ll. 18–20)[22]

The music of bird-song breaks into the Dreamer's silence, the loneliness he has felt, and hearing the song is sweet to him. The song effects an emotional change, a shift, within him that prepares him for greater joy.[23]

As the Dreamer continues his exploration of the dreamscape, he sees the birds that he at first had only heard.

> Fowles þer flowen in fryth in fere,[24]
> Of flaumbande hwes, both smale and grete.
> Bot sytole-stryng and gyternere
> Her reken myrþe moght not retrete;
> Fir quen those bryddes her wynges bete,
> Thay songen wyth a swete asent. (ll. 88–93)

The colors of these birds, which are of all different sizes ("small and great"), are so bright that the narrator calls the colors "flaming hues."[25] They inspire him to make a comparison, one that is both synedochical and antithetical at once, so that he claims that neither a musician's stringed instrument nor a musician himself could reproduce the joy of the sound and song of the birds. For it is not only the sound of the birds' singing, but the sound of their wings in flight that produces the harmony that the Dreamer so enjoys.

The metaphorical description of the birds that the Dreamer is hearing and seeing suggests that a further emotional shift is taking place within the Dreamer. Whereas in the enclosed garden he was mourning his loss, in the dreamscape, with the birds, he begins to experience sweetness ("so *swete* a sang") and mirth ("myrþe"). Just as the birds are uplifted by their wings, so the Dreamer's eyes are uplifted to see them, and his heart seems to be uplifted, too.

The purpose of such bird watching in paradise appears to be to alleviate anxiety and console the Dreamer's sorrowing heart.[26] As the poem progresses, it becomes clear that the poet was a birdwatcher, attentive to the behavior of birds not only in nature, but also in biblical and literary tradition. His observations, reproduced in verse, involve readers in imaginary bird watching along with the Dreamer. Thus the consolation of the Dreamer can extend to the poet's audience as well.

Avian Metaphors and Bird Symbolism

Three key figures in *Pearl* are compared to birds: the Dreamer, the Pearl-Maiden, and Mary, the Queen of Heaven. The Dreamer is metaphorically identified with a tamed hawk and a dazed quail, the Pearl-Maiden with a "flawless bird that can brightly flame," and Mary with the phoenix of Arabia. The comparisons, when understood in context, convey subtle nuances that reveal the Dreamer's hopes and fears.

It is the narrator who compares the Dreamer, whom he represents in the poem as himself remembered at an earlier time, to a mild ("hende") or tamed hawk when he first sees the Pearl-Maiden standing under the crystal cliff.

> More þen me lyste my drede aros:
> I stod ful stylle and dorste not calle;
> Wyth y3en open and mouth ful clos
> I stod as hende as hawk in halle.
> I hoped þat gostly wat3 þat porpose;[27]
> I dred onende quat schulde byfalle,
> Lest ho me eschaped þat I þer chos,
> Er I at steuen hir mo3t stalle. (ll. 181–88)

Strong emotional undercurrents surface in this passage. The Dreamer speaks of his fear ("drede") first: it makes him hold still and keep silent, staring. At the same time, he hopes ("hoped") that there is a greater spiritual purpose in the vision of the Pearl-Maiden that he is beholding. Still, his fear seems to be greater than his hope, and he specifically fears that he will lose his beloved again ("Lest ho me eschaped"). So he resolves to delay her.

Of all the birds in all the world, why does the narrator compare the Dreamer to a hawk, and a tamed one at that? The hawk is a courtly bird, associated with noblemen hunting both in reality, in the lush landscapes of the poet's fourteenth-century England, and in medieval literary romances. As John Bowers has suggested, the poet may have had a London-Cheshire connection and could be considered a Ricardian poet affiliated, at least to

72 Moral Purpose

some degree, with the royal court; so a courtly metaphor would be appropriate here because of the way that it related to the poet's own experience and to that of his audience.[28] The idea that a lover might be transformed into a hawk literally (not just metaphorically, as here) and back again is also part of the tradition of medieval literary romance.[29]

However, the hawk to which the Dreamer is compared is not only mild ("hende") but appears to be bound, even trapped, inside a nobleman's castle ("in halle"). The Dreamer is not free to fly where he wishes. He is trapped by what he feels, by what he sees, and by what he cannot forget: the loss of his beloved Pearl-Maiden.[30]

The Dreamer's desire for the Pearl-Maiden increases as he looks at her and talks with her. But in the course of their conversation, the Pearl-Maiden reveals that, following her fall ("schede," a likely reference to her death), she has experienced a spiritual marriage to the Lamb (ll. 409–20) that has, in essence, transformed her perspective of all worldly concerns as well as her own identity: for she has been crowned a queen in heaven (line 415). The Dreamer cannot accept this, and he begins to make a series of objections to the Pearl-Maiden's marital state, beginning by saying she cannot be a queen in heaven since Mary is the Queen of Heaven—and her role is unique.

> 'Blysful,' quod I, 'may þys be trwe?
> Dysplese3 not if I speke errour –
> Art þou þe quene of heuenez blwe,
> Þat al þys worlde schal do honour?
> We leuen on Marye þat grace of grewe,[31]
> Þat ber a barne of vyrgyn flour.
> Þe croune fro hyr quo mo3t remwe
> Bot ho hir passed in sum fauour?
> Now, for synglerty o hyr dousour,
> We calle hyr Fenyx of Arraby,
> Þat freles fle3e of hyr fasor,[32]
> Lyk to þe quen of cortaysye.' (ll. 419–32)

To emphasize the uniqueness of Mary in her role as Queen of Heaven, as well as her sweetness, the Dreamer compares her to the phoenix of Arabia: a traditional comparison.[33] On the one hand, this praise glorifies Mary and emphasizes that she, like the phoenix, is unique. On the other hand, the Dreamer articulates it specifically to undermine the Pearl-Maiden's claims.

The phoenix legend enters western literary traditions directly from Ovid's *Metamorphoses* XV.

> Haec tamen ex aliis generis primordia ducunt,
> una est, quae reparet seque ipsa reseminet, ales:
> Assyrii phoenica vocant; non fruge neque herbis,
> sed turis lacrimis et suco vivit amomi.
> haec ubi quinque suae conplevit saecula vitae,

ilicet in ramis tremulaeque cacumine palmae
unguibus et puro nidum sibi construit ore,
quo simul ac casias et nardi lenis aristas
quassaque cum fulva substravit cinnama murra,
se super inponit finitque in odoribus aevum.   400
inde ferunt, totidem qui vivere debeat annos,
corpore de patrio parvum phoenica renasci;
cum dedit huic aetas vires, onerique ferendo est,
ponderibus nidi ramos levat arboris altae
fertque pius cunasque suas patriumque sepulcrum   405
perque leves auras Hyperionis urbe potitus
ante fores sacras Hyperionis aede reponit.[34]

(All these creatures, however, derive their origin from something other than themselves. There is one living thing, a bird, which reproduces and regenerates itself, without any outside aid. The Assyrians call it the Phoenix. It lives, not on corn or grasses, but on the gum of incense and the sap of balsam. When it has completed five centuries of life, it straightaway builds a nest for itself, working with unsullied beak and claw, in the topmost branches of some swaying palm. Then, when it has laid a foundation of cassia, and smooth spikes of nard, chips of cinnamon bark and yellow myrrh, it places itself on top and ends its life amid the perfumes.

Then, they say, a little Phoenix is born anew from the father's body, fated to live a like number of years. When the nestling is old enough and strong enough to carry the weight, it lifts the heavy nest from the high branches and, like a dutiful son, carries its father's tomb, its own cradle, through the yielding air, till it reaches the city of the sun, where it lays its burden before the sacred doors within Hyperion's Temple.)[35]

The classical story was later interpreted allegorically by western Christian commentators who found it rich in signifying power. Because Ovid's text was widely used in schools for educational purposes, it became influential as it continued to be interpreted morally and allegorically.[36]

In medieval English literature, for example, the phoenix becomes a commonplace comparison to Christ, Mary, or a uniquely beautiful woman. The fire-bird appears in the Old English *Phoenix* to praise Christ, Albertus Magnus's *De laudibus beatae Mariae virginis* VII.iii.1 to praise Mary, and Chaucer's *Book of the Duchess* 982 to praise the Lady White. When the *Pearl*-poet alludes to it, he does so in one of the Dreamer's speeches, making the Dreamer use it to express his awe of Mary and his doubt of the Pearl-Maiden's claims to a new, queenly status. But the poet may be influenced by the wider range of meaning that the symbol of the phoenix had. For in the complex symbolic world of the medieval imagination, the phoenix consistently signifies transformation and resurrection, themes clearly relevant to the poet's theological work in *Pearl*.[37]

In her dialogue with the Dreamer, the Pearl-Maiden is eager to help the Dreamer understand her transformation from an earthly maiden to a heavenly bride (ll. 409–20). Yet the Dreamer struggles to accept that she is spiritually married to the Lamb. He questions his beloved, and he specifically inquires about *what kind of thing* the Lamb may be.

> Why, maskellez bryd þat bry3t con flambe,
> Þat reiatéz hatz so ryche and ryf,
> Quat kyn þyng may be þat Lambe
> Þat þe wolde wedde vnto hys vyf? (ll. 770–74)

The Dreamer begins his question by calling the Pearl-Maiden "maskelle3 bryd," a phrase that has been translated in diverse ways. The Middle English Dictionary gives "spotless" or "flawless" as modern English equivalents for "maskellez."[38] Translators of *Pearl* render the phrase variously: Sophie Jewett gives "unblemished bride"; Hillman, "spotless bride"; Marie Borroff, "immaculate being"; J.R.R. Tolkien, "immaculate bride"; Vantuono, "spotless bride"; and Finch, in a free translation, "purest pearl."[39] The phrase clearly presents a linguistic crux to the translator because the terms in it have more than one denotation in Middle English and can embrace a range of meaning and signification in the original language that is inevitably narrowed in modern English. It is notable that while the translation of the adjective varies, only Borroff and Finch give something other than "bride" for the noun. It seems that only Borroff's "being" attempts to find a middle way between "bride" and the other possibility, given as "bird" in the following translation: "Why, flawless bird that can brightly flame, / who has royal dignities so rich and plentiful, / what kind of thing may be that Lamb / that he would wed you as his wife?"

For "bryd" (also spelled "brid") means both "bride" and "bird" in Middle English. In late-medieval England, "bryd" could be applied to a beloved woman; the Middle English Dictionary gives "a term of endearment, sweetheart" as one definition of the term.[40] As Charles Osgood notes in his edition of the poem (1906), "The poet doubtless intends a pun. The context unmistakably points to the meaning bride, but *flambe* (see l. 90) shows also that he is thinking of 'bird.' Cf. l. 429 and n[ote]."[41] Certainly "flawless bird" is at least one of the meanings the poet wishes his audience to understand in this phrase. The Dreamer's punning here is actually a serious game, a *double-entendre* that reveals his conflicting emotions and an interior shift toward greater objection even than was implied in his praise of Mary-as-phoenix. In the earlier case, he praised Mary as a means to undercut the Pearl-Maiden's claim to be queen in heaven; now he calls the Pearl-Maiden "bryd," which could be an acceptance of her claim to be married on the one hand or, on the other, an assertion that she is still his "sweetheart."

The reference to the Pearl-Maiden's ability to "brightly flame" does resonate with the description of the birds the Dreamer saw when he first entered the dreamscape, as Osgood suggested, but it also connects to the comparison of Mary to the phoenix. For the phoenix is the only bird that burns itself in an immolating fire, flaming brightly, as a means to resurrect itself and be reborn. This, of course, is the Dreamer's greatest hope with respect to the Pearl-Maiden: that she would be resurrected, restored, and returned to him.

Yet the Pearl-Maiden's purpose in visiting the Dreamer in this vision is to help him to see a bigger, heavenly picture. For though, according to medieval Christian theology, she and all Christians will be resurrected, there is no marriage between Christians in heaven,[42] only the great marriage between the Lamb and his bride, the Church.[43] To help the Dreamer understand this, the Pearl-Maiden reveals to the Dreamer that she has requested that he be able to see a vision of the New Jerusalem.

The description of the city of the heavenly Jerusalem begins to unfold in section XVII of the poem, and at the end of section XVIII the Dreamer describes his reaction to the magnitude of the New Jerusalem that he has seen so far:

> Anvnder mone so great merwayle
> No fleschly hert ne my3t endeure,
> As quen I blusched vpon þat baly,
> So ferly þerof wat3 þe fasure.
> I stod as stylle as dased quayle
> For ferly of þat frelich fygure,[44]
> Þat felde I nawþer reste ne trauayle,
> So watz I rauyste wyth glymme pure. (ll. 1081–88)

The dreamer has gone from describing himself as a *hende* hawk to describing himself as a "dazed quail." His astonishment and awe are emotions that cause him to imagine himself very humbly indeed. Whereas a hawk is a courtly bird, and the Pearl-Maiden's appearance made him feel like a mild, even tamed hawk in her presence, the vision of the New Jerusalem makes him feel dazed and grounded—grounded in the sense that he is lowly and earth-bound.

For in nature, quails are birds that spend much of their time on the ground, and when frightened, they rush to cover. The quail is not a hunter, but a hunted game-bird. In fact, it is often the prey of the hawk. In medieval bestiary tradition, the quail is interpreted allegorically: "The quail mother attacked by the hawk as she nears the earth represents the Christian who will be attacked by the devil if he approaches worldly things."[45]

The Dreamer makes clear that he does not feel either a sense of peace ("reste") or striving ("trauayle"), but a sense of being ravished by radiance ("So watz I rauyste wyth glymme pure"). So the Dreamer's comparison of himself to a quail, as ordinary and humble a metaphor as this might be, nevertheless reveals his emotions and a significant emotional shift on his journey through the vision toward consolation.[46] He is being brought back down to earth, for he has been soaring in his *somnium*, beholding things too great and wonderful for words, and he is on the verge of awakening to new understanding.[47]

Bird's Eye View of the New Jerusalem

The Dreamer's vision of the New Jerusalem is really quite extraordinary, not only intrinsically, but specifically in terms of the many different perspectives of the heavenly city that he is able to perceive. His perspective is multidimensional.[48] The way the city is described in the poem seems to necessitate that the viewer be able to fly: to be able to soar around the walls and above them and look down and through the city. The similar description in Revelation may be one reason the early Christian Church identified John, the fourth evangelist and the author of Revelation, as an eagle in the developing iconographic tradition.[49] In *Pearl*, it appears that the Dreamer, whether he knows it or not, has "imp'd his wing"[50] on John's in order to see what he is seeing.[51]

It seems that the final bird in the dream vision of *Pearl* is actually invisible, a presence only implied by repeated reference to John, whom medieval Christians regarded as both the evangelist (the author of John's gospel) and the revelator (the author of Revelation). John is consistently represented as an eagle in traditional Christian iconography, and the *Pearl*-poet's medieval audience would know this very well from art, architecture, and manuscript illuminations. So the audience might very well imagine an eagle representing John when repeatedly reading or hearing the name in the context of the description of the New Jerusalem.[52]

This eagle, though undescribed, is not unimaginable.[53] In fact, the eagle is repeatedly named in the poem, John, for this is one of the poet's concatenation words in section XVII. The meaning of "John" is "the grace of God." The name, its meaning, and its iconographic tradition function as contexts for the final avian symbolism of the poem. Just as John beheld the vision of the New Jerusalem, like a soaring eagle whose piercing sight sees everything below him, so too the Dreamer beholds the New Jerusalem as if from the Eagle's perspective, and so he gains, upon waking, the awareness of the possibility of taking refuge in the shadow of God's wings.[54] In other words, he gains the possibility of receiving consolation for his loss and being changed emotionally as well as spiritually by his dream vision.

Following the Birds to the Lamb

The initial, literal appearances of birds in *Pearl* have a significant emotional impact on the Dreamer. In the narrative transition between the enclosed garden and the dream landscape, the joyful song and colorful flight of the birds awaken the Dreamer's heart to the possibility of gladness in the midst of his sorrow. They bring hope.

Later, three important characters are associated metaphorically with specific birds. The Dreamer is compared to a tamed hawk and a dazed quail; the Pearl-Maiden is compared to a "flawless bird that can brightly flame"; and Mary, Queen of Heaven, is compared to the phoenix of Arabia. In each case, the avian metaphors reveal the emotional conflict within the speaking character who articulates these comparisons: the Dreamer. For it is the narrator who compares the Dreamer, himself remembered at an earlier time, to hawk and quail; the Dreamer questioning the Pearl-Maiden who creates a *double-entendre* with "bride/bird" when questioning her marriage to the Lamb; and the Dreamer, again, who honors Mary as unique phoenix but specifically in order to express his doubt about the Pearl-Maiden's elevation to the status of a queen in heaven.

It is possible that the *Pearl*-poet may have wanted his medieval audience to imagine another bird, the eagle, which stood for John, the evangelist and revelator, in Christian iconography. It seems that this eagle, though named ("John") repeatedly in *Pearl*, remains without a description within the poem itself because the Dreamer is not looking at it but, like Dante in *Purgatorio* or Chaucer in the *House of Fame*, flying with it and seeing the New Jerusalem from the Eagle's perspective.

Near the end of *Pearl*, however, it is not a bird, but the Lamb who finally brings the Dreamer the consolation that he needs. When he sees the Lamb, the Dreamer actually laughs aloud for joy!

> Delyt þat Hys come encroched
> To much hit were of for to melle
> Þise aldermen, quen He aproched,
> Grouelyng to His fete þay felle.
> Legyounes of aungelez togeder uoched
> Þer kesten ensens of swete smelle.[55]
> Þen glory and gle watz nwe abroched;
> Al songe to loue þat gay juelle.
> Þe steuen mo3t stryke þur3 þe vrþe to helle
> Þat þe vertues of heuen of joye endyte.
> To loue þe Lombe his meyny inmelle
> Iwysse I la3t a gret delyt. (ll. 1117–28)

The Dreamer's emotions have radically shifted from dark sorrow to bright delight. As he says himself here, "Indeed, I laughed with great delight!" He is laughing aloud as he has not done before in *Pearl*.

As he continues to gaze upon the Lamb, even greater emotional shifts take place.[56] By beholding the Lamb's wounded side, open and bleeding (lines 1131–40), the Dreamer beholds the suffering he already knows Jesus experienced to make salvation and redemption available to everyone, including him. According to medieval Christian theology, and the worldview it inspired among ordinary lay-people, the death of Christ on the Cross made the reconciliation of God and man possible, as well as a future resurrection and, ultimately, the reunion of the saints in heaven. When he sees the Lamb's bleeding side, the Dreamer asks who did that spiteful deed (line 1138). The answer, from a medieval Christian point of view, is every human being who has ever sinned, which includes the Dreamer. In the Dreamer's perceptions of the Lamb's pain are the beginnings of empathy, of realizing that even the God-Man himself was willing to suffer, to die to conquer death. But the Lamb's response to suffering is not like the Dreamer's. The Lamb's response is joy (ll. 1141–45), the expression on his face "gloryous glade" ("gloriously glad").

Although the Dreamer's eyes will soon fall on his Pearl-Maiden, and "delyt" will drive into his eyes, his ears, and his "man's mind" (ll. 1153–54) and motivate him to act impulsively, attempting to cross the stream he has expressly been forbidden to cross (and thus he will wake without seeing more of heaven), still this visionary moment, beholding the Lamb, transforms his emotional state to delight. He will meditate upon it long after. It changes him from resisting the will of God to surrendering to the pleasure of the Prince. As a result, he will come to call Christ not only his lord, but his friend (line 1204). So it is that bird watching in *Pearl*, which ultimately leads to a vision of the Lamb, helps to draw the Dreamer—and with him, if they so desire, the readers of *Pearl*—toward true consolation. Such consolation is not only an experience of emotions that change from grief to joy, but a recognition of Christian truth that leads the Dreamer to redemption and greater faith in God.

Notes

1. For a history of the scholarly debate over *Pearl*'s genre, whether elegy or allegory, see René Welleck, *The Pearl: An Interpretation of the Middle English Poem*, Studies in English by Members of the English Seminar of the Charles University, Prague (Praze, Czech Rep.: Riváce, 1933); Laurence Eldredge, "The State of *Pearl* Studies since 1933," *Viator* 6 (1975): 171–94; Malcolm Andrew, *The Gawain-Poet: An Annotated Bibiography, 1839–1977* (New York, NY: Garland Publishing, 1979); and Robert Blanch, "The State of *Pearl* Criticism." *Chaucer Yearbook* 3 (1996): 21–33. In "The Pearl-Maiden's Two Lovers," I first described my elegiac interpretation but later argued for an allegorical interpretation as well in "The Signifying Power of *Pearl*." For scholarship on *Pearl* by two other "new allegorists," see Meyer, *Medieval Allegory and the Building of the New Jerusalem* and Chance, "Allegory and Structure in *Pearl*."
2. John Conley, "Pearl and a Lost Tradition," *Journal of English and Germanic Philology* 55 (1955): 332–47. Repr. in *The Middle English Pearl: Critical Essays*, ed. John Conley (South Bend, IN: University of Notre Dame Press, 1970), 50–72. See also Ian Bishop, *"Pearl" in Its Setting*.
3. William Davenport, "Desolation, not Consolation: *Pearl* 19–22," *English Studies* 55 (1974): 421–23.
4. Nicholas Watson, "The Gawain-Poet as Vernacular Theologian," 299.

5. Aers, "The Self Mourning: Reflections on *Pearl*," 54–73 and Stanbury, "The Body and the City in *Pearl*," 30–47. It is George Edmondson, in "*Pearl*: The Shadow of the Object, the Shape of the Law," *Studies in the Age of Chaucer* 26 (2004), 29–63, who characterizes Aers's reading as Freudian and Stanbury's as feminist.
6. Aers, "Self in Mourning," 56.
7. Stanbury, "The Body and the City," 42.
8. A partial exception is Paul Reichardt's "Animal Similes in *Pearl*," in *Text and Matter: New Critical Perspectives of the Pearl-Poet*, ed. Robert J. Blanch, Julian N. Wasserman, and Miriam Youngerman Miller (Troy, NY: Whitston, 1991), 17–30. Reichardt has argued that the Dreamer's comparisons of himself to a hawk, a doe, and a quail can be contextualized by medieval bestiary traditions.
9. For an excellent discussion of the multiple symbolic transformations of the pearl, see A.C. Spearing, *The Gawain-Poet: A Critical Study* (Cambridge: Cambridge University Press, 1971), 128–29, 134–37.
10. Although modern critics are uncertain whether the John who authored the Gospel also authored Revelation (or even if John was the author), medieval tradition accepted John as the author of both books.
11. William Vantuono provides a comprehensive list of scriptural quotations and allusions in the poem in his edition: *Pearl: An Edition with Verse Translation* (South Bend, IN: University of Notre Dame Press, 1995), 178–80.
12. Some negative use of avian imagery certainly occurs in Dante's *Inferno*, Canto 5, when the lustful lovers are compared to birds blown about by the wind and who therefore have no control over their flight as well as in Canto 13, which features the half-woman, half-bird harpies who punish those who have committed suicide. In contrast, the *Pearl*-poet never uses avian imagery or symbolism negatively in *Pearl*. Avian imagery naturally becomes more positive as Dante journeys through purgatory and heaven.
13. Matt. 6:25–25. For a general introduction to the role of birds in the Bible, see Alice Parmelee, *All the Birds of the Bible: Their Stories, Identifications, and Meaning* (New Canaan, CT: Keats Publishing, Inc., 1959). There are also many references to birds in the poetic books of the Bible, including Psalms (Pss. 50:11, 84:3, 102:6, 104:12, 105:40 and Proverbs (Prov. 23:5, 26:2, 30:17, 30:31), and elsewhere. See Joyce G. Baldwin, "Birds," in *A Dictionary of Biblical Tradition in English Literature*, ed. David Lyle Jeffrey (Grand Rapids, MI: William B. Eerdmanns Publishing Company, 1992), 88–89.
14. See Beryl Rowland, *Birds with Human Souls* (Knoxville, TN: University of Tennessee Press, 1978); Willene Clark and Meredith McMunn, *Beasts and Birds of the Middle Ages: The Bestiary and its Legacy* (Philadelphia, PA: University of Pennsylvania Press, 1991); and Elizabeth Eva Leach, *Sung Birds: Music, Nature, and Poetry in the Later Middle Ages* (Ithaca, NY: Cornell University Press, 2007).
15. David Ployd, "The Unity of the Dove: The Sixth Homily on the Gospel of John and Augustine's Trinitarian Solution to the Donatist Schism," *Augustinian Studies* 21:1 (2011): 57–77.
16. See Pss. 17:8, 36:7, 57:1, 63:7, and 91:1.
17. Beal, "The Pearl-Maiden's Two Lovers," 9–15 or chap. 1 of this book. Other scholars have briefly mentioned the *Pearl*-poet's likely awareness of Christian traditions of avian imagery and symbolism. Sandra Pierson Prior agrees that the

Pearl-poet would have been well aware of the iconography of the Holy Spirit as dove; James Earl, who makes a very plausible argument for the influence of Saint Margaret on the *Pearl*-Poet's representation of the Pearl-Maiden, notes that the dove descends on Saint Margaret at her death—which suggests her connection to the Holy Spirit.

18. Boethius, *Consolation of Philosophy*, trans. by W.V. Cooper, The Temple Classics (London: J.M. Dent and Company, 1902). For the Latin, see *Boethius: The Theological Tractates; The Consolation of Philosophy*, trans. and ed. H. F. Stewart, E. K. Rand, and S. J. Tester, Loeb Classical Library 74 (Cambridge, MA: Harvard University Press 1973).
19. Similarities between the *Romance of the Rose* and *Pearl* are noted by Pilch, "The Middle-English *Pearl*: Its Relation to the *Roman de la Rose*," trans. Hyprath, 163–84; A.C. Spearing, *Medieval Dream Poetry* (Cambridge: Cambridge University Press, 1976), 111–28; and Sandra Pierson Prior, *The Fayre Formez of the Pearl-Poet* (East Lansing, MI: Michigan State University Press, 1994), 21–25. See also Richard Newhauser, "Sources II: Scriptural and Devotional Sources," in *A Companion to the Gawain-Poet*, ed. Derek Brewer and Jonathan Gibson (Woodbridge: D.S. Brewer, 1997), 257–76.
20. Scholars have observed the influence of this episode on Chaucer's *House of Fame*; see explanatory notes to the *House of Fame* in *The Riverside Chaucer*, 3rd. ed, gen. ed. Larry D. Benson (Oxford: Oxford University Press, 1986), 994–1002. It is also worth noting that Chaucer was influenced considerably by literary traditions of avian representation as one of his other dream vision poems, *Parliament of Fowls*, shows. *Parliament* is a complete avian allegory in which the dreamer is led by Scipio Africanus through the celestial spheres to the temple of Venus where he witnesses, through a window, three tercel eagles seeking the love of a formel eagle in the presence of Nature, who ultimately allows the formel eagle to delay her choice of mate by one year.
21. "Then they lead me, with them, up to the Grifon's breast, where Beatrice stood, and turned towards us. They said: 'See that you do not spare your eyes: we have set you in front of the bright emeralds, from which Love once shot his arrows at you.' A thousand desires, hotter than flame, kept my eyes fixed on those shining eyes, that in turn stayed fixed on the Grifon. The dual-natured creature was reflected in them, just like the sun in a mirror, with the attributes now of the human, now of the divine. Reader, think how I marvelled, in my mind, to see the thing itself remain unmoving, and yet its image changing." (Dante, *Purgatorio*, XXX, trans. A.S. Kline). Kline's translation is available online (http://www.poetryintranslation.com/PITBR/Italian/DantPurg29to33.htm - accessed 4 February 2014).
22. As noted in previous chapters, the Middle English quotations of *Pearl* are from Andrew and Waldron, eds., *Poems of the Pearl Manuscript*, 5th ed.
23. The *Pearl*-poet's knowledge of medieval romance conventions may have influenced his decision to use bird-song to affect the Dreamer's emotional state as he enters the new, paradisial garden of his dream-vision. In the *Romance of the Rose*, for example, enchanting bird-song reaches Amans' ears when he first enters the Garden of Love (cf. lines 45–86, 629–80, 681–717).
24. This line appears to come from the stock phrases of the medieval English poetic movement known as the "alliterative revival" of the fourteenth century. Compare to the lyric poem, "Fowles in the frith" (available online at http://www.luminarium.org/medlit/medlyric/fowles.php—accessed 4 February 2014.) For

more on the alliterative revival, see the literary-critical work of Elizabeth Salter, "The Alliterative Revival," *Modern Philology* 64 (1966): 146–50 and Thorlac Turville-Petre, *The Alliterative Revival* (Woodbridge: Boydell & Brewer, 1977) as well as Derek Pearsall, "The Alliterative Revival: Origins and Social Backgrounds," in *Middle English Alliterative Poetry and Its Literary Background: Seven Essays*, ed. David Lawton (Cambridge: D.S. Brewer, 1982), 34–53 and "The Origins of the Alliterative Revival," in *The Alliterative Tradition in the Fourteenth Century*, ed. Bernard S. Levy and Paul Szarmach (Kent, OH: Kent State University Press, 1981), 1–24. See also Christine Chism, *Alliterative Revivals* (Philadelphia, PA: University of Pennsylvania Press, 2002), which discusses the revivification of the body in several Middle English alliterative poems, including *Sir Gawain and the Green Knight* (but not *Pearl*) and the authoritative force of the words of a speaking ghost.

25. Later in the poem, a form of this adjective, "flaming," will be used to describe the Pearl-Maiden herself.
26. One possible subtext for the development of a bird-watching theme in *Pearl*, which may have inspired the biblically informed *Pearl*-poet, is Matt. 6:25–26: "Do not worry about your life ... consider the birds of the air!" Note that Matthew's Gospel is the primary one upon which the poet draws for the Parable of the Pearl of Great Price, the Parable of the Laborers in the Vineyard, and allusions to the Beatitudes (Matt. 22:1–14, 20–1–16, 5:1–10).
27. The Dreamer hopes for this vision to have "gostly ... porpose"—another claim in the poem hinting to readers that there is not only a literal but an allegorical or spiritual sense of the dream vision.
28. For a discussion of *Pearl* and courtly connections, see Bowers, *The Politics of Pearl: Court Poetry in the Age of Richard II* (Woodbridge: D.S. Brewer, 2000).
29. An example of this is *Yonec*, one of the lovely *Lais* of the twelfth-century Anglo-Norman poet, Marie de France. In this Old French poem, the lady's lover can literally transform from a free-flying hawk that comes through the window of the tower where she is imprisoned into a gentle knight lying beside her in bed where she is waiting for him. For an English version of *Yonec* in verse, see Marie de France, *The Lais of Marie de France*, trans. Robert Hanning and Joan Ferrante (Grand Rapids, MI: Baker Books, 1978, repr. 2004); in prose, see *The Lais of Marie de France*, trans. Glyn S Burgess and Keith Busby (London: Penguin Books, 1986, repr. 2003).
30. In "Animal Similes in *Pearl*," Reichardt has argued that the Dreamer's comparisons of himself to a hawk, a doe, and a quail can be contextualized by the medieval bestiary tradition. Specifically, he suggests that these three animal images reveal "the Dreamer's emotional and spiritual character" (17), with the hawk standing for his desire to seize the object of his desire, the doe his anxious wish "to avoid what is unpleasant and painful" (20), and the quail his attachment to carnal pleasures since it was "proverbially linked to fleshliness and earth-bound existence" (22). While I find this thesis intriguing, it seems unlikely to me that the Dreamer's comparison of himself to a hawk is meant to evoke the demonic or devilish, as Reichardt suggests, though the bestiary tradition did metaphorically connect the *hunting* hawk (not the tamed hawk in the hall) to the work of the ultimate predator, the devil. For further discussion, see chapter 5 of this book.
31. In saying Mary "grew from grace," the Dreamer makes not only a theological statement, but one that puns on Mary's mother's name, which was believed in the Middle Ages to be Anne, meaning "grace."

82 Moral Purpose

32. In ME, "freles," means "flawless" but is amended to "fereles" by Andrew & Waldron, meaning "without equal." The homonymic relationship between these two words may be another instance of the *Pearl*-poet's famous use of *double-entendre*.
33. As Charles Osgood points out in his edition of *Pearl*, in his note on the allusion to the phoenix, "The Phoenix was a not uncommon medieval symbol of the birth of Christ and of the resurrection of Christ and of man. More rarely in reference to the incarnation, Mary was called the Phoenix … More rarely still is the Phoenix a type of singular beauty and sweetness, as here." Salzer cites fewer than six examples, none of which resembles these lines as closely as does Chaucer [in *The Book of the Duchess* ll. 429–31]. The nearest is from Milchsack, *Hymeni et Sequentiae* (1886) no. 21.180: "Haec est fenix unica, capillos cujus auri color et verticem miratur olor." In an OF lyric (*Herr. Arch.* 42.281), she is "la gloriouse fenix, Meire et fille a dous pellicant." Raynouard, *Lexique Rom.* s.v. *fenixi*, cites from the Povençal poet Bistors an instance in which a lady is addressed as "bels fenics." In the *Romance of the Rose* 9437 (ed. Michel) is mentioned the *prodefame*, who is rarer than the phoenix. See *The Pearl: A Middle English Poem*, ed. Charles Osgood (Boston and London: D.C. Heath & Co., 1906), 71–72.
34. The complete Latin text of Ovid's *Metamorphoses* is available online (http://www.thelatinlibrary.com/ovid/ovid.met15.shtml - accessed 14 October 2013). For a scholarly edition in print, see *Ovid: Metamorphoses*, ed. and trans. Frank Justus Miller (Cambridge, MA: Harvard University Press, 1964).
35. Ovid, *Metamorphoses*, trans. Rolfe Humphries (Bloomington, IN: University of Indiana Press), 345. A.S. Kline's translation (2000) is also available online (http://www.poetryintranslation.com/PITBR/Latin/Metamorph15.htm#_Toc64106008 - accessed 14 October 2013).
36. One such text is the *Ovide moralisé*, an early fourteenth-century allegorical interpretation of Ovid's *Metamorphoses* produced in France in Old French. See *Ovid in the Middle Ages*, ed. James G. Clark, Frank T. Coulson, and Kathryn L. McKinney (Cambridge: Cambridge University Press, 2011) for further discussion of the reception of the *Metamorphoses* and its four-fold interpretation.
37. For a view of the *Pearl*-poet's theology, see Jim Rhodes, *Poetry Does Theology: Chaucer, Grosseteste, and the Pearl-Poet* (South Bend, IN: University of Notre Dame Press, 2001).
38. "Maskelles," *Middle English Dictionary Online* (http://quod.lib.umich.edu/cgi/m/mec/med-idx?type=id&id=MED27012 - accessed 16 October 2013). Like "freles" and "fereles," mentioned earlier, there is something of a homonymic relationship between "maskellez" and "makeles," the later word equivalent to the modern English "matchless" and containing the *double-entendre* "without peer" and "without mate." The Dreamer describes the Pearl-Maiden as "makeles" at line 780. Vantuono's glossary to his edition even lists these two words, "maskellez" and "makeles," together as if they are interchangeable (237).
39. *Pearl: A Middle English Poem – A Modern Version in the Metre of the Original*, trans. Sophie Jewett (New York, NY: Thomas Crowell & Co., 1908), 65; *The Pearl: A New Translation and Interpretation*, trans. Mary Vincent Hillmann (South Bend, IN: University of Notre Dame Press, 1961), 45; *Pearl: A New Verse Translation*, trans. Marie Borroff (New York, NY: W.W. Norton, 1977), 20; *Sir Gawain and the Green Knight, Pearl and Sir Orfeo*, trans. J.R.R. Tolkien

(New York, NY: Ballantine Books, 1975), 151; *Pearl: An Edition with Verse Translation*, trans. Vantuono (South Bend, IN: University of Notre Dame Press, 1995), 62; *The Complete Works of the Pearl Poet with Translation and Introduction*, trans. Casey Finch with facing-page Middle English Texts ed. Malcolm Andrew, Ronald Waldron, and Clifford Peterson (Berkeley and Los Angeles, CA: University of California Press, 1993), 80.

40. "Brid," *Middle English Dictionary Online* (http://quod.lib.umich.edu/cgi/m/mec/med-idx?type=id&id=MED6006 - accessed 16 October 2013).
41. Osgood, ed., *The Pearl: A Middle English Poem*, 85 n. 769.
42. Cf. Matt. 22:30.
43. Cf. Rev. 21.
44. *Fresh*: In Middle English, *freuch*. The Middle English word may also be rendered "noble" (when emended to *frelich* according to Moorman and Gordon) "delicate," "delightful" (from *frough* according to Osgood) or "brilliant" (see the Middle English Dictionary). *Figure*: In Middle English, "fygure" (cf. LL *figura*) is a word that may point toward the allegorical sense of the passage.
45. *The Medieval Bestiary* (http://bestiary.ca/beasts/beast256.htm - accessed 16 October 2013).
46. The poem has been interpreted as a consolation by many literary scholars, including those who popularized the notion: V.E. Watts, "*Pearl* as a Consolatio," *Medium Ævum* 32 (1963): 34–36, and Ian Bishop, *The Pearl in Its Setting* (Oxford: Basil Blackwell, 1968). In contrast, Davenport and Watson see the poem as a *contra-consolatio*, another way of reading the poem as narrating failure. See their essays, "Desolation, not Consolation: *Pearl* 19–22," *Review of English Studies* (1974): 421–23 and "The *Gawain*-Poet as Vernacular Theologian," 293–314 respectively.
47. For discussion of medieval dream theory and *Pearl*, see A.C. Spearing, *Medieval Dream-Poetry* (Cambridge: Cambridge University Press, 1976); Kathryn L. Lynch, *The High Medieval Dream Vision: Poetry, Philosophy and Literary Form* (Stanford, CA: Stanford University Press, 1988); Peter Brown, *Reading Dreams: The Interpretation of Dreams from Chaucer to Shakespeare* (Oxford: Oxford University Press, 1999).
48. See Sarah Stanbury, *Seeing the Gawain-Poet: Description and the Art of Perception* (Philadelphia, PA: University of Pennsylvania, 1991) for further discussion.
49. Matthew was represented as an angel, Mark as a lion, and Luke as an ox. For an introductory discussion, see Alva William Steffler, *Symbols of the Christian Faith* (Grand Rapids, MI: Eerdmans, 2002), 87–88. See also Elizabeth Edwards Goldsmith, *Sacred Symbols in Art* (New York, NY: G.P. Putnam's Sons: The Knickerbocker Press, 1911), 137–45.
50. Recall Gerard Manly Hopkins's poem, "Easter Wings": "For if I imp my wing on Thine / Affliction shall advance the flight in me" (ll. 19–20).
51. While Saint John the Evangelist is most often portrayed as an eagle or as a human being with an eagle near him while he writes, there exists an iconographic tradition in Christian art that depicts St. John sitting on the wings of an eagle. Whether the *Pearl*-poet was familiar with this tradition is unclear; he may have drawn on it, or he may have independently invented it and incorporated the concept into his dream vision poem (though the former seems more likely giving the poet's traditional, medieval way of thinking). For an excellent overview of medieval Christian iconography in illustrated books, see Leslie D. Ross, *Text,*

Image, Message: Saints in Medieval Manuscript Illustrations, Contributions to the Study of Art and Architecture (Santa Barbara, CA: Praeger Publishers, 1994).

52. The interplay of reading (or listening), memory, and the medieval imagination has been well discussed by Mary Carruthers. See her study, *The Book of Memory: A Study of Memory in Medieval Culture*, 2nd ed. (Cambridge: Cambridge University Press, 2008) and *The Medieval Craft of Memory: An Anthology of Texts and Pictures*, ed. Mary Carruthers and Jan Ziolkowski (Philadelphia, PA: University of Pennsylvania Press, 2002).
53. Indeed, it makes sense here to recall Dante's encounter with Saint Lucy in the form of an eagle in his dream-within-a-dream as well as Chaucer's flight in *House of Fame* for comparison.
54. In medieval architecture, passages from Revelation are engraved in the ceiling of the Chapel of Berkeley Castle, where the *Pearl*-poet's contemporary, John Trevisa, served as priest. Among other things, these passages describe the darkening of the heavenly lights and a flying eagle warning of the angelic trumpets whose sounding will bring woe to the earth at the end of time. See D.A. Trotter, "The Anglo-Norman Inscriptions at Berkeley Castle," *Medium Aevum* 59 (1990): 114–20. For further discussion, see my book, *John Trevisa and the English Polychronicon* (Tempe, AZ and Turnhout: ACMRS and Brepols, 2013).
55. The angels are imagined to be censing those gathered to worship much as an incense-bearer might a medieval churchgoing audience.
56. It is worth remembering here how, in *Purgatorio*, Dante the pilgrim gazed on Christ in the form of the Griffin, experienced shifting emotions, and ultimately perceived a Christian truth about Christ: his nature as the God-Man—fully human and fully divine.

4 Anagogical Revelation
Imagining Spiritual Marriage to Christ

The exquisitely beautiful, fourteenth-century, Middle English poem *Pearl* can be interpreted as a revelation. The poem has been called a dream vision, an elegy, an allegory, and a consolation (as well as a *contra-consolatio*, a courtly love story, a dialogue, a debate, a hagiographical account, and even a spiritual quest), and the poem certainly participates in multiple genres. However, several literary scholars also have noted its debt to the biblical book of Revelation and likely relationship to illustrated apocalypse manuscripts of the later Middle Ages.[1] As Cynthia Kraman has observed so insightfully: "For critics who do not notice the highly literary and personal quality of *Pearl*, the genre discussion of *Pearl* is rather overwrought, heightened by expectations that it will conform to a single type of literature, unaware that a new and original literature is being created before their eyes."[2] As Kraman goes on to show, *Pearl* can be read as a revelation, solidly centered in the tradition of Judeo-Christian apocalyptic literature, even if it also participates in other medieval genres and stylistic conventions.[3] Furthermore, it can be so not only partially, at the conclusion of the poem when the Dreamer beholds a vision of the New Jerusalem, but entirely, from the beginning to the end.

This chapter considers *Pearl* as a revelation because this genre is particularly relevant to a question that has sprung up in recent interpretation of the poem: what is the nature of the God of *Pearl*? This God, represented as Christ in the form of a bleeding lamb in the poem, has been understood in various ways by different readers. In his essay on the *Pearl*-poet as vernacular theologian, for example, Nicholas Watson has argued that 1) "the God revealed in *Pearl* takes no notice of how hard individuals have labored, only the 'coeunaunt,'" 2) that he "takes no more interest in most aspects of his servants' inner lives than a hunter does in the death agonies of a deer," and 3) that he "is not primarily concerned with inner transformation, but outer submission."[4] Watson's remarks paint a picture of a judgmental, even callous, God in the poem, one that is consonant with his view that the Dreamer is not consoled at the end of the poem, remaining sorrowful but believing he will take his place in heaven because he has submitted.[5]

Publishing his reflections two years before Watson, but still in response to a trend in scholarship consonant with Watson's interpretation, Lawrence

Clopper argued differently: "In characterizing the God of the *Gawain*-poet, I intend to respond to his critics who have found that God to be cantankerous, annoying, and overly human. ... Specifically, I want to contest the idea that the poet anthropomorphizes the deity to such an extent that he gives him a number of common human failings."[6] Clopper goes on to emphasize God's merciful covenant with humanity as well as his transcendent "otherness."

As even a brief glance at these two diverging viewpoints suggests, the nature of God revealed in *Pearl* is an interpretive crux in the poem—a debated aspect worth reconsidering—in terms of medieval literary and cultural contexts. When the evidence of the poem is examined in these contexts, interpretation need not be a choice between a harshly judgmental God or a covenantally merciful one; there is a third possibility. As this study will show, the God of *Pearl* can perhaps be best understood in the context of contemplative Christianity and the affective piety medieval people developed in relationship to their understanding of the sufferings of Christ.

In what follows in this chapter, consideration of the visionary genre of the poem and the cultural context represented by the experiences of medieval contemplative Christians will establish the foundation for a new understanding of the poem. Then, close examination of the Pearl-Maiden's claim to be married to Christ will show how the poem connects to the cultural practices of medieval affective piety. Finally, review of the poem's conclusion, the point of which is often missed or dismissed, will suggest why the poet's focus on the memorial of the Eucharist matters and how it helps to reveal the loving nature of God.

Dream Vision and Revelation

Pearl is visionary literature. While the poem's affiliations with certain genres can be debated, the attentive reader inevitably notes that the plot features a man grief-stricken over the loss of his pearl, who falls asleep in a garden, whose spirit then "springs into space," at which point he walks in a fantastical dreamscape. There he encounters the Pearl-Maiden, and after a long conversation beholds a vision-within-his-dream, which she has requested for him, of the New Jerusalem and a procession of saints led by the bleeding-but-joyful Lamb. After this, he suddenly awakens to remember and reflect. In literary scholarship, the man is typically called the Dreamer (though occasionally "the Jeweler" as well) because the catalytic action he takes at the start of the narrative is falling asleep and beginning to dream. Furthermore, most of the poem is taken up by the dream, framed by the brief scenes of falling asleep and then remembering the dream after awakening. As simple as these generic conventions may appear, they do in fact make this poem a dream vision, one that shares these aspects in common with other dream visions of the period.

Granting that the poem is a dream vision, a reader may yet wonder if it is also a revelation. As J.R.R. Tolkien insightfully has observed, the literary dream vision and the dream vision of lived experience overlap:

> This was one of the reasons for the popularity of visions: they allowed marvels to be placed within the real world, linking them with a person, a place, a time, while providing them with an explanation in the fantasies of sleep, and a defense against critics in the notorious deception of dreams. ... We are dealing with a period when men, aware of the vagaries of dreams, still thought that amid their japes came visions of truth. And their waking imagination was strongly moved by symbols and the figures of allegory, and filled vividly with the pictures evoked by the scriptures, directly or through the wealth of medieval art. ... The narrated vision in the more serious medieval writing represented, if not an actual dream, at least a real process of thought culminating in some resolution or turning point of the interior life– as with Dante and in *Pearl*. ... It is overwhelmingly more probable that [*Pearl*] too was founded on a real sorrow and drew its sweetness from a real bitterness.[7]

Pearl does represent itself as the authentic, if highly wrought, recollection of a vision that a man truly experienced. Certainly the three landscapes of the poem—the garden in which the Dreamer falls asleep in the beginning, the paradisial dreamscape he explores in the middle, and the heavenly city of Jerusalem he perceives in his vision-within-a-dream in the last third of the poem—constitute a meaningful, transformative progression culminating in revelation based upon Revelation.[8] It is worthwhile to consider further, then, just how *Pearl* is situated in relation to both dream vision and revelation.

The dream vision genre of literature was at the height of its power in the later Middle Ages. Drawing on powerful examples from the Bible and dream theory from Augustine, Cicero's *Dream of Scipio,* and Macrobius' *Commentary on the Dream of Scipio*, medieval poets were inspired in their writing about dreams: French poets Guillaume de Lorris and Jean de Meun produced the *Romance of the Rose*; the Italian poet Dante produced the *Divine Comedy*.[9] Meanwhile, English writers caused dream vision poems to proliferate. There were Chaucerian dream visions,[10] frame narrative dream visions,[11] allegorical dream visions,[12] alliterative revival dream visions,[13] and fifteenth-century dream visions, some of them Scottish in origin.[14] The genre's popularity was matched by its versatility, which permitted poets to explore a great diversity of issues, from love to the afterlife to women's issues to moral living to the proper responsibilities of kings.[15]

Because dreams and visions were, in their most rarefied forms, associated with divine intervention in the human soul and prophetic experiences that pierced the fabric of time, dream vision poems had a certain amount of authority attributed to them by their writers and accepted by their medieval readers. Such poems were largely exempted from the normal degree of scrutiny applied to formal treatises on theological and social subjects because, after all, they were dreams, and what man could control what he dreamed? Dream visions that made bold propositions could escape censure by virtue of the fact that they were memories of fantasies that occurred while the poet (or the narrator or the protagonist) was asleep.

Yet by the very nature of sleep, dreams—and dream vision poems about them—allowed poets to explore what was taking place in the soul. Allegorical or abstract figures that appeared in these dream visions allowed poets to represent virtues, vices, and emotions as dramatic actors interacting within the dreamer, taking him on a journey from one place (which represented one state of the soul) to another (which represented another state of the soul, often a more elevated state). This is a standard pattern in medieval dream visions that draws on classical tradition. As Kevin Marti remarks on the dream vision in general (but note how Dante's *Divine Comedy* in particular supplies the paradigm):

> The dreamer experiences an assent toward a vision of heaven in stages that figure simultaneously as the stages of an interior journey to the core of his own creativity. By visualizing more and more abstract representations of some earthly object or person, the dreamer manages to perceive its immaterial counterpart in the heavenly realm of Platonic form. The importance of these stages of abstraction in textual and other cultural form is rooted in ancient schemes for the return of the soul to God after death (*regressus animae*) and for the resurrection of the body.[16]

Of course, inner transformation can be accomplished not only through ascent, but also through descent, as the tradition of St. Patrick's Purgatory visions demonstrates.[17]

Just as it may be considered dream vision literature, so also may *Pearl* be considered a revelation that participates in the genre conventions of apocalyptic literature. The term "apocalypse" comes from the Greek, and etymologically, it means "to unveil," "to uncover," or "to reveal," and so is synonymous with "revelation." In the Middle Ages, biblical literature provided inspiration and impetus for the creation of illustrated apocalypse manuscripts as well as works of art and literature imitative of biblical models.

Thus the proto-apocalyptic narratives of the Jewish Bible (Is. 24–27, 333–35, Jer. 33:14–26, Ezek. 38–39, Joel 3:9–17, Zach. 12–14, and most influentially, Dan. 7–12) and those of the Christian New Testament (Matt. 24, The Parable of the Sheep and the Goats, Mark 13, 2 Thess. 2, and, most significant of all, the book of Revelation) inspired written and visual commentary, the genre of non-canonical apocalyptic books by pseudo-eponymous authors linked to biblical characters (such as James, Peter, Stephen, and Paul) as well as ecclesiastical figures like Methodius, and Latin and vernacular prose and poetry that engage with doctrinal concepts and imagery that are essentially apocalyptic. They are concerned, prophetically, as one twelfth-century, Calabrian monk, Joachim of Fiore, wrote, with "things past, the knowledge of things to come, the opening of what is sealed, the uncovering of what is hidden."[18] Because the biblical book of Revelation describes the New Jerusalem as a "bride adorned for her husband,"[19] and because the relationship between Christ and the Church was imagined as one between a Bridegroom and his Bride, the Song of Songs was also widely incorporated into apocalyptic literature.

Revelation in the Middle Ages, however, was not only a narrower literary genre of dream vision based specifically on biblical precedent, but also an experience. It was deliberately sought in prayer by medieval Christian contemplatives, who sometimes have been called "mystics."[20] The contemplative tradition stressed the importance of humility, considered the first rung on the ladder that led up into the heavens where God is, and the progressive journey into God. Spiritual formation on this journey included purgation, illumination, and, finally, unification with the divine. The whole process could involve visionary experiences in prayer, and the final step, unification, was understood as a spiritual marriage between the individual Christian soul and her bridegroom, Christ. Often the language of the Song of Songs was used to evoke the tender intimacy contemplatives sensed in their relationship to Christ.[21]

Both the genre of literary revelation and the prayerful experience of revelation bear on the interpretation of *Pearl*. For the Dreamer experiences a purgative and illuminating dream vision, that prepares him for unification with the divine (though he does not experience it in the space and time recorded by the poem), and the Pearl-Maiden reveals, through her dialogue with the Dreamer, that she has herself experienced a spiritual marriage to Christ. In the process, the nature of the God of *Pearl* is revealed.

Pearl and the Practices of Contemplative Christians[22]

In order to understand the Pearl-Maiden's claims that she has been married to Christ, it is important to consider the late-medieval, contemplative Christian practices of *lectio divina* ("divine reading"), the four senses of scripture, experiences in contemplative prayer, the three-fold path to union with God, and affective piety in general. The practice of *lectio divina* was encouraged by the early Church Fathers: Augustine, Jerome, Ambrose, and Gregory as well as Origen and Cassian. "Divine reading" was actually a series of practices that could include beginning in silence, reading aloud, meditating, praying, contemplating and eventually applying the truths of scripture. Such intensive reading helped train contemplative Christians to read scripture for its multiple meanings.

The four recognized levels of scriptural interpretation compelled the devout to pursue contemplative reading that could foster deeper understanding of biblical passages. The four levels are aptly summed up in a Latin phrase: *litera gesta docet; allegoria quod credas; moralis quid agas; quo tendas anagogia* ("the literal (sense) teaches deeds; the allegorical what you believe; the moral what you do; the anagogical where you are going").[23] To derive the meaning from these senses required time and thought, which the founders of the monastic orders, particularly Saint Benedict, fully recognized. To accommodate *lectio divina*, Benedict's Rule permitted two hours of private scripture readings to monks, but three during the season of Lent; St. Caesarius of Arles likewise permitted two hours of private readings to nuns in his Rule.[24]

By the twelfth century, the stages of *lectio divina* were codified in a letter to a fellow monk by Guigo II, a Carthusian monk, and the letter circulated as a treatise known in Latin as the *Scala Paradiso* or the *Scala Claustralium*.[25] Guigo advised that the *lectio divina* include reading, meditation, prayer, and contemplation. His letter begins in this fashion:

> When I was at hard at work one day, thinking on the spiritual work needful for God's servants, four such spiritual works came to my mind, these being: reading; meditation; prayer; contemplation. This is the ladder for those in cloisters, and for others in the world who are God's Lovers, by means of which they can climb from earth to heaven. It is a marvelously tall ladder, but with just four rungs, the one end standing on the ground, the other thrilling into the clouds and showing the climber heavenly secrets. This is the ladder Jacob saw, in Genesis, that stood on the earth and reached into heaven. ...
>
> Understand now what the four staves of this ladder are, each in turn. Reading, Lesson, is busily looking on Holy Scripture with all one's will and wit. Meditation is a studious in searching with the mind to know what was before concealed through desiring proper skill. Prayer is a devout desiring of the heart to get what is good and avoid what is evil. Contemplation is the lifting up of the heart to God tasting somewhat of the heavenly sweetness and savor. Reading seeks, meditation finds, prayer asks, contemplation feels. ...
>
> Reading puts, as it were, whole food into your mouth; meditation chews it and breaks it down; prayer finds its savor; contemplation is the sweetness that so delights and strengthens.[26]

For Guigo, then, as well as for other Christian contemplatives in monastic environments, the practice of *lectio divina* connected his earthly experience with heavenly realities, as Jacob's dream of the ladder did for him at Bethel (Genesis 28). The stages of *lectio* were active, entailing commitments to seek, find, ask, and feel, and they were metaphorically akin to eating because they provided food for the soul.[27]

It is especially notable that Guigo anticipates that both those living inside the cloisters, oath-bound to the monastic life, and those living outside of them, as lay Christians in the world, would practice *lectio divina*: "This is the ladder for those in cloisters, and *for others in the world who are God's Lovers,* by means of which they can climb from earth to heaven" (emphasis added). While the *Pearl*-poet's status as a monastic or lay Christian is unknown, the visionary poem *Pearl* gives strong evidence that he practiced divine reading, for he paraphrases scripture throughout the poem, using it to compose, create, and interweave the four levels of meaning that he found in the Bible into his dream vision. Furthermore, the Dreamer's ascent through three ever-rising landscapes—the earthly garden, the paradisial dreamscape, the heavenly vision of Jerusalem—act metaphorically like Jacob's ladder, the *scala paradiso* connecting earth to heaven and heaven to earth. The apotheosis of the poem, the grand vision of the New Jerusalem based upon Revelation 21, shows just how deeply the poet has meditated on scripture.

Ruminating on scripture, eating its truth, and becoming stronger thereby provided a context for contemplative prayer.[28] The beginning of the *lectio* involved reading, followed by meditation—the engagement of the mind in rumination and imaginative placement of the self at, for example, the side of the manger where the baby Jesus lay or the foot of the Cross where he was crucified[29]—and oral prayer while contemplating drew the prayerful Christian into quieter, closer relationship to Christ. In the emotional union it facilitated, contemplation might not require any thought at all.[30] Indeed, contemplative prayer focused on the centering experience of being in the presence of God and being united with Him.

Through prayer and other practices, contemplative Christians proceeded on a three-fold path into God: purgation, illumination, and unification. In the purgative stage, they experienced repentance and forgiveness, a spiritual cleansing that prepared them for illumination. In the illuminative stage, their hearts and minds gained greater understanding of God and divine things. Both stages might be repeated many times, and writers on the contemplative life agree that the Christian seeking to move on to unification with God might never do so in this life. Understanding this context, it is possible to recognize that the Pearl-Maiden's reported experience of spiritual marriage to Christ represents unification with God after her death while the Dreamer's parallel, but very different, experience shows that he is passing through the purgative stage and has not yet experienced unification, which the Pearl-Maiden says is only possible if he crosses the stream between them, and to do that, he would have to die (ll. 313–24).[31] Nevertheless, some contemplatives did believe that they could experience unification with the divine in life. The metaphor for understanding such unification was spiritual marriage.

The tradition of imagining spiritual marriage in the Middle Ages has its roots in the Hebrew Bible and the Christian New Testament.[32] It was further developed within the early church, particularly by the example of Augustine and the theory of sexual hierarchy articulated by Jerome in *Against Jovinian*, which emphasized the chaste ideal in a sexually immoral world; it was further emphasized in medieval virgin martyr legends.[33] Allegorical commentaries on the Song of Songs, beginning with Origen in the second century, infused Christian contemplation with a sensual and passionate language for imagining the soul's union with the divine.[34] By the twelfth century, Bernard of Clairvaux could celebrate the spiritual marriage of the soul to Christ extravagantly in his sermons on the Song of Songs without objection from his monastic audience of any conflict between the literal and spiritual sense of his text.

Bernard of Clairvaux, in his second sermon on the Song of Solomon, provides an allegorical exegesis of the kiss mentioned in the first verse of that great epithalamion that shows a clear set of connections, a continuum of relation, between *lectio divina*, meditation on the senses of scripture, experiences of contemplative prayer, and the desire to pass through the stages of purgation and illumination to unification with God:

> All the prophets are empty to me. But he, he of whom they speak, let him speak to me. Let him kiss me with the kiss of his mouth. ... His living and effective word is a kiss; not a meeting of lips which can sometimes be deceptive about the state of the heart, but a full infusion of joys, a revelation of secrets, a wonderful and inseparable mingling of the light from above in the mind on which it is shed, which, when it is joined with God, is one spirit with him ... O happy kiss, and wonder of amazing self-humbling which is not a mere meeting of lips, but the union of God with man![35]

In these words, Bernard reveals his own extensive practice of *lectio divina*, his own meditation on Scripture, and through his allegorical exegesis of the Song of Songs shows how it led to an understanding of intimate, contemplative prayer—in which he could hear the voice of God—and the "kiss" experienced in this state that leads to the union of God with man.

Similarly to Bernard of Clairvaux, many medieval Christian women left written records that show that their own contemplative prayer life led, in a striking number of cases, to distinctive visions of their souls being married to Christ. Contemplative women who recorded their experiences of spiritual marriage include Angela of Foligno, Catherine of Siena, Birgitta of Sweden, Margery Kempe, and Teresa of Avila.[36] While their spiritual visions met with a mixed reception by their contemporaries, rarely were they dismissed as heretical or unorthodox by the Church because of a clear tradition establishing precedent for their visions in scripture and church exegetical tradition.

Spiritual devotion to Jesus, and visionary experiences of spiritual marriage to him in prayer, can better be understood as part of the overall movement of affective piety in the Church in the later Middle Ages. Affective piety was the compassionate, co-identifying, emotional response of believing Christians to the sufferings of Christ on the Cross, which, through scripted (and unscripted) prayers, hymns and lyrics, as well as interpretations of Augustine's writings and applications of Franciscan theology, encouraged contemplatives to imagine themselves beside Mary, the weeping mother of Jesus, at the foot of the Cross.[37] As Sarah McNamer has argued, late medieval meditations on the Passion are "richly emotional, script-like texts that ask their readers to imagine themselves present at scenes of Christ's suffering and to perform compassion for that suffering victim in a private drama of the heart."[38] McNamer sees this as a specifically historical and gendered experience of believing women, devoted to the suffering humanity of Christ, one in which loving and being loved by God was experienced as not a theological concept, but a lived reality.

Pearl aligns with this understanding of the gendered experience affective piety, with the female Pearl-Maiden showing a greater ability to meditate on Christ's Passion as well as, ultimately, to enter into a spiritual marriage with Christ, experiences that are denied the male Dreamer, at least temporarily. More importantly, careful study shows that spiritual devotion to Jesus, the suffering Christ on the Cross, was closely related to the contemplative journey into God and unification with the divine imagined as spiritual marriage. Thus it should come as no surprise that the Pearl-Maiden's revelation of her spiritual marriage to Christ is intimately connected to her highly imagistic, even visionary, meditations on his Passion.

Spiritual Marriage and Christ's Passion in *Pearl*

The practices of late-medieval, contemplative Christians, especially the felt responses fostered by affective piety, meant that love expressed as compassion for the suffering of Christ on the Cross was a central spiritual experience for "God's Lovers." Using language from the Song of Songs, contemplatives imagined themselves as lovers and Christ as beloved, but role-reversal was possible within this intimate relationship, and Christ could equally be imagined as lover and the believing soul as beloved. Within the cultural, spiritual, and emotional framework of contemplative spirituality, it is worth noting that the record of medieval Christian perceptions of God does not primarily reveal him as judgmental or callous, transcendently "Other" or covenantally merciful. Instead, they reveal him as intimately loving. *Pearl* is a visionary poem that can be interpreted in this tradition.

Specifically, *Pearl* reveals perceptions of God in stages meant to draw the character of the Dreamer—and along with him, the readers or hearers of the poem—into a contemplative Christian understanding of God's love. In the first stage, we see God from the perspective of the Dreamer, who is angry and overwrought because of the loss of his beloved Pearl-Maiden. Gradually, however, readers are presented with another perspective: that of the Pearl-Maiden. When she speaks, she reveals her spiritual marriage to Christ, her identity as both lover and beloved, and she also repeats the words God has spoken to her soul. These words are direct quotations from the Song of Songs: they are the love-song of the Lamb remembered, as an echo, in the Pearl-Maiden's own speech.

94 *Anagogical Revelation*

The final stage of the progressive revelation of God within the poem takes place within the context of the Dreamer's vision of the New Jerusalem, where he sees the Lamb himself, with a wide-open, bleeding wound but, nevertheless, a joyous countenance. This iconic representation of the Lamb, which has been anticipated by the Pearl-Maiden's detailed recollections of Christ's Crucifixion in the earlier sections XIV and XV of the poem, begins to awaken the Dreamer's compassion for the suffering of someone other than himself. While the Dreamer cannot keep his focus on the Lamb, but is instead distracted by the sight of his beloved Pearl-Maiden in the heavenly procession, upon awakening, the Dreamer takes time to reflect upon his visionary experience. The conclusion of the poem shows that a definitive shift has taken place in the Dreamer's perception of God.

The Dreamer's original feelings about the loss of the Pearl-Maiden, whom he regards as his own, are manifestly negative. After speaking of his "deuely dele" (l. 51), his desolating or devastating grief, he adds: "Þagh kynde of Kryst me comfort kenned/My wreched wylle in wo ay wragte" (ll. 54–55). The Dreamer makes it clear in these two lines that he knows about the comfort available to him through the example and the person of Christ, but his will—his volition—is in anguish. It is not just the Dreamer's heart that has been broken by the loss of the Pearl-Maiden, but also his freedom of choice that has been violated: her death happened against his will and desire.[39]

When the Dreamer enters into the bejeweled landscape of his dream, the beauty stuns him so much that he admits that the splendor "Bylde in me blys, abated my balez,/Fordidden my stresse, dystryed my paynez" ("Built in me bliss, abated my woes/Ended my distress, destroyed my pains") (ll. 123–24). The dream, like a wish-fulfillment fantasy, temporarily relieves his woe, distress, and pain. It also serves to emphasize that the Dreamer has been experiencing these emotions to a stunningly deep degree.

Finally, when the Dreamer first sees the Pearl-Maiden, he experiences "abaysment" (l. 174), amazement or confusion as well as bewilderment and "drede" (ll. 181, 186), that is, fear, particularly at the thought of what might happen if she "eschaped" or eluded him again (l. 187). The Dreamer's first words to the Pearl-Maiden when he sees her further expound his feelings.

> 'O perle,' quoþ I, 'in perlez py3t,
> Art þou my perle þat I haf *playned*,
> *Regretted* by myn one on ny3te?
> Much *longeyng* haf I for þe layned,
> Syþen into gresse þou me agly3te.
> *Pensyf, payred,* I am *forpayned,*
> And þou in a lyf of lykyng ly3te,
> In Paradys erde, of stryf vnstrayned.
> What Wyrde hatz hyder my juel vayned,
> And don me in þys *del* and gret daunger?
> Fro we in twynne wern towen and twayned,
> I haf ben a *joylez* juelere.' (ll. 241–52, emphases added)

Anagogical Revelation 95

In this passage, the Dreamer clearly expresses to the Pearl-Maiden that he has mourned over her, been filled with regret and longing for her, felt overmastered by his own thoughts, and been wasted-away and afflicted, deep in sorrow and longing and joylessness. The Dreamer, with unabashed truthfulness, tells the Pearl-Maiden exactly how he feels. The Pearl-Maiden, who is clearly not a professional psychologist, does not respond with reflective listening or even with empathy for the Dreamer. Instead, she says, "Sir, ye haf your tale mysetente" ("Sir, you have misunderstood your story") (l. 257). When the Pearl-Maiden informs the Dreamer that he has misunderstood ("mysetente") his own experience, she shows there is another perspective to consider.

In this moment, when the Pearl-Maiden challenges the Dreamer's perceptions of reality, it is not superiority but spiritual friendship that she shows him. As he has been truthful with her, she is now truthful with him. She seeks to contextualize his great grief not in his individual, emotional reality but in the transcendent, spiritual reality of Christian belief in God's promise of hope for life after death. She tells him that she holds him much to blame if he believes the Lord would tell a lie who has loyally promised to raise his life up again even though Fortune made his flesh die (ll. 304–306). When she explains that he cannot be with her unless he dies, he asks if she is judging him to grief again and expresses his fear that he will lose her once more. He is clearly anxious about re-experiencing "durande doel" ("enduring grief") (l. 356)—a lasting, almost inescapable sorrow. To this, the Pearl-Maiden replies that it would be better for the Dreamer to bless himself and love God, whether in "well or woe" (l. 341), as anger gains him nothing.

This is just the beginning of the Pearl-Maiden's expression of the truth she has experienced on the other side of dying. Her consolation is not the consolation that the Dreamer is seeking. She chooses to reveal what has comforted and consoled her: intimacy with Christ.

> 'A blysful lyf þou says I lede;
> Þou woldez knaw þerof þe stage.
> Þow wost wel when þy perle con schede
> I watz ful 3ong and tender of age;
> Bot my Lorde þe Lombe þur3 Hys godhede,
> He toke myself to Hys maryage,
> Corounde me quene in blysse to brede
> In lenghe of dayez þat euer schal wage;
> And sesed in alle Hys herytage
> Hys lef is. I am holy Hysse.
> Hys prese, Hys prys, and Hys parage
> Is rote and grounde of alle my blysse.' (ll. 409–20)

The Pearl-Maiden tells the Dreamer that her blissful life is the consequence of her marriage to her Lord, the Lamb, who has crowned her queen. The Lamb and his inheritance are, she says, the root and ground of all her bliss.

96   *Anagogical Revelation*

More than halfway through the poem, the Pearl-Maiden will find it necessary to affirm, again, that she is married to Christ. As if it were not enough that she has already asserted "I am wholly His," now, in response to a question to the Dreamer, she must say that the Lamb beats out everyone else who even tries to compete with him:

> 'My makelez Lambe þat al may bete,'
> Quoþ scho, 'my dere Destyné,
> Me ches to Hys make, alþa3 vnmete
> Sumtyme semed þat assemblé.
> When I wente fro yor worlde wete,
> He calde me to hys bonerté:
> "Cum hyder to me, my lemman swete,
> For mote ne spot is non in þe."
> He gef me my3t and als bewté;
> In hys blod he wesch my wede on dese,
> And coronde clene in vergynté,
> And py3t me in perlez maskellez.' (ll. 756–68)

In the process of defending her marriage to Christ to the Dreamer, the Pearl-Maiden reveals Christ's words to her, his intimate communication with her soul, which, in this passage, is a Middle English paraphrase (although not an exact translation) of words from the Latin Vulgate Bible:

> Tota pulchra es amica mea
> et macula non est in te. (Songs of Songs 4.7–8)
> (All beautiful is my friend,
> and no spot is in you.)
>
> "Cum hyder to me, my lemman swete,
> For mote ne spot is non in þe." (ll. 763–64)[40]

The Pearl-Maiden here remembers how the Lamb wooed her, the exact phrasing of his invitation to her to come to him, and his perception of her as his sweet lover, without blemish or spot. The innocence that the Lamb sees in the Pearl-Maiden, she clarifies within two lines, is actually made possible by the Lamb himself, who washes her garments in his own blood.

Underlying this washed-in-the-blood imagery in the poem is a passage from Revelation, "et dixi illi domine mi tu scis et dixit mihi hii sunt qui veniunt de tribulatione magna et laverunt stolas suas et dealbaverunt eas in sanguine agni,"[41] which in turn draws on Isaiah, "Et venite et arguite me dicit Dominus si fuerint peccata vestra ut coccinum quasi nix dealbabuntur et si fuerint rubra quasi vermiculus velut lana erunt."[42] In the poem, the Pearl-Maiden makes a vivid connection between her spiritual marriage to Christ—to being chosen by him as his "make"[43] and wooed by his love-song—and having her clothes, which represent the state of her soul, washed in his blood. In the process, she is given the gifts of strength and beauty, crowned in a state of clean virginity, and adorned with pearls.

The source of the blood is the Lamb himself, and the Judeo-Christian significance of the blood is its power to atone for sin and make union between God and humanity possible. The Pearl-Maiden's focus on blood here is a precursor to her extensive meditation on Christ's Passion in the next section of the poem. When the Dreamer asks her, "Quat kyn þyng may be þat Lambe / Þat þe wolde wedde vnto hys vyf?" (ll. 771–72), it gives her the opportunity to describe the Crucifixion. She begins the story on Mount Zion:

> 'On þe hyl of Syon, þat semly clot,
> Þe apostel hem segh in gostly drem
> Arayed to þe weddyng in þat hyl-coppe,
> Þe nwe cyté o Jerusalem.' (ll. 789–92)

Strikingly, this passage forms a bridge between the Pearl-Maiden's affirmation of her spiritual marriage and her meditation on Christ's Passion. In this transition, the Pearl-Maiden specifically mentions the "gostly drem" vision of St. John the Revelator, who once saw a group of people "arayed to þe weddyng" (l. 791). This image suggests the larger Church, whose members corporately make up the Bride of Christ, just as the Pearl-Maiden's soul does individually. This hilltop gathering for a wedding, on Mount Zion, recalls Isaiah 51 and 62, in which God comforts Israel by the name "Zion" and promises she shall be called *beulah* ("married").

In the very next stanza of the poem, the Pearl-Maiden begins to tell the story of the Crucifixion, calling Christ "My Lombe," "my dere Juelle," and "my lemman fre," all words of adoration in the tradition of affective piety. Not coincidentally, the Dreamer has been applying similar terms to her, but she, by example, wants to show him to apply these terms of endearment and praise to their Lord, her Bridegroom.

> 'Of Jerusalem I in speche spelle.
> If þou wyl knaw what kyn He be –
> My Lombe, my Lorde, my dere Juelle,
> My Joy, my Blys, my Lemman fre –
> Þe profete Ysaye of Hym con melle
> Pitously of Hys debonerté:
> "Þat gloryous Gyltlez þat mon con quelle
> Wythouten any sake of felonye,
> As a schep to þe sla3t þer lad watz he;
> And, as lombe þat clypper in hande nem,
> So closed he hys mouth fro vch query,"
> Quen Juez Hym iugged in Jerusalem.' (ll. 793–804)

The Pearl-Maiden's reference to Isaiah clearly emphasizes Christ's identification with an innocent lamb; the allusion to the Lamb's silence, medieval

Christians understood, was a prophetic prediction of the silence of Jesus in the face of his accusers in his nighttime trial.[44]

What follows, in the rest of section XIV of the poem, is the Pearl-Maiden's detailed recollection of Christ's Passion. It is unlike the lengthy retelling of the Parable of the Workers in the Vineyard, although this discourse has similarly been inspired by a question from the Dreamer. In the parable paraphrase, the Pearl-Maiden sought to reveal the nature of salvation as a gift, which could not be earned, based on the number of hours a believing soul worked in the world for Christ, only received. Here, by remembering the death of Christ on the Cross, the Pearl-Maiden reveals the source and the means of salvation. As she does so, she will again call Christ "my Lemman swete" (l. 829). As with medieval Christian contemplatives in late-medieval England, so here too with the Pearl-Maiden: the tradition of affective piety causes identification with the suffering of the human Christ, inspiring love to be shown through the performance of compassion in the heart of "God's lover." It even leads to an invitation to others (in this case, the Dreamer and the readers of the poem) to see inwardly, imaginatively, this vision and to respond, emotionally, with similar devotion.

Although the Pearl-Maiden appears to be trying to lead the Dreamer into contemplative Christian practice, her effort does not take effect immediately. So she reveals that she has asked for him to behold a vision of the New Jerusalem. The Dreamer need not simply recall, inwardly, the vision of Christ's Passion that she has described. Instead, he can see for himself—as St. John did—the New Jerusalem and the Lamb within the heavenly city. At this point, the Pearl-Maiden moves from explaining how salvation works (the parable) and who is its source (Christ on the Cross) to how it matters in eternity, its eternal results: the unification of the saints with their loving God in heaven.

A Vision of the New Jerusalem and the Memorial of the Eucharist

The New Jerusalem that the Dreamer beholds, described in sections XVII–XVIII of the poem, has long been recognized as an elaborate poetic paraphrase of Revelation 21. It reveals the poet's own practice of *lectio divina* and can be considered in light of the four senses of scripture, which medieval readers understood to be hidden within the biblical text. It is the privileged landscape within which the Dreamer beholds the Lamb himself, the Lamb who could be considered, historically, the scapegoat onto whom sin was transferred for atonement in ancient Israel; allegorically, Jesus at the time of the Crucifixion; morally, the invitation to believing contemplatives to apply the modes of affective piety; and anagogically, the promise of future unification of Christians with God in heaven at the marriage feast of the Lamb.[45]

The representation of the Lamb in *Pearl* is strikingly iconographic: an image meant to inspire devotional, emotional response on the part of the viewer.[46] The poet emphasizes a whiteness about this Lamb that is pearlescent, a Lamb who is again called "Juelle" (l. 1124), which is highly significant in the symbolic nexus of meaning of the poem overall.[47] The poet also highlights a vivid contrast between the Lamb's wide, wet wound gushing blood from his side (ll. 1135–40) and his initially inexplicably glad countenance (ll. 1141–44). The Dreamer cannot understand who could do something so spiteful as to wound the Lamb. He wonders, "Who did þat spyt?" (l. 1138), but he recognizes that "Ani breste for bale a3t haf forbrent / Er he þerto hade had delyt" (ll. 1139–40).[48] Recognizing the hurt caused by the wound, he cannot comprehend how the Lamb can look about with "glentez glorious glade" (l. 1144), never showing in his expression the suffering caused by his bleeding side.[49]

It is this crucial moment, when he sees the bleeding Lamb, for which the Pearl-Maiden has sought to prepare the Dreamer, so that he could compassionately co-identify with the suffering Christ. He needs this experience, spiritually and emotionally, in order to heal from the loss of his beloved Pearl-Maiden and direct his greatest love toward God, not a woman, and so be illuminated, purged, and unified with the divine, just as the young woman he loved has been. But he does not keep his focus on the Lamb. He becomes distracted when he sees the one he calls "my lyttel quene" (l. 1147), whom he still thinks of his own, despite what the Pearl-Maiden has first revealed and then affirmed about her marriage to Christ. Then "luf-longyng" (l. 1152), not for Christ, but for her, drives him toward the stream he has been forbidden to enter or cross.[50] When he attempts a crossing, he awakens suddenly to reflect upon the meaning of his experience.

In the conclusion of the poem, the narrator indicates that a significant shift has taken place in his emotional state and his perception of God. Whereas he has been emotionally overwrought and regarded the loss of his pearl with anger (somewhat as Jonah regarded the loss of his vine), perceiving "Wyrde" as a thief (l. 273), now he sees the Prince as "a God, a Lorde, a frende ful fyin" (l. 1204). He does not call Christ "my lemman," as the Pearl-Maiden did, and it is not certain that by "Lorde" he also means "Bridegroom," but his post-visionary contemplation has led him to another stage of relationship to the divine: friendship with God. It is highly significant that he concludes the poem by turning to a meditation on the Eucharist, "þat in þe forme of bred and wyn / Þe preste vus schewez vch a daye" (ll. 1209–10). For this sacrament is an integral part of the contemplative life, in which all repentant Christians can participate as "homly hyne" (l. 1211), that is, humble servants.[51]

For medieval Christian contemplatives, *humilitas* was the first rung of the ladder that leads the devoted believer into God. To take the Eucharist humbly was a place to begin.[52] Because it was the memorial of Christ's Passion, it was also an invitation to meditate with tears of contrition, felt love of God, and identification with the saints who were at the foot of Christ's Cross—as well as with Christ himself—when he died. It was the central experience of affective devotion. For the Crucifixion represented the betrothal of Christ and his Bride. But the Eucharistic memorial was also a foreshadowing of the marriage feast of the Lamb that is to come in heaven, when the wedding itself will be celebrated. That the narrator, remembering his dream, recalls the Eucharist at the conclusion of the poem and includes "vus"—the readers and listeners of *Pearl*—suggests that he is closer to seeing himself as part of the Bride of Christ.[53] He now takes on the Pearl-Maiden's role of inviting others to see themselves this way as well, which may explain why he calls all of us, not just the beloved Pearl-Maiden whom he lost, "precious perlez vnto His pay" (l. 1212).

Conclusions

Medieval Christian doctrine certainly taught that God's nature is just and capable of judgment, merciful and honoring of the covenantal relationships established with Israel and the Church, but also that God's nature is as loving as a bridegroom is toward his beloved bride. The humanity of Christ, and the profound emotional response his suffering on the Cross called forth from "God's lovers" in the later Middle Ages, became a religious movement that scholars subsequently identified as affective piety. This tradition forms a cultural and literary context in which to better understand *Pearl*. When contextualized by this tradition, the nature of God portrayed in *Pearl* is revealed as intimately loving. This loving God extends an invitation to all—the Dreamer, the Pearl-Maiden, and the awakened poet himself, as well as the readers and hearers of the poem—to be embraced by his love. The God of *Pearl* desires the inner transformation of his people through identification with the sufferings of Christ, and this leads, not as the primary goal (which is actually loving union with the divine), but simply as a natural result, to the soul's willing submission to God's providential purposes.

Notes

1. In 1953, E.V. Gordon provided a list of probable allusions to the biblical book of Revelation in an appendix to his edition (165–67). Subsequent scholars who have argued for the importance of understanding *Pearl* as revelation or in the context of medieval apocalyptic literature include Barbara Nolan, *The Gothic Visionary Perspective* (Princeton, NJ: Princeton University Press, 1977); Muriel A. Whitaker, "*Pearl* and Some Illustrated Apocalypse Manuscripts," *Viator* 12 (1981): 183–96; Rosalind Field, "The Heavenly Jerusalem in *Pearl*," 7–17; Richard Emmerson and Bernard McGinn, eds., *The Apocalypse in the Middle Ages* (Ithaca, NY: Cornell University Press, 1993); Stanbury, "The Body and the City in *Pearl*," 30–47; and Cynthia Kraman, "Body and Soul: *Pearl* and Apocalyptic Literature," in *Time and Eternity*, ed. Gerhard Jaritz and Gerson Moreno-Riaño (Turnhout: Brepols, 2003), 355–62. See also Ann R. Meyer, *Medieval Allegory and the Building of the New Jerusalem*, especially chap. 5 and 6.
2. Kraman, "Body and Soul," 360–61.

3. Robertson and Chance have both argued that Pearl can be interpreted according to the four levels of meaning seen in medieval scriptural interpretation. See Robertson, "The Pearl as Symbol," 44–61 and Chance, "Allegory and Structure in *Pearl*," 31–59. I also have argued that *Pearl* can be considered elegy, allegory, consolation, and revelation as well in "The Signifying Power of *Pearl*," 27–58, or compare to the introduction to this volume. See also Elizabeth Kate Schirmer, "Genre Trouble: Spiritual Reading in the Vernacular and the Literary Project of the Pearl-Poet," (Diss., University of California Berkeley, 2001), in which additional scholarship on genre questions is reviewed.
4. Nicolas Watson, "The *Gawain*-Poet as Vernacular Theologian," 305.
5. Note that Watson makes his remarks in response to lines 345–48 of the poem, when the Pearl-Maiden says to the Dreamer that though he "daunce as any do" (l. 345) yet he must abide God's judgment. NB: As elsewhere in this book, all Middle English quotations of *Pearl* are from Andrew and Waldron, ed., *Poems of the Pearl Manuscript*, 5th ed.
6. See also Lawrence Clopper, "The God of the *Gawain*-Poet," *Modern Philology* (1996): 1–18.
7. J.R.R. Tolkien, "Introduction: *Pearl*," in *Sir Gawain and the Green Knight, Pearl, and Sir Orfeo*, trans. J.R.R Tolkien (New York, NY: Ballantine/DelRey, 1975), 14–16.
8. On the landscapes of *Pearl*, and to understand these landscapes in cultural and literary context, see Derek Pearsall and Elizabeth Salter, *Landscapes and Seasons of the Medieval World* (Toronto: University of Toronto Press, 1973), 56–75; Henri Lefebvre, *The Production of Space*, trans. Donald Nicholson-Smith (Oxford: Blackwell Publishing, 1974), and William Alexander McClung, *The Architecture of Paradise: Survivals of Eden and Jerusalem* (Berkeley and Los Angeles, CA: University of California Press, 1983) as well as Laura L. Howes, ed., *Place, Space, and Landscape in Medieval Narrative* (Knoxville, TN: University of Tennessee Press, 2007) as well as John Finlayson, "*Pearl*: Landscape and Vision," *Studies in Philology* 71 (1974): 314–43; Elizabeth Petroff, "Landscape in 'Pearl': The Transformation of Nature," *The Chaucer Review* 16 (1981): 181–93, and Barbara Newman, "The Artifice of Eternity: Speaking of Heaven in Three Medieval Poems," *Religion and Literature* 37 (2005): 1–24.
9. A useful bibliographic essay surveying primary works and scholarly investigations of the genre is Kevin Marti, "The Dream Vision," in *A Companion to Old and Middle English Literature*, ed. Laura Lambdin et al. (Westport, CT: Greenwood Press, 2002).
10. Chaucer's four dream poems include the *Book of the Duchess, House of Fame, Parliament of Fowls*, and *Legend of Good Women*. Chaucer also incorporated dream visions into larger narratives; examples include Troilus's dream, which Chaucer relates tragically, and the Nun's Priest's Tale, which he relates comically. The Wife of Bath's interpretation of her dream of blood as being about a wealth of gold is apparently meant ironically. The standard edition of these poems is *The Riverside Chaucer*.
11. Gower's *Confessio Amantis* is a key example. Whereas Chaucer uses a pilgrimage to form the frame narrative of the Canterbury Tales, Gower uses a dream vision.
12. William Langland's *Vision of Piers Plowman* was a very popular allegorical dream vision from this period; it exists in four versions (labeled A, B, C, and Z by medieval literary scholars) and many manuscripts.

13. Four of these are the anonymously authored *Winner and Waster, The Parliament of Three Ages, Mum and the Sothsegger,* and *Death and Life. Piers Plowman* obviously fits in this category as well.
14. These include Lydgate's *Temple of Glass* and the Scottish *Kingis Quair*. See Julia Boffey, *Fifteenth-Century English Dream Visions: An Anthology* (Oxford: Oxford University Press, 2003).
15. Although the popularity of the genre waned in the next century, three women writers used it to good effect: Aemelia Lanyer, Rachel Speght, and Elizabeth Melville. See Colleen Erin Shea, *Early Modern Women's Dream Visions: Male Literary Tradition and Female Authorial Voice* (M.A. Thesis, Dalhousie University, 1999). Available online: http://www.collectionscanada.gc.ca/obj/s4/f2/dsk1/tape9/PQDD_0023/MQ50096.pdf.
16. Kevin Marti, "Dream Vision," in *A Companion to Old and Middle English Poetry*, ed. Laura Lambdin and Robert Lambdin (Westport, CT: Greenwood, 2002), 179. For further consideration of the literary genre of dream vision, see Kathryn Lynch, *High Medieval Dream Vision: Poetry, Philosophy and Literary Form* (Stanford, CA: Stanford University Press, 1988), J. Stephen Russell, *English Dream Vision* (Athens, OH: Ohio State University Press, 1988), which is available online (https://ohiostatepress.org/index.htm?/books/book%20pages/russell%20 english.htm), and Stephen Kruger, *Dreaming in the Middle Ages* (Cambridge: Cambridge University Press,1992). See also Peter Brown, *Reading Dreams: The Interpretation of Dreams from Chaucer to Shakespeare* (Oxford: Oxford University Press, 1999).
17. Marie de France translated a version of a dream vision of St. Patrick's Purgatory. The standard modern edition and translation of it gives a good overview of the genre: Michael Curley, ed. and trans. *Saint Patrick's Purgatory: A Poem by Marie de France* (Binghamton, NY: Medieval and Renaissance Texts and Studies, 1993, 1997.) See also Eileen Gardiner, *Visions of Heaven and Hell before Dante* (New York, NY: Italica Press, 1989).
18. Trans. by McGinn from Joachim of Fiore, *Expositio in Apocalysim* (Venice, 1527; repr. Frankfurt am Main: Minverva, 1964) in Emmerson and McGinn, *The Apocalypse in the Middle Ages*, 19.
19. Rev. 21:2.
20. Watson has suggested that the term "mysticism" has largely outlived its usefulness for scholars. He points to the ahistorical nature and use of the term, the tendency of devotional and historical exploration of mystics to be conflated with one another, and the modern belief in the unifying nature of the "quality of experience" of the "Middle English mystics" as problematic factors in the study of "mysticism," which ought to lead to the abandonment of the term. See Watson, "Middle English Mystics," in *The Cambridge History of Medieval English Literature*, ed. David Wallace (Cambridge: Cambridge University Press, 1999), 539–65. My essay uses the term "contemplative Christians" or just "contemplatives" instead, a group that includes both regular and lay believers who devoted themselves to Christ and certain spiritual practices.
21. For discussion, see Matter, *The Voice of My Beloved* and Astell, *The Song of Songs in the Middle Ages*.
22. The paragraphs in this section, now slightly revised, were originally published in my chapter, "Moses and Christian Contemplative Devotion," in *Illuminating Moses: A History of Reception from Exodus to the Renaissance*, ed. Jane Beal (Leiden: Brill, 2014), 304–309.

23. This medieval phrase occurs in various places, including a sermon of Jacobus de Fusignano, a Dominican friar and later bishop (fl. 1280s–1330s), in Siegfried Wenzel, *The Art of Preaching: Five Medieval Texts and Translations* (Washington, DC: Catholic University of America Press, 2013), 60–61.
24. Beryl Smalley, *The Study of the Bible in the Middle Ages* (South Bend, IN: University of Notre Dame Press, 1964, repr. 1978), 29.
25. It was later translated into Middle English under the title *Ladder of Foure Ronges*. For an edition, see the one included in Barry Windeatt, *English Mystics of the Middle Ages* (Cambridge: Cambridge University Press, 1994), 248–52; see also Guigo II the Carthusian, "Ladder of Monks" and "Twelve Meditations," trans. Edmund Colledge and James Walsh, *Cistercian Studies Series 48* (Kalamazoo, MI: Cistercian Publications, 1979).
26. This translation is by Julia Bolton-Holloway. See "*The Ladder of Four Rungs*: Guigo II on Contemplation" (http://www.umilta.net/ladder.html - accessed 25 March 2014).
27. See Michael Casey, *Sacred Reading: The Ancient Art of Lectio Divina* (Liguori, MI: Liguori/Triumph Publications, 1996) and chapters 3–6 in Guglielmo Cavallo and Robert Chartier, eds., *A History of Reading in the West* (Oxford: Blackwell Publishing Ltd., 1999).
28. For discussion of the related practices of monastic reading and prayer, see Paul Griffiths, *Religious Reading: The Place of Reading in the Practice of Religion* (Oxford: Oxford University Press, 1999); Mary Carruthers, *The Craft of Thought: Meditation, Rhetoric and the Making of Images, 400–1200* (Cambridge: Cambridge University Press, 1998); Jean Leclercq, *The Love of Learning and the Desire for God: A Study of Monastic Culture*, trans. Catharine Misrahi, 3rd ed. (Bronx, NY: Fordham University Press, 1982), and Paul Saenger, "Silent Reading: Its Impact on Late Medieval Script and Society," *Viator* 13 (1982): 367–414. See also Joseph Dyer, "The Psalms in Monastic Prayer," in *The Place of the Psalms*, ed. Nancy van Deusen (Albany, NY: SUNY Press, 1999), 59–89.
29. The late-medieval mystic Birgitta of Sweden, in her *Revelations*, wrote of being meditatively present at the birth of Jesus; fourteenth-century anchoritess Julian of Norwich in her *Revelation of Love* recalled vivid meditations of Christ's Passion during an illness she experienced in her thirty-third year.
30. This is reflected in the concept of the *via negativa* inherited by the *Pearl*-poet's contemporary, the author of the *Cloud of Unknowing*, from the late fifth- or early sixth-century *Mystical Theology* of Pseudo-Dionysius.
31. Lynn Staley Johnson has made the argument that the Pearl-Maiden has not died literally, but instead metaphorically, to the world, by entering a convent. See Johnson, "*Pearl* and the Contingencies of Love and Piety," 83–112.
32. For direct Old Testament references to God as Bridegroom and Israel as Bride, see, for example, Is. 54 and 62, Ezek. 16, and Hos. 1–3. For New Testament references to Christ as the Bridegroom, see how Jesus is depicted as referring to himself as such in the synoptic Gospels (Matt. 9:15, Mark 2:19, Luke 5:34), the parable of the wise and the foolish virgins (Matt. 25), John the Baptist's recognition of Jesus as the bridegroom (John 3:27–30), the apostle Paul's allegorical meditation on marriage, especially as it is a picture of the relationship between Christ and the Church (Eph. 5:21–32), and Rev. 21.
33. In the tenth century, Hrotsvita of Gandersheim would write a number of plays celebrating the same plot: virgins resist attacks on their purity by vile men and are, miraculously, preserved in both life and chastity with the consequence that

the men are frequently converted to Christianity (though often only after first being made to look ridiculous). As Karen A. Winstead has shown in her anthology, *Chaste Passions: Medieval English Virgin Martyr Legends* (Ithaca, NY: Cornell University Press, 2000), the stories of virgin martyrs had wide currency in England between the thirteenth and fifteenth centuries, with such famous saints as St. Lucy, St. Cecilia, St. Margaret, St. Agnes, and St. Katherine being just a few of those that were well-known. The Pearl-Maiden has been compared to at least one of these virgin martyrs, St. Margaret. See James Earl, "Saint Margaret and the Pearl Maiden," *Modern Philology* 70 (1972): 1–8.

34. See Matter, *The Voice of my Beloved* and Astell, *The Song of Songs in the Middle Ages*.
35. Bernard of Clairvaux, *Selected Works*, trans. and forward by G.R. Evans, introduction by Jean LeClercq, Classics of Western Spirituality (New York, NY: Paulist Press, 1987), 216–17.
36. For discussion of this phenomenon in cultural context, see Bernard McGinn, *The Flowering of Mysticism, 1250–1350* (New York, NY: Crossroad Publishing Company, 1998), the third volume in his series on the Presence of God; R. N. Swanson, *Religion and Devotion in Europe, c. 1215–c.1515* (Cambridge: University of Cambridge Press, 1995, repr. 1997), esp. chap. 5 "Devotion"; Monica Furlong, *Visions and Longings: Medieval Women Mystics* (Boston, MA: Shambala, 1997); Elizabeth Alvilda Petroff, ed., *Body and Soul: Essays on Medieval Women and Mysticism* (Oxford: Oxford University Press, 1994), and Steven Fanning, *Mystics of the Christian Tradition* (London: Routledge Press, 2001), esp. chap. 4 "The Western Church in the Middle Ages." For a discussion of spiritual marriage in another late-medieval, West Midlands text, see Heather Reid, "Female Initiation Rites and Women Visionaries: Mystical Marriage in the Middle English Translation of 'The Storie of Asneth,'" in *Women and the Divine in Literature Before 1700*, ed. Kathryn Kerby-Fulton (Victoria: University of Victoria Press, 2009), 137–52.
37. See Rachel Fulton, *From Judgment to Passion: Devotion to Jesus and the Virgin Mary, 800–1200* (New York, NY: Columbia University Press, 2005).
38. Sarah McNamer, *Affective Piety and the Invention of Medieval Compassion* (Philadelphia, PA: University of Pennsylvania Press, 2010), 1. Two related studies relevant for consideration of *Pearl* in the context of late-medieval contemplative devotion are Barbara Newman, "What Did It Mean to Say "I Saw"? The Clash between Theory and Practice in Medieval Visionary Culture," *Speculum* 80 (2005): 1–43 and Seeta Chagnati, *The Medieval Poetics of the Reliquary: Enshrinement, Inscription, Performance* (New York, NY: Palgrave Macmillan, 2008), esp. chap. 4, "Enshrining Form: *Pearl* as Inscriptional Object and Devotional Event."
39. Examination of the Dreamer's grief, as well as his overall psychological state, is well expressed in Aers, "The Self Mourning," 53–73. See also Stanbury, "The Body and the City in *Pearl*," 30–47, 115.
40. The source of these words in Revelation is noted by editors Andrew and Waldron. For a more expansive discussion, see also Richard Newhauser, "Sources II: Scriptural and Devotional Sources," 257–76.
41. Rev. 7:14.
42. Is. 1:18.
43. The Middle English Dictionary shows how broad a meaning this term may have: "(a) Either of a married human couple, mate, husband, wife; (b) either of a

non-human couple, bird, animal or fish; a mate; (c) either of a betrothed human couple; also, lover, paramour, mistress; (d) *fig.* a person as bride of Christ; also, Christ as bridegroom; (e) consort; queen."

44. On the silence of Jesus, see Matt. 17:11–14, Mark 14:60–61, and Luke 23:8–10.
45. On the marriage feast of the Lamb, see Rev. 19:6–9.
46. For discussion of artistic sources that may have influenced the poet's depiction at this stage in the poem, see Whitaker, "*Pearl* and Some Illustrated Apocalypse Manuscripts," 183–96.
47. For discussion of the Lamb's pearl-like qualities, see A.C. Spearing, *The Gawain-Poet: A Critical Study*, 128–29, 134–37, which gives an excellent discussion of the multiple symbolic transformations of the pearl. See also White, "Blood in *Pearl*," 1–13.
48. Although the Dreamer recognizes that anyone ought to burn in his breast for sorrow at what he sees, he does not say that he experiences this himself. He is getting closer to compassion for the suffering Christ, but he is not there yet.
49. Compare to Heb. 12:2, which speaks of how Jesus, for the joy set before him, endured the Cross, despising its shame.
50. The sexual tension inherent in the Dreamer's desire at this moment, and other moments in the poem, has been explored in Gross, "Courtly Language in *Pearl*," 79–92; Bullón-Fernández, "'Byyonde the Water,'" 35–49; Gilbert, "Gender and Sexual Transgression," 53–70; and Cox, "*Pearl's* 'Precios Pere': Gender, Language, and Difference," *Chaucer Review* 32 (1998): 377–90 as well as my own "The Pearl-Maiden's Two Lovers," 1–21 and chapter 1 of this book.
51. Sklute noted that the narrator does not have to approach the godhead because it is "present for him in the Eucharist whose essential mystery is in its offer of the bliss of heaven here on earth." See Larry Sklute, "Expectation and Fulfillment in *Pearl*," *Philological Quarterly* 52 (1973): 663–79. However, it might be more accurate to say that the narrator does approach God through the Eucharist, for eating the bread, the body of Christ, unifies the believer with Christ. The sacrament at once looks back in time to the Crucifixion and forward in time to the consummation of history in the Last Judgment and the marriage feast of the Lamb.
52. Others have commented on Eucharistic symbolism and significance in *Pearl*, beginning with Robert Garrett, *Pearl: An Interpretation*, Publications in English (Seattle, WA: University of Washington Press, 1918), who claimed, without persuading the majority of scholars, that the poem's primary meaning was Eucharistic. See also Robert Ackerman, "The Pearl-Maiden and the Penny," in *The Middle English Pearl: Critical Essays*, ed. John Conley (Notre Dame, IN: University of Notre Dame Press, 1970), 149–62; John Gatta, "Transformation Symbolism and the Liturgy of the Mass in *Pearl*," *Modern Philology* 71 (1974): 243–56; Laurence Eldredge, "Imagery of Roundness in William Woodford's *De Sacramento Altaris* and its Possible Relevance to the Middle English *Pearl*," *Notes & Queries*, N.S. (1978): 3–5; and Heather Phillips, "The Eucharistic Allusions in *Pearl*," *Mediaeval Studies* 47 (1985): 474–86. In addition, see Jennifer Garrison, "Liturgy and Loss: *Pearl* and the Ritual Reform of the Aristocratic Subject," *Chaucer Review* (2010): 294–322, who challenges David Aers' assertion that the poem's conclusion is "theologically superficial and psychologically superficial" (Aers, "The Self Mourning," 70) as well as John Bowers' claim that it is a "gratuitous assertion of the Real Presence" (*The Politics of Pearl: Court*

Poetry in the Age of Richard II [Cambridge: Cambridge University Press, 2001], 53). Compare Garrison's points to Alan J. Fletcher, "*Pearl* and the Limits of History," *Studies in Late Medieval and Early Renaissance Texts in Honour of John Scattergood,* ed. Anne Marie D'Arcy and Alan J. Fletcher (Dublin: Four Courts, 2005), 148–70. For the larger cultural context in which to situate Eucharistic allusion in *Pearl*, see Caroline Walker Bynum, *Holy Feast and Holy Fast: The Religious Significance of Food to Medieval Women* (Oakland: University of California Press, 1987).

53. In *Pearl and Contemplative Writing*, Lagerholm notes, "In recounting events, the use of the active voice, the first person pronoun, is prevalent in *Pearl*. As an indication of his spiritual state, the Dreamer addresses God as 'my Lorde' (ll. 285 and 362). The Pearl-Maiden, by contrast, says "our Lorde" (l. 304). However, when she speaks of her Divine Spouse, she refers to him in a more intimate tone: 'my Lorde the Lombe' (l. 413) or as in l. 796: "my Lemman fre.' The difference, it seems, lies in the fact that the Maiden addresses Christ as 'my' to indicate her soul's union with him. The Dreamer, on the other hand, places himself first and ties the external world to himself. In fact, it is only towards the end of the narrative that he becomes an 'object' for the first time. He uses 'we' rather than 'I.' 'He gef *vus* to be His homly hyne' (l. 1211, italics added), which is a sign of inner spiritual growth" (39).

5 Beyond the Four Levels of Meaning
Folktale Genre Patterns in *Pearl*

The exquisitely beautiful, fourteenth-century, Middle English poem *Pearl* signifies at many different levels of meaning and participates in different generic conventions. The poem has been called a dream vision, and as we have seen, it can be interpreted as an elegy, an allegory, a consolation, and a revelation. The poem certainly participates in multiple genres. In this final chapter, my purpose is to suggest the ways that *Pearl* moves beyond the four levels of meaning and participates in three sub-genres of the larger category of folktale: the parable, the fable, and the fairy-tale.

The parable features human characters, often in an agricultural context, and uses images from the lived experience of the anticipated audience to reveal hidden truth about the spiritual world. The parables of Jesus, which appear in the gospels,[1] were of this kind. Medieval audiences were familiar with them not only orally, because certain ones were read aloud in churches throughout the liturgical year, but visually, for they were represented in church windows, sculpture and architecture, and manuscripts as well as, ultimately, their own imaginations.[2]

In contrast, the fable often uses talking animal characters to comment on social injustice and unequal power dynamics in hierarchal cultures. It typically concludes with a proverbial moral lesson. The fables of Aesop were generally known in late-medieval English culture, and they were widely referred to, even in sermons in church, but they were perhaps best known to medieval readers and listeners who attended school, for they were a standard part of Latin language learning and translation exercises.[3] Aesopian fables naturally influenced the oral folktale traditions of England and Europe, and their influence can be seen in later, written collections of fables, such as those by Marie de France.[4]

The fairy-tale encompasses not only human characters and animal creatures, but also supernatural beings, interweaving magic with the plot in order to address the psychological experiences of human beings: hopes, fears, wishes, and dreams.[5] Though the genre rapidly developed between the seventeenth and nineteenth centuries—in the writings of such key figures as Charles Perrault, Madame d'Aulnoy, the Brothers Grimm, and Hans Christian Andersen—and was revivified in the twentieth century by two key figures, Walt Disney and J.R.R. Tolkien (albeit in vastly different ways), the roots of the fairy-tale are in the medieval interpretations of the primal fairy-tale, the classical love-story: Cupid and Psyche.

By exploring the poet's use of folktale conventions in *Pearl*, I hope to show more about the Pearl-Maiden's complex self-understanding, expressed in relationship to the Parable of the Workers in the Vineyard, and the Dreamer's central spiritual conflict, expressed in recurring animal metaphors in the poem, which are connected to the fable tradition. A careful reading of *Pearl* suggests that the poet aims to reconcile the heart of the Dreamer (and the reader) to Christian truth by transforming fairy-tale expectations for human love like that found in the Cupid and Psyche myth (that, in the *Pearl*-poet's day, were cultivated by medieval romance) and re-forming them around the central love-story of Christian history, that of Christ and his Bride. Significantly, it appears that the experiences shared by the Pearl-Maiden and the Dreamer—in the presence of the Lamb—are intended to form a model to which the *Pearl*-poet's readers are invited to respond.

Parabolic Allusions in Pearl: Image and Truth

Pearl has parabolic qualities, and it calls self-referential attention to these qualities through multiple allusions to the parables of Jesus. The poem particularly draws on the parables of Matthew 13 in multiple references to the Parable of the Pearl of Great Price, which greatly informs the imagery and themes of the poem, and the related Parable of the Treasure Hidden in a Field (also known as the Parable of the Merchant). Other parables from Matthew 13 appear to be relevant to the poem, especially the Parable of the Sower, which occurs first in Matthew 13 and presents a paradoxical paradigm for interpretation of all the biblical parables of Jesus. The Parable of the Seine Net, which occurs directly after the parables of the Treasure Hidden in the Field and the Pearl of Great Price in Matthew 13, may be visually invoked in the manuscript illustrations of Cotton Nero A.x. associated with *Pearl*: all four of the illustrations appear together, sequentially [from folios 41r to 42v], as a preface to the poem. The briefest allusion to a parable in *Pearl* is the one to the Parable of the Growing Seed, from Mark 4, in line 40; the longest re-telling is of the Parable of the Workers in the Vineyard, from Matthew 20,[6] which is elaborately articulated and interpreted by the Pearl-Maiden in lines 491–88 (or, more narrowly, lines 501–76). In order to understand the parabolic nature of *Pearl*, it is helpful to define the term "parable."

The word "parable" entered the English language in approximately 1275, and it appears widely in psalters and Wycliffite Bibles in the years 1350–1380, the period to which *Pearl* dates.[7] Etymologically, it comes from the Old French *parabole*, which comes from the Latin *parabola*, which in turn comes from the Greek *parabole*. The Greek word combines the preposition "para," meaning *alongside*, with the noun "bole," meaning a *throwing, casting, beam*, or *ray*; the noun is related to the verb "ballein," meaning *to throw*. Thus, etymologically, the word derives from the phrase "to throw beside" and means, in Greek, Latin, French, and English, "a comparison" or even "a juxtaposition." From the idea of "comparison" or "metaphor," the word "parable" acquires fuller meaning: in Latin, it means not only *comparison*, but also *word*; in French, it is connected to "parler," meaning *to speak*.

According to the Middle English Dictionary, the use of the English word "parable" in literature reveals at least three working definitions of the word in the late medieval period. It can denote a speech or discourse (including a scornful speech or taunt), a proverb or wise saying, or an allegorical or metaphorical narrative, usually with a didactic purpose.[8] In this latter category, it is naturally associated with the sayings and stories of Jesus in the Gospels.[9]

In his 1850 book, which was printed fourteen years before the first edition of *Pearl* (Morris, EETS), Friedrich Gustav Lisco stated that in the parables of Jesus, "the *image borrowed from the visible [material] world* is accompanied by a *truth from the invisible [spiritual] world*" and that the parables of Jesus are not "mere similitudes which serve the purpose of illustration, but are internal analogies where *nature becomes a witness for the spiritual world*."[10] Indeed, the poet who authored *Pearl* seems to be working with this idea, which, though articulated by Lisco in the nineteenth century, nevertheless represents an understanding consonant with fourteenth century ways of thinking. For the visible, material images of net, seed, pearl, treasure, and vineyard in the poem clearly correspond to the unseen realities of the spiritual world, the kingdom of God.

However, the correspondence is not a one-to-one relationship between a metaphoric vehicle and simple, real-world tenor. Instead, the parables in *Pearl* must be understood in two broader contexts: their medieval allegorical interpretation and their liturgical use. The parabolic images in *Pearl* become symbols that resonate with extra-textual and inter-textual significance.

In his book, *Medieval Allegories of Jesus' Parables*, Stephen Wailes brings together the major medieval allegorical interpretations of forty of Jesus's parables, including the three interrelated Parables of the Hidden Treasure, the Pearl of Great Price, and the Seine Net from Matthew 13 and the Parable of the Workers in the Vineyard from Matthew 20. These traditional interpretations give guidance to readers about the potential allegorical significance of the parabolic images used by the *Pearl*-poet. For the detection of allegorical significance need not be a guessing game when ecclesiastical tradition sets forth both the possibilities and limits of allegorical interpretation.

Traditionally, the image of "treasure" in Jesus's Parable of Hidden Treasure was interpreted in three ways: as the treasure of the gospel in the field of the world (Chrysostom), as the treasure of the Bible in the field of the Church (Jerome), and as the treasure of Christ himself hidden in the field of human flesh (Hilary of Poitiers). In other words, the treasure is the "word," whether understood as the truth of the Gospel, the message of the Bible, or the Incarnate Person of Christ. Gregory the Great saw the treasure as *coeleste desiderium*, a longing for heaven in the field of the human soul.

In a related interpretation, Arnobius the Younger sees the treasure as eternal life in the field of paradise. Arnobius writes, "The man is he who in this world, having sold all, gains Christ and eternal life."[11] Thus the means, the word-who-is-Christ, is co-identified with the end, eternal life, for when one obtains the first, one gains the second as well.[12] Wailes comments:

> ... all authorities treat this text as a counsel of personal perfection. Although the idea of radical almsgiving was never lost from the medieval discussion, it was far more common to take the phrase "sells all that he has" in the sense of a full conversion from worldly to spiritual values.[13]

Thus the major medieval allegorical interpretations of the Parable of the Hidden Treasure point toward giving away all that one has to obtain Christ and eternal life. A minor or less common interpretation, voiced by Hugh of Saint-Cher in the thirteenth century and Ludoph of Saxony in the fourteenth century, interprets the treasure as virginity in the field of human flesh—an idea that may be tied to the belief in Christ's virginity and Incarnation. Both the more and less common interpretations are clearly consonant with the over-arching themes of *Pearl*.

Like the Parable of the Hidden Treasure, the Parable of the Pearl of Great Price has standard allegorical interpretations associated with it. The first and foremost of these is Origen's. Origen interpreted the *bonas margaritas* or "fine pearls" as human wisdom before the Incarnation and the pearl of great price as Christ himself. Origen's influence resulted in a common tendency in later medieval commentators to see the pearl as Christ. Clearly, there is continuity between the parables of the Hidden Treasure and of the Pearl of Great Price, for both have parabolic images—the treasure and the pearl—that are given Christological interpretation.

The "good pearls," and indeed "all" the merchant has, are seen not only as human wisdom (Origen) but also as the observances of the old Law (Jerome and Hilary of Poitiers), which is exemplified by the conversion of Paul; the teachings of the prophets and philosophers (Thomas Aquinas); and temporal, worldly things, which include both material possessions and worldly pleasures and even the merchant's very self (Gregory the Great). The pearl of great price is understood to be eternal blessedness (Gregory), the sweetness and radiance of our eternal home, heaven (Haimo of Auxerre), and, again, Christ himself (Origen et alia). Thus when the Pearl-Maiden says to the Dreamer, "I rede þe forsake þe worlde wode / And porchace þy perle maskelles" ("I counsel you to forsake the mad world / and purchase the pearl that is matchless"),[14] she is quite obviously suggesting that the Dreamer can become like the merchant of the parable, selling all he has—giving even his very self—to gain Christ and the kingdom of heaven.

The concept, present in the parable, of selling all one has, was given various interpretations (as already noted), but it could also be seen as a practical call to the vow of poverty and withdrawal from the world to the contemplative life (Peter Chrysologus and Gottfried of Admont). This is surely significant because the Pearl-Maiden counsels the Dreamer not simply to sell all he has to purchase the pearl, but to *forsake the mad world*. Her words are reminiscent of language used by medieval Christian contemplatives withdrawing from the secular world to the contemplative life.

It is worth noting that there is a less common strand of interpretation of the Parable of the Pearl of Great Price, seen in homilies by Pseudo-Bede and Bruno of Segni, in which the merchant actually signifies Christ and the pearl signifies the Church that Christ loves. Both the more and the less common readings are relevant to *Pearl*, for the pearl in the midst of the Pearl-Maiden's breast clearly corresponds to Christ, salvation, and eternal life while the Pearl-Maiden herself is represented as a *sponsa Christi*, an individual Bride of Christ, who is part of the Church universal, the corporate Bride of Christ. Thus, if the Dreamer heeds the Maiden's admonition to forsake the world and purchase the pearl, he becomes not only like the merchant of the parable, but like Christ, and he gains the true pearl, which is not only Christ, but Christ's Church. Gaining the pearl does not mean possessing his Pearl-Maiden for his own selfish purposes, as he seems to wish for so much of the duration of the poem, but rather becoming a part of the corporate Bride of Christ himself.

The Parable of the Seine Net that follows the parables of the Hidden Treasure and Pearl of Great Price in Matthew 13 is not directly alluded to in *Pearl*. Yet I would like to suggest that the mysterious fish, which appear in the stream in three of the four illustrations that preface *Pearl* in its unique manuscript, Cotton Nero A.x (but are never mentioned in the poem), may be the illustrator's way of evoking the third parable from the conclusion of Matthew 13. Juxtaposed with the two earlier parables in Matthew 13, the Parable of the Net serves as a *contra-distinctio*.

In the medieval commentary tradition, whereas the treasure and the pearl represent Christ, salvation, and eternal life in heaven, and the merchant represents the human soul that obtains them, the net represents death. It "catches" the fish, which represent human beings. The fishermen (who are usually interpreted to be Christ and his angels) sort through them, throwing the bad fish back into the sea but keeping the good fish: a vivid picture of the Last Judgment.

In the illustrations that precede *Pearl*, the fish are swimming freely in the stream, which may indicate that the time of the Last Judgment has not yet come—neither has the net been cast nor the culling begun. Yet the ambiguous facial expressions drawn on these fish may suggest moral complexity, particularly the good and evil that co-exist in the hearts of men. That the Dreamer is depicted as pointing directly at a fish in the stream in the second illustration suggests the illustrator's imperative: that those who see this pointing finger must at least meditate on what the fish might signify. Although there are many ways the significance of these fish can be explained (and I have explored some of those ways elsewhere),[15] if the meaning is in fact connected to the Parable of the Seine Net, then it seems to me that the illustrator, like the poet, is actively inviting the reader-viewer of *Pearl* to engage with the text. Such dynamic, interactive engagement may catalyze new self-awareness in the audience.

Catalyzing new awareness in the Dreamer certainly seems to be one of the Pearl-Maiden's goals in her re-telling of the Parable of the Workers in the Vineyard, which occurs in sections IX and X of the poem.[16] The original, biblical parable appears in the Gospel of Matthew:

> The kingdom of heaven is like to an householder, who went out early in the morning to hire labourers into his vineyard. And having agreed with the labourers for a penny a day, he sent them into his vineyard. And going about the third hour, he saw others standing in the market place idle. And he said to them: Go you also into my vineyard, and I will give you what shall be just. And they went their way. And again he went out about the sixth and the ninth hour, and did in like manner. But about the eleventh hour he went out and found others standing, and he saith to them: Why stand you here all the day idle? They say to him: Because no man hath hired us. He saith to them: Go you also into my vineyard.
>
> And when evening was come, the lord of the vineyard saith to his steward: Call the labourers and pay them their hire, beginning from the last even to the first. When therefore they were come, that came about the eleventh hour, they received every man a penny. But when the first also came, they thought that they should receive more: and they also received every man a penny. And receiving it they murmured against the master of the house, Saying: These last have worked but one hour, and thou hast made them equal to us, that have borne the burden of the day and the heats. But he answering said to one of them: Friend, I do thee no wrong: didst thou not agree with me for a penny? Take what is thine, and go thy way: I will also give to this last even as to thee. Or, is it not lawful for me to do what I will? is thy eye evil, because I am good? So shall the last be first, and the first last. For many are called, but few chosen.[17]

Medieval biblical expositors interpreted this parable allegorically, reading Christ's words in three distinct ways: as an allegory of the ages of the world, as an allegory of the ages of man, and as an allegory of spiritual growth. Origen, for example, read the parable in the first two ways. In his first interpretation, the hours of the day in the parable stand for the ages of the world from Adam to Noah, Noah to Abraham, Abraham to Moses, Moses to Christ, and Christ to the present (and, eventually, to the Last Judgment).[18] In a second interpretation, further developed by Gregory the Great, the hours stand for the ages of man: *pueritia* (childhood), *adolescentia* (adolescence), *juventus* (prime of life), *senectus* (old age), and *aetas decrepita* (extreme old age or decrepitude).[19] The allegory of spiritual growth was developed by later, lesser-known readers. In the twelfth century, Odo of Morimond, a Cisterician living in a monastery on the Rhine in Burgundy, identifies the five hours as five stages: the illumination of faith, hope, the works of charity, humility, and perfection.[20] Likewise, the twelfth century, French Cisterican monk, Isaac of Stella, read the parable as an allegory of spiritual growth, albeit of a slightly different kind. In his view,

> At dawn, our conscience accuses us, and in the third hour, filled with compunction, we reject our sinful past; in the sixth hour, we amend our behavior and accept bodily discipline; in the ninth hour, we move beyond the active life to contemplation, and the eleventh hour holds our final achievement, the vision and enjoyment of God.[21]

Various elements of the parable were interpreted allegorically as well. The murmuring workers were seen as Jews (and compared to the older brother of the Parable of the Prodigal Son), the vines were seen as the saints, and the denarius was consistently interpreted as *eternal life*, though Augustine saw it as standing for the resurrection of the dead as well. Commentators saw further significance in the fact that the denarius was a unit of ten, and so, in their view, stood for keeping the commandments of the Decalogue with Christ's help.

Strikingly, the Pearl-Maiden reads the parable morally, for its direct application to herself, but when considered in the context of the tradition of medieval allegorical and homiletic interpretation, her words take on additional significance:

> 'More haf I of joye and blysse hereinne,
> Of ladyschyp gret and lyuez blom,
> Þen alle þe wy3ez in þe worlde my3t wynne
> By þe way of ry3t to aske dome.
> Wheþer welnygh now I con bygynne –
> In euentyde into þe vyne I come –
> Fyrst of my hyre my Lorde con mynne:
> I wat3 payed anon of al and sum.
> 3et oþer þer werne þat toke more tom,
> Þat swange and swat for long 3ore,
> Þat 3et of hyre noþynk þay nom,
> Paraunter no3t schal to-3ere more.' (ll. 577–88)

Given the three strands of medieval interpretation of this parable, it seems the Pearl-Maiden could be saying that she lived in the last age of the world, from Christ to the Last Judgment; that she was baptized as an infant (or converted to Christianity as an adult) and lived in Christ's service only a short time before she died; or that she renounced the world and entered the monastic life and so, with only the illumination of faith—and not many works or much spiritual progress through the stages of the contemplative life that would lead her to perfection—died in faith and yet still received salvation, and more than salvation: the joy and bliss of "great ladyship" and "life's bloom" in heaven. The Pearl-Maiden is expressing a complex view of her own identity in terms taken from the biblical parable.

The picture of the Pearl-Maiden's experience of great joy in heaven relates to Isaac of Stella's idea that the eleventh hour corresponds to the vision and enjoyment of God.[22] The Pearl-Maiden's indication that others—by implication, the Dreamer—have not yet, and will not yet, experience the same thing is important at this moment in the unfolding dialogue of *Pearl*, especially in light of what happens later in the plot of the poem. The Pearl-Maiden is further ahead on the contemplative journey; the Dreamer is catching up. Her spiritual progress is a model to him.

It is, of course, relevant that the Parable of the Workers in the Vineyard was preached on Septuagesima Sunday, which occurred approximately 70 days before Easter. In some medieval church traditions, a scroll with the "alleluia" was buried, and the word was not uttered again in church until Easter.[23] This symbolic act essentially foreshadowed the upcoming season of Lent. Medieval Septuagesima Sunday sermons focus on the human need to amend sinful behavior, which related to the Lenten emphasis on doing spiritual good works: fasting, prayer, and works of mercy.[24] Mary Raschko has noted the irony:

> The Parable of the Laborers in the Vineyard makes this task [of medieval preachers emphasizing spiritual good works] challenging in so far as it suggests that those who exert comparatively little effort, either on the literal level of physical labor or interpreted allegorically as spiritual labor, receive the same reward in heaven as those who labor throughout their lives. While the *Pearl*-poet forces the reader to confront this discrepancy between divine and human logic without making it more palatable, homilists looked for a way to reconcile the teachings of the parable with conventional religious and social practices. In this effort, a number of vernacular homilists counter-intuitively interpreted the parable as an illustration of how good works merit reward.[25]

It is striking that the Pearl-Maiden's self-understanding does not participate in this irony at all. Instead, she articulates a vision of herself as a recipient of abundant, unmerited grace.

Indeed, the Pearl-Maiden is depicted in the poem as a living symbol of Christ's words: "the first shall be last, and *the last shall be first*."[26] She is a picture of joy and bliss—the tenor of the unspoken, metaphoric word, "alleluia."[27] Just as her discourse connects her to the Parable of the Workers in the Vineyard and Septuagesima Sunday, her close association with the pearl symbol connects her to the Parable of Great Price and its liturgical moment, for it was read in the liturgy of the Common of Virgin-Martyrs.[28]

The oral transmission and interpretation of the parables of Jesus in sermons in churches at specific moments in time during the liturgical year made the parables, as well as their associated meanings and liturgical seasons, familiar to a broad swath of English layfolk. The *Pearl*-poet was able to draw on this rich set of discourses, which circulated aurally (as well as in writing), when crafting his poem and allowing the Pearl-Maiden to express her complex self-understanding in relation to them. In essence, the parables of *Pearl* would have resonated with many significant, associated meanings based on their known contexts for readers and hearers of the poem. This is true not only for the parabolic allusions in *Pearl*, but for the fable motifs as well.

Fable Motifs in *Pearl*: Deception and Innocence

Although *Pearl* as a whole cannot fairly be characterized as a fable, the poet has interwoven fable motifs in his masterpiece, and it appears he has been influenced by his knowledge of specific Aesopian fables.[29] Two key features of the fable, the use of talking animal characters and the critique of injustice within a social hierarchy, appear in *Pearl* in modified form, but significantly, their traditional, generic purposes are transformed. Whereas animal characters in classical and medieval fables tend to embody human characteristics (e.g., the sly fox, the silly goose), in *Pearl*, animal metaphors tend to reflect human emotional states.

The one animal character who does appear in *Pearl*, the Lamb, so greatly surpasses the generic conventions of fabulous characters that he serves as a symbol not simply of one quality, such as innocence, but many (holiness, sacrifice, majesty, etc.), for the iconic picture of the Lamb in *Pearl* is a picture of Christ. The Dreamer, who is compared to three different animals—the hawk, the doe, and the quail[30]—articulates a critique of perceived injustice in the social hierarchy of the kingdom of God, but ultimately, the theophany of the Lamb presents a new ideal of justice based upon the all-sufficient grace of God. The Lamb's appearance to the Dreamer critiques the Dreamer's critique, altering the Dreamer's objections by showing him a new reality.

The Dreamer's self-understanding is much different than the Pearl-Maiden's, in part because Aesopian fables rather than Christian parables are shaping it. In addition, his feelings are driving him to misread scripture and interpret both his identity and truth in light of those misreadings. Yet despite his struggles, by the end of the poem, he has made significant spiritual progress.

The term "fable" actually appears in *Pearl*, used by the Dreamer in his response to the Pearl-Maiden's retelling of the Parable of the Workers in the

Vineyard, precisely to object to the unfairness of the Lord's paying all the workers equally:

> "Me þynk þy tale vnresounable;
> Goddeȝ ryȝt is redy and euermore rert,
> Oþer Holy Wryt is bot a fable." (ll. 590–93)

Other parts of scripture, the Dreamer suggests, state that God will reward each person according to what he has done, according to his good deeds and the merit of his works. The paradox of the parable, in his view, makes no sense.

In the Dreamer's usage, the term "fable" appears synonymous not simply with an "imaginative narrative" or an "idle or foolish tale," but with "a false statement intended to deceive."[31] The Middle English word derived from the Old French word of the same spelling, which in turn derived from the Latin *fabula*: a first declension, feminine noun simply meaning "story," "tale," or even "play." Yet in late-medieval, Middle English parlance, "fable" came to be contrasted with truth, whether historical or (in this case) spiritual.[32] The Dreamer's use of it is in this latter sense. The irony, of course, is that he is using one part of "Holy Writ" to call another part a "fable."

The parables of Jesus could indeed be considered "fables," in the first sense of the definition of the term: they are short, imaginative narratives meant to convey a moral. However, as they are told by Jesus, no orthodox medieval Christian could ever regard them as ultimately untruthful. So the poet uses the Dreamer's frustration to present a subtle critique of his culture's tendency to dismiss imaginative narratives as untrue simply because they are not historical. Deeper spiritual and theological truth is hidden in imaginative writings than may be expressed in the factual details of a historical account or a theological exposition. In this sense, *Pearl* itself is a fable.[33]

Indeed, *Pearl* participates in the generic conventions of the fable, adapting traditional associations of animals with certain traits from the fable tradition and using them in animal metaphors that describe the Dreamer. Comparing the animal metaphors in *Pearl* to specific Aesopian fables concerning the hawk, the doe, and the lamb can provide context for understanding the poet's intentions in using animal metaphors and suggest ways the poet may have wished to impact his audience.

Like biblical stories, Aesopian fables had wide currency in late-medieval England, and their transmission cut across the divide between those readers who were literate in Latin and those who were not. They were shared informally in families and between friends as part of medieval, storytelling culture. Preachers used them as *exempla* in their sermons.[34] Following classical educational practice inherited from ancient Greece and Rome, medieval teachers used fables to instruct their students in the schools, where they were used to improve students' rhetorical and linguistic abilities.[35] Fables were treated as translation exercises, and students turned them from Latin into vernacular languages, including French and English.

Because of the fables' moral content—especially the proverbs and axioms with which they usually concluded—the fables were also thought to be morally instructive. Far from being merely comic stories intended to entertain children, fables in the schools were intended to edify and instruct: "As modern readers of medieval vernacular texts, we need to accustom ourselves to the impressive number of curricular addenda and interpretive options available to medieval fable readers, so that we can more fully appreciate the interests and accomplishments of vernacular fabulists and incorporate those elements into their translations."[36] Teachers and students had at their disposal quite a variety of fables to interpret, for the earliest fable collections originated with Aesop, reputedly a blind slave in sixth-century B.C. Greece, and were transmitted by two men: Phaedrus and Babrius. Phaedrus translated the *Aesopica* into Latin during his lifetime (15 B.C.–50 A.D.) in a collection known as the *Romulus*, which existed in both prose and verse versions, while Babrius wrote the fables down in Greek in the second century A.D. and took them to Rome. Fables translated by Phaedrus circulated more widely in Western Europe.

England proved highly receptive to the fable tradition beginning with the Anglo-Saxons, when Latin fables circulated and influenced vernacular literature in Old English. Fables proved particularly appealing after the Norman Conquest, when they provided a voice for social critique and covert political commentary.[37] Among the noted fabulists working in medieval England from the twelfth to the fifteenth century were Marie de France, Walter of England, John Lydgate, and Robert Henryson. The *Pearl*-poet, like Chaucer in his "Nun's Priest's Tale," appears to have been vividly aware of the translation of the Latin fable tradition into the vernacular, participating in that culture of translation through allusion—and transforming the possibilities of its use in the process.

Once translated, Aesopian fables circulated in the larger vernacular culture in both written and oral forms. Thus the *Pearl*-poet's animal metaphors can allude to the fable tradition, for the poet could have a reasonable expectation that his intended audience would be familiar with a wide variety of Aesopian fables. Indeed, specific ones may have been in his mind or the minds of the readers and hearers of *Pearl*. To consider this possibility, it will be valuable to look more closely at the animal metaphors used to describe the Dreamer and then at the character of the Lamb.

The Dreamer's response to his first sight of the Pearl-Maiden, standing on the other side of the stream, is fear and shock: "drede."[38] His reaction to his fear is, oddly enough, hope that her sudden appearance has a spiritual purpose or import (line 185).[39] But fear—"dred"[40]—not hope, ultimately has the upper hand in his heart. As J.J. Anderson remarks: "Predictably, the Dreamer's sighting of the Maiden produces a powerful response in him. The struggle between his desire to cross the stream to speak to her, and his fear that if he tries to do so, he will lose her (lines 169–88) is heightened. His emotions, together with the shock of seeing her (line 174), leave him in the state of paralysis (lines 182–4)."[41] The Dreamer specifically fears that the

Pearl-Maiden might escape him; he does not want to lose her again. In the midst of this emotional turmoil, the Dreamer compares himself to a hawk:

> More þen me lyste my drede aros:
> I stod ful stylle and dorste not calle;
> Wyth y3en open and mouth ful clos
> I stod as hende as hawk in halle.
> I hoped þat gostly watz þat porpose;[42]
> I dred onende quat schulde byfalle,
> Lest ho me eschaped þat I þer chos,
> Er I at steuen hir mo3t stalle. (ll. 181–88)

This comparison has been interpreted variously. Spearing first said, not without sympathy to the Dreamer's feelings, that the comparison was "comic in effect."[43] Looking to the bestiary genre, Reichardt saw the hawk as standing for the Dreamer's wish to seize the object of his desire; he notes that the hawk could stand for the devil.[44] Remein sees Reichardt's interpretation as misleading:

> This hawk is not a salivating, wild, carrion bird nor is it even a trained hawk diving after a sparrow. ... Since the hawk in this simile is specifically "in halle" – perhaps the implied scene, since it is not a hawk on the hunt, is that of a rare hunting bird presented as a gift to a King in a lavish court setting – it would seem that these courtly valences apply ... a hawk *indoors* is a bird of high nobility, well-controlled, on another level entirely.[45]

Remein clearly prefers to emphasize the courtly connotations of the comparison. But it is Bogdanos who noted that the image of the "hawk in halle" is "a descriptive stroke recalling court and countryside, the romance and the beast fable."[46] If the metaphor participates in the beast fable tradition, which of Aesop's fables circulating widely in the Middle Ages might provide context and aid in interpretation?

The fable known as "The Nightingale and the Hawk," or, in Latin, "Luscinia et Accipiter," is certainly one promising possibility.

> In nidum lusciniae cum sederet accipiter, ut specularetur auritum, parvos in illo invenit pullos. Supervenit luscinia et rogabat illum parcere pullis. Ait accipiter, "Faciam quod vis, si mihi bene cantaveris." Et quamvis se praecederat animo, tamen metu pavebat; denique coacta et dolore plena cantavit. Acceptor, qui praedam captaverat, ait, "Non bene cantasti"; apprehenditque unum de pullis eius, et devorare coepit. Ex diverso venit auceps, et, calamo silenter levato, acceptorem, contracto visco, in terram deiecit. Qui aliis insidiantur, timere debent ne capiantur.[47]

In this little story, the nightingale tries to save the life of her chick from the hawk with a song. He, however, is more interested in filling his belly. Medieval readers tended to interpret the nightingale as an allegorical figure of the fate of the poor artist, the hawk as a figure of a demanding lord.[48] Dissatisfied with the injustice of the hawk's betrayal, they noted the hawk's eventual capture and the moral of the story: whoever practices deceit should be afraid lest he himself be captured! For when the hawk flies off, he is captured in turn by the fowler. The fowler, medieval commentators claimed, stood for the wicked devil himself.[49]

To the extent that this fable may provide context for the Dreamer's comparison of himself to a "hawk in the hall," it seems that the Dreamer *qua* hawk is not the Dreamer as devil, but Dreamer as one who has been captured by the devil's deceptive wiles.[50] The Dreamer thought that his Pearl-Maiden was completely lost to him, and he grieved inordinately over her death, but her sudden appearance before him in his dream demonstrates that he was deceived. Despite her death, the Pearl-Maiden lives, as her revelations to him in his dream shock him into realizing. She is not completely lost to him. She is not, in fact, lost at all.

The underlying notion that the Dreamer has been tormented by the deception of the devil in his time of loss, vulnerability, and grief is reinforced when he compares himself to a dazed quail (line 1085). While no medieval Aesopian fables particularly feature quail as characters, the medieval bestiary tradition does interpret their significance, glossing the figure of the quail as a Christian vulnerable to the attack of the devil.[51] Between the first and second bird metaphors, the Dreamer's self-understanding has changed from seeing himself as a captured predator to a vulnerable bird of prey. His self-characterization in both cases is consistent with medieval fable and medieval bestiary traditions associated with hawk and quail respectively. It is consistent with the theme of vulnerability to the devil's snares.

The Pearl-Maiden also characterizes the Dreamer using an animal metaphor. She does not compare him to a bird, however, but to a wounded doe. She does so because she sees his pain, his "doel-dystresse,"[52] and she wants to encourage him to change his focus: to bless himself, love God in all circumstances, and realize that he will suffer if it is necessary, but it is better to patiently abide in God's will than to resist it with anger.

>'Thow demeȝ noȝt bot doel-dystresse,'
>Þenne sayde þat wyȝt. 'Why dotȝ þou so?
>For dyne of doel of lureȝ lesse
>Ofte mony mon forgos þe mo.
>Þe oȝte better þyseluen blesse,
>And loue ay God, in wele and wo,
>For anger gayneȝ þe not a cresse.
>Who nedeȝ schal þole, be not so þro.
>For þoȝ þou daunce as any do,

>   Braundysch and bray þy braþeȝ breme,
>   When þou no fyrre may, to ne fro,
>   Þou moste abyde þat He schal deme.' (ll. 336–48)

Using the feminine noun to describe a deer—as doe, not stag—stands out because, of course, the Dreamer is a man. The Pearl-Maiden's comparison does not seem intended to belittle or emasculate the Dreamer, for the Pearl-Maiden, however stern in her truth-telling, is the Dreamer's spiritual friend and not given to insulting him in an *ad hominem* manner. The feminine "doe" may have been chosen because it corresponds to the Dreamer's *anima*, his spirit (a feminine noun in Latin), or in order to invoke connotations of feminine weakness (in contrast to masculine strength). After all, from a Christian perspective, in weakness, there is great strength, as the Pearl-Maiden herself exemplifies.[53] In addition, "doe" may have been chosen by the poet in part because he is alluding to an Aesopian fable.

The fable of "The One-Eyed Doe" (or, in Latin, "Cervus Oculo Captus") is a particularly relevant context for the Pearl-Maiden's metaphor, and strikingly it is consistent with the theme of the Dreamer's vulnerability to the devil's deception.

> Cervus, altero oculo captus, iuxta mare pasci consueverat ita ut integrum oculum in terram haberet versum; nihil enim periculi videbatur e mari impendere. Cum autem forte navis praetereveheretur, qui in illa erant, directa in cervum sagitta, incautum confixere. Ille ictus, "Me miserum," inquit, "quantopere deceptus fui, qui a terra metui, undis fretus, e quibus mihi mors immittitur."[54]
>
> (A deer, blind in one eye, was in the habit of grazing beside the sea so that its whole [*sic* "seeing"] eye could be turned to the land; for nothing of danger did it see [*or* anticipate] coming from the sea. When, however, by chance a ship sailed by, those who were in it directed arrows toward the deer, [and] the incautious animal was struck. The stricken one cried, "Woe is me! I was greatly deceived, who feared danger from the land, [but] trusted the waves, out of which death was sent to me.")[55]

In this modern Latin version of the fable, the doe complains, "deceptus fui," (*I was deceived*). She had only one eye and kept it fixed where she thought the danger would come: from the land. But she was struck by an arrow shot by a sailor on a ship on the sea.

The Pearl-Maiden's allusion dovetails nicely with her earlier comments to the Dreamer about his over-reliance on his sight (lines 286–300): his belief that she is actually present in the dream-vision valley because he sees her with his eyes. In fact, human sight is unreliable in gauging spiritual realities. Since "faith comes by hearing,"[56] listening with a discerning heart and mind is far more important. Nevertheless, if the Dreamer is going to look more closely than he listens, the Pearl-Maiden decides she will ask for him to have a new sight: a vision of the heavenly Jerusalem and the Lamb within it.

It goes without saying that the iconographic significance of the Lamb of God in *Pearl* far exceeds that of any lamb in an Aesopian fable in majesty, in meaning, and in apocalyptic implication. Yet the Lamb nevertheless may participate, to a degree, in the fabulous tradition, especially to the extent that Aesopian fables associated the figure of the lamb with innocence, vulnerability to the wolf's attack, and critique of an unjust social order in which the humble were badly mistreated by the powerful. These qualities are evident in the fable known as "The Wolf and the Lamb" (or, in Latin, "Agnus et Lupus").

> Ad rivum eundem lupus et agnus venerant,
> Siti compulsi. Superior stabat lupus,
> Longeque inferior agnus. Tunc fauce improba
> Latro incitatus iurgii causam intulit:
> "Cur," inquit, "turbulentam fecisti mihi
> aquam bibenti?" laniger contra timens:
> "Qui possum, quaeso, facere quod quereris, lupe?
> A te decurrit ad meos haustus liquor."
> Repulsus ille veritatis viribus
> "Ante hos sex menses male," ait, "dixisti mihi."
> Respondit agnus, "Equidem natus sum non eram."
> "Pater hercle tuus," ille inquit, "male dixit mihi,"
> atque ita correptum lacerat iniusta nece.
> Haec propter illos scripta est homines fibula
> Qui fictis causis innocentes opprimunt.
>
> (Impelled by thirst, a wolf and a lamb had to come to the same brook. Upstream stood the wolf, much lower down the lamb. Then the spoiler, prompted by his wicked gullet, launched pretext for a quarrel: "Why," said he, "have you roiled the water where I am drinking?" Sore afraid, the woolly one made answer: "Pray, how can I, wolf, be guilty of the thing you charge? The water flows from you downstream to where I drink." Balked by the power of truth, the wolf exclaimed, "Six months ago you cursed me." "Indeed," replied the lamb, "at that time I was not yet born." "Well, I swear, your father cursed me," said the wolf, and, with no more ado, he pounced upon the lamb and tore him, and the lamb died for no just cause. This fable was composed for those persons who invent false charges by which to oppress the innocent.)[57]

In this fable, the wolf tries to deceive the lamb with his lies, but the lamb, in his innocence, simply answers the lies with truth. As a result, the enraged wolf seizes the lamb and tears him apart.

The wolf, in this fable, is like the fowler and the sailor previously discussed: medieval readers understood him as representative of the devil or his agents. The context for this medieval understanding was a parable of Jesus, in which the devil is compared to a wolf, and other scriptures that compare the devil's agents (such as false prophets) to wolves.[58] Sometimes medieval commentators also interpreted the wolf as a type of unjust lord or unjust judge. This can be seen in Marie de France's axiomatic interpretation of her version of the fable:

> Issi funt li riche seigneur,
> Li vescunte e li jugeür,
> De ceus qu'il unt en lur justise:
> Faus acheisuns par coveitise
> Treovent asez pure us confundre;
> Suvent les funt a pleit somundre.
> La char lur toient e la pel,
> Si cum li lus fist a l'aignel.
>
> (And this is what our great lords do, the viscounts and the judges, too, with all the people whom they rule: false charge they make from greed so cruel. To cause confusion they consort and often summon folk to court. They strip them clean of flesh and skin, as the wolf did to the lambkin.)[59]

This fable, and the moral commentary associated with it, provides a context particularly relevant to the Pearl-Maiden's retelling of Christ's journey to the Cross, which included persecution by unjust judges and lords (e.g., Pharisees, Pilate, and Herod) who were essentially wolf-like in their false accusations and brutal treatment of the innocent Lamb of God.[60] Jesus, however, answered only with silence or truth when accused.

The fable of "The Wolf and the Lamb" provides a striking counterpoint to the fables of "The Nightingale and the Hawk" and "The One-Eyed Doe." In all three stories, a figure for the devil appears—the fowler with his birdlime, the sailor with his arrow, the wolf with lying tongue and savage teeth—and attempts to destroy his chosen prey. Each figure apparently achieves his aim, but with an important difference in the prey: whereas the hawk and the doe are deceived, the innocent lamb is not. The lamb responds to falsehood with truth even in the face of imminent suffering and death. As relevant contexts for the animal metaphors of *Pearl*, these Aesopian fables reinforce the themes of the dream vision. The Dreamer has been deceived in his time of grief, but the Lamb of God provides a shining example of how to resist the devil: in silent innocence or truthful speech. The Dreamer and the Pearl-Maiden are both aware of the Dreamer's spiritual problem, as their characterizations of the Dreamer as tamed hawk, dazed quail, and pierced doe demonstrate, but hearing the truth about his spiritual condition is not enough for the Dreamer. He has to see something that transforms his perspective. That is why his vision of the Lamb of God is necessary and, in the end, more than fabulous. It is the happy ending to a fairy-tale the Dreamer didn't know he was in—and the beginning of something new.

Fairy-Tale Qualities in *Pearl*: Expectation and Transformation

Although *Pearl* has not been considered a fairy-tale *per se* until now, it does in fact have fairy-tale qualities. *Pearl* has been considered in relation to medieval courtly romance, for it does contain elements of romance, while the term "fairy-tale" may seem anachronistic when applied to *Pearl*. The term "fairy-tale" was invented in French (*conte du fee*) by Madame d'Aulnoy in the seventeenth century and only subsequently translated into English, gaining wide currency in the nineteenth century when it was associated with the *märchen* of the Brothers Grimm and the *eventyr* of Hans Christian Anderson. Nevertheless, the genre existed even before the English name for it did, and studying fairy-tale qualities in *Pearl* can reveal new aspects of the poem, especially in comparison to other late-medieval folktale genres.

Fairy-tales, like parables and fables, are short stories, but they are distinguished from other folkloric genres by key characteristics. While virtually all scholars agree that fairies need not be part of the tale for it to be a fairy-tale, the story must have some element of Faërie in it: some aspect of magic or the supernatural. Common literary characteristics of the fairy-tale include:

- Set in an indefinite time period ("Once upon a time …")
- Archetypal characters (innocent princess, heroic prince, evil stepmother, wicked witch, fairy-godmother)
- Magical characters (elves, dwarves, giants), magical beasts (talking birds), and magical flora and fauna (giant beanstalks) as well as magical objects (wands, mirrors, spinning wheels)
- Plots shaped by the quest or hero's journey (often including prohibitions and the breaking of prohibitions, the accomplishment of impossible tasks with magical help, and poor, younger sons and daughters triumphing over opposition through determination, trickery, and/ or sheer, unreasonable good luck—in order to win the castle, a royal spouse, and unimaginable riches and so as to become the happy parents of good offspring)
- Themes focused on the struggle between good and evil, wish-fulfillment fantasies (for delectable food, true love, extraordinary wealth, social status, and even revenge), and the growth of the protagonist from childhood to maturity
- Characterization focused on the dynamic *transformation* of the main characters from one state to another (while other characters may remain static, flat, or unchanging)
- Style that tends to be simple, concise, and repetitive, with patterns of events, characters, or symbols that recur in threes or sevens
- Tone that may be surprisingly dark but then turns, as happy endings occur quite frequently in the genre (although, of course, not always)

In addition to these characteristics, folklore scholars have noted common plot patterns and motifs, functions, and character types.[61] Feminist readers have analyzed the re-inscription of real-world patriarchy in fairy-tales, the problems of gender inequality, sexual objectification, and oppression that fairy-tales reveal and the ironic, but nevertheless radical, empowerment of female protagonists that often occurs in fairy-tale plots.[62] Psychoanalytic readers have used Freudian concepts (id, ego, and superego) to see the conflicts in our consciousness played out in fairy-tales or Jungian archetypes to interpret fairy-tales as evidence of the collective unconscious expressing deepest human fears and desires.[63]

Bruno Bettelheim, in *The Uses of Enchantment*, has argued that fairy-tales help fulfill one of our deepest human needs: to make sense of our chaotic existence and find meaning in our lives.

> For a story truly to hold the child's attention, it must entertain him and arouse his curiosity. But to enrich his life, it must stimulate his imagination, help him to develop his intellect and to clarify his emotions, be attuned to his anxieties and aspirations, give full recognition to his difficulties, while at the same time suggesting solutions to the problems which perturb him. In short, it must at one and the same time relate to all aspects of his personality—and this without ever belittling but, on the contrary, giving full credence to the seriousness of the child's predicaments, while simultaneously promoting confidence in himself and his future. In all these and many other respects, of the entire "children's literature"—with rare exceptions—nothing can be as enriching and satisfying to child and adult alike as a folk fairy tale.[64]

It is this insight, taken together with the other characteristics of fairy-tale, that is particularly relevant to discerning the purpose of the fairy-tale qualities in *Pearl*.

The Dreamer of *Pearl* begins his story like any sorrowful, disappointed, or rejected medieval lover: in a garden consumed by grief. Like the protagonist of most fairy-tales, he begins at a suitably low point, so he can move up. Once his spirit springs into space (line 61), and he finds himself moving through a magical landscape, his heart lifts, and his feelings change. Then, at last, he sees the Pearl-Maiden across the stream. Suddenly, both he and the reader journeying with him are inside the world of fairy-tale expectations.[65]

To a certain extent, the Dreamer's adventure is set in an indefinite time period. Yes, it was August "in a high season" that he fell asleep in the garden, but in what year is never stated. The time or season of the setting of his dream is not particularly clear, either—perhaps spring. Both Dreamer and Maiden could be characterized as archetypal figures. Unnamed as they are, they are called by their particular roles: he, a dreamer and a jeweler; she, a maiden and a beloved pearl. The landscape through which the Dreamer has journeyed is suggestive of Fäerie: trees have blue trunks and silver leaves while the streambed is bejeweled. The Maiden herself is a figure of supernatural beauty, "blysnande whyt" ("blazing white"),[66] transfigured like Christ and yet clearly a beautiful woman.

In other romances (*Sir Orfeo*) and dreams (*Roman de la Rose*), the moment of meeting between man and woman in an enchanted landscape would instantly generate in medieval readers expectations of loving reunion—or further complications that postpone it, heightening desire.[67] When they see one another in the forest for the first time after a long separation, Orfeo and his beloved Herodis are separated by the Fäerie hunt. Amans may fall in love with the Rose at the pool of Narcissus, but it will be many hundreds of lines before he will take possession of his beloved.[68] In the case of *Pearl*, like *Sir Orfeo* and the *Roman de la Rose*, further complications ensue, for the Dreamer is faced with a fairy-tale prohibition: he must not cross the stream. His quest to recover his pearl is at an impasse and can progress no further for the moment.

The Dreamer looks at the Maiden with a deep longing, a profound wish, to be reunited with her. But in order for him to grow into spiritual maturity, his wish-fulfillment fantasy, so clearly expressed in his multiple assertions that he is ready and willing to cross the stream to be with her, must be transformed. While most fairy-tale heroes grow by overcoming obstacles to obtain the beloved, the Dreamer is in a new genre, for the specifically Christian nature of the fairy-tale of *Pearl* suggests that the focus of his desire is on the wrong beloved: the Pearl-Maiden, not Christ. In order for his true wish, which is for unfailing love, to be fulfilled, he must shift from seeking what he believes he wants, the Pearl-Maiden, to seeking the One who is capable of fulfilling his heart's desire.

This, of course, adds a new layer of complexity that many "simple, concise" fairy-tales do not have. Even so, the fairy-tale quality of transformation of the main character is achieved by it, in the context of significant repetition (threes, twelves, and so on) and symbolism. The Dreamer is changed, multiple times and in multiple ways, on his dream vision journey. Emotionally, he makes a shift from profound grief in the garden to renewed hope and happiness in the wondrous landscape of his dream. Spiritually, he is enlightened by the vision of the New Jerusalem and the Lamb who, though suffering from a wounded side, is nevertheless uplifting a joyful countenance.[69] When he awakens, the Dreamer understands that the Lord, from whom he had been alienated, is his friend (line 1204).

Although there has been debate over whether the Dreamer is actually consoled at the end of *Pearl*, the ending of *Pearl* is in fact happy—in that it is blessed—though naturally it is not the happy ending that the Dreamer expected at first. It is not only that his feelings have changed—they have—but that he is able to accept the truth he could not bear before. His attention does shift from the singular Pearl of his dream to the Eucharist, to the bread and wine that is the body and blood of Christ (lines 1209–10). His awareness opens to the realization that we are all precious pearls to the

Prince (lines 1211–12). By identifying all people as God's pearls, he implicitly acknowledges that the great love he has for his Pearl is superseded by the even greater love that God has for all of his children, all of his beloveds, all of his lovers: everyone.

The fairy-tale of *Pearl* is ultimately a Christian version of the Cupid and Psyche myth,[70] only the man and the woman of *Pearl*, the Dreamer and the Maiden, do not stand respectively for the mythic lovers. Instead, the Lamb is Amor ("God is Love"),[71] and the Maiden is Psyche, and the Dreamer is assured through the Eucharist he speaks of at the poem's conclusion that he, too, is embraced in the beloved: part of the Church, part of the Bride of Christ. Rather than being the lover who is constantly seeking, he becomes the beloved who is sought and treasured, loved and esteemed. The Dreamer is changed, and his transformation leads to a new spiritual maturity.

It appears at the conclusion of *Pearl* that the Dreamer is at last able to put childish ways behind him and begin to love, not selfishly, solely to have his own needs and desires met, but sacrificially, like the bleeding Lamb, and to receive the love of God that heals his broken heart in the fallen world. He relinquishes his emotional possessiveness of his singular pearl, not only to receive the Pearl of Great Price, salvation, but to see that he is himself a beloved pearl to God and to wish that all people would truly see themselves that way: a new wish with far deeper and richer implications for eternity than the love of one man for one woman—however wonderful he knows such love to be. The Dreamer's recognition of spiritual truth is what makes the ending of *Pearl* happy and blessed.[72]

J.R.R. Tolkien wrote in "On Fairy-Stories" that fairy-tales have four qualities, which, strikingly, are all about the effects of fairy-tales on readers: fantasy, recovery, escape, and consolation.[73] Although *Pearl* has only some of the literary qualities of the fairy-tale genre as it is defined today, the poem has the power to catalyze all of the reader-response effects that Tolkien identified in his famous essay. The dream vision of *Pearl* engages the reader's mind in fantasy, prompting the creation of mental images that have the inner consistency of reality, which in turn connects the reader to the Divine. For just as the Maker made humans, and humans are made in the image of God, so humans also make and create many things, including the mental images that fantasy invites.[74]

Pearl provides the possibility of recovery to readers. Recovery, in Tolkien's view, is the return and renewal of health. It is also, and particularly, about the restoration of "a clear view," or "seeing things as we are (or were) meant to see them":[75]

> We need, in any case, to clean our windows, so that the things seen clearly may be freed from the drab blur of triteness or familiarity – from possessiveness. Of all faces, those of our familiars are the ones both most difficult to play fantastic tricks with, and most difficult really to see with fresh attention, perceiving in their likeness and

unlikeness that they are faces, and yet unique faces ... We say we know them. They have become like the things which once attracted us by their glitter, or their colour, or their shape, and we laid hands on them, and then locked them in our hoard, acquired them, and in acquiring, ceased to look at them.[76]

Tolkien's idea, that possessiveness is opposed to recovery and that we cannot see clearly even the beloved faces of those most familiar to us when we think we own them, resonates with the Dreamer's experience in *Pearl*—and with the reader's experience in journeying along with the Dreamer, seeing things from his perspective, until surprised by the ending of the poem into re-reading and looking at the whole from different angles.

Escape, too, is part of the opportunity *Pearl* provides:

Escape is evidently as a rule very practical, and may even be heroic. In real life it is difficult to blame it, unless it fails ... Why should a man be scorned if, finding himself in prison, he tries to get out and go home? Or if, when he cannot do so, he thinks and talks about other topics than jailers and prison walls?[77]

For Tolkien, then, the fairy-story provides the reader with a practical means of escape from the bleak realities of "Real Life," and such escape, in his view, is not irresponsible. The reader who escapes can be a hero, journeying with the hero of the story, not only (or even especially) because he shares the protagonist's adventure, but because he has succeeded, although a prisoner, in experiencing freedom. As Tolkien says, "There are other things more grim and terrible to fly from than the noise, stench, ruthlessness, and extravagance of the internal combustion engine. There are hunger, thirst, poverty, pain, sorrow, injustice, death."[78] For both medieval and modern readers of *Pearl*, for those who share the Dreamer's experience of death and the loss of those they have loved in this life, *Pearl* provides escape from sorrow.

Consolation comes at the happy ending of fairy-stories, according to Tolkien, and in the sudden, joyous turn of events in an otherwise sad tale. Tolkien calls this turn "eucatastrophe," and he opposes it to the dyscatastrophe of sorrow and failure—though dyscatastrophe may be "necessary to the joy of deliverance. ... Joy beyond the walls of the world, poignant as grief."[79]

Like other fairy-tales, *Pearl* presents readers with *eucatastrophe*: that sudden, joyous turn of events. The Dreamer's vision of the iconic bleeding Lamb is the eucatastrophe. Although he will not instantly grasp the implications of it, although he will break the prohibition, stumble toward the stream, and attempt to reunite with his "lyttel quene"[80] (line 1147) among the saints in procession with the Lamb, nevertheless, the Dreamer begins the process of change at that moment of beholding. For Christ's death on the Cross, symbolized by the Lamb with the pierced side, makes the Dreamer's suffering meaningful. For the Lamb redeems redeems suffering and makes possible hope for life on earth and unending life in heaven. From a Christian perspective, this is the real happy ending—and, of course, it doesn't end.

Conclusions

The folktale genre elements in *Pearl*—parabolic allusions, fable motifs, and fairy-tale qualities—suggest that the *Pearl*-poet was drawing in his work not only on the elevated four levels of meaning, used by the educated *literati* of his day to interpret scripture and compose poetry, that signified at the literal and allegorical levels simultaneously, but also on the spoken word heard in his culture and known by vernacular English speakers: his audience for *Pearl*. The *Pearl*-poet used parabolic allusions to help articulate the Pearl-Maiden's complex self-understanding and fable motifs to reveal the Dreamer's central spiritual problem: that he had been deceived by doubt in a time of vulnerability and grief. The poet's use of fairy-tale qualities is equally subtle, overturning the Dreamer's fairy-tale expectations in order to achieve his spiritual transformation. The poet could have had a reasonable hope that his anticipated audience would understand (with some effort) what he was trying to signify because the culture of storytelling in late-medieval England involved a nexus of texts (both written and spoken) that were woven into the fabric of daily life and held in the minds of those who read them, heard them, and re-told them.

The parables of Jesus and many of the fables of Aesop were known to the *Pearl*-poet's anticipated, vernacular English audience in the context of a multilingual culture. This audience consisted of Christian men, women, and even children who went to church and heard the parables and fables in sermons or went to school (or knew someone who went to school) and heard them there (or from there). While courtly romances circulated more frequently and obviously among the upper echelons of medieval society, "fairy-stories"—short tales of magic and wonder, many essentially based on the Cupid and Psyche myth of love facing nearly insurmountable obstacles[81]—were invented, shared, and re-discovered at all levels of society. Medieval readers or listeners traveling with the Dreamer through the bejeweled, Fäerie landscape of his dream, and when first encountering the Pearl-Maiden, had every reason to think they were about to see a moment comparable to loving encounters in *Sir Orfeo* or *La Roman de la Rose*.

Instead, in the end, the *Pearl*-poet demonstrates that his fairy-tale is a divine romance, a Christian one aimed at reconciling the reader's heart to God just as much as the Dreamer's. For the eucatastrophe of *Pearl*, the sudden happy turn of events when the Dreamer beholds the bleeding Lamb and begins to get the barest inkling that great joy is possible in the midst of profound sorrow, is an invitation to the audience. We, too, can come to see things more clearly.

Notes

1. The Synoptic gospels contain the majority of the parables of Jesus. The five most popular parables in the Middle Ages were the Parable of the Prodigal Son (Luke 15:11–32), the Parable of the Good Samaritan (Luke 10:25–37), the Parable of the Workers in the Vineyard (Matt. 20:1–6), the Parable of the Rich Man and Lazarus (Luke 16:19–31), and the Parable of the Wise and Foolish Virgins (Matt. 25:1–13). The Parable of the Sower, the only story that Jesus is recorded as explaining in detail to his disciples, became paradigmatic for medieval allegorical exegesis of the parables, which saw significance in even the smallest details of the words of Jesus. See Matt. 13:1–23.
2. On the cultivation of images in the medieval imagination from external sources of inspiration in medieval culture, see Mary Carruthers, *The Craft of Thought: Meditation, Rhetoric, and the Making of Images, 400–1200* (Cambridge: Cambridge University Press, 1998, repr. 2003).
3. On the Aesopian fable tradition in medieval education, see Edward Wheatley, *Mastering Aesop: Medieval Education, Chaucer, and his Followers* (Gainesville, FL: University of Florida Press, 2000).
4. For an edition, see Marie de France, *Fables,* ed. and trans. Harriet Spiegel (Toronto: University of Toronto Press, 1994, repr. 2000).
5. See Bruno Bettelheim, *The Uses of Enchantment: The Meaning and Importance of Fairy-Tales* (New York, NY: Vintage Books, 1977).
6. The parallel passages from the other two synoptic Gospels are in Luke 8: 1–15 and Mark 4: 1–20.
7. On the date of *Pearl*, see Susanna Fein, "Twelve Line Stanza Forms." The *terminus ad quem* is 1400; the *terminus a quo* is 1348. Fein dates the poem to 1380, *pace* Bowers, who dates it to 1390.
8. "Parable," MED (MED http://quod.lib.umich.edu/cgi/m/mec/med-idx?size=First+100&type=headword&q1=parable&rgxp=constrained).
9. "Parable" is also associated with related words and synonyms, such as "example," the word in line 499 of *Pearl* that is used to introduce the Parable of the Workers in the Vineyard. Note that the poem uses the Middle English version of the word: "sample."
10. Friedrich Gustav Lisco, *The Parables of Jesus* (Philadelphia, PA: Daniels and Smith Publishers, 1850), 9–11. Italics added for emphasis.
11. Quoted in Stephen L. Wailes, *Medieval Allegories of Jesus' Parables* (Berkeley and Los Angeles, CA: University of California Press, 1987), 120.
12. Only Nicholas of Lyra and Ludolph of Saxony read the parable as reflecting the development of the early church. For these fourteenth-century commentators, "the field represents active labor and merciful works in the governance of the Church, with the treasure symbolizing the heavenly reward for such exertions" (Wailes, *Medieval Allegories,* 118).
13. Wailes, *Medieval Allegories,* 120.
14. *Pearl*, 743–44.
15. See the extended discussion of the manuscript illustrations in chapter 1 of this book.
16. The Pearl-Maiden has been compared to a preacher and her discourse on the Parable of the Workers in the Vineyard to a sermon by Jane Chance, J.J. Anderson, and Davis Aers. See Chance, "Allegory and Structure in Pearl: The Four Senses of the *Ars Praedicandi* and Fourteenth-Century Homiletic Poetry," in *Text*

and Matter: New Critical Perspectives of the Pearl-Poet, ed. Robert J. Blanch, Miriam Youngerman Miller, and Julian N. Wasserman (Troy, NY: Whitston, 1991), 31–60. J. J. Anderson, *Language and Imagination in the Gawain-poems* (Manchester: Manchester University Press, 2005), 31, 35. Even those who doubt the efficacy of the Maiden's speech sometimes refer to the maiden's discourse as homiletic. For example, when David Aers describes the Maiden's failure to change the Dreamer's will, he compares her instruction to a homily, arguing that "No homily, however forceful, can bend the will of another." See Aers, "The Self Mourning," 64. For discussion, see the second chapter in Mary Raschko, *Rendering the Word*, esp. 75–76.
17. Matthew 20:1–16 (Douay-Rheims).
18. Wailes, 139. A variation of this "ages of the world" scheme appears in the writings of the twelfth century Benedictine Gottfried of Admont, who interpreted the hours in this way: Incarnation of Christ (owner goes out), redemption (contract at dawn), Pentecost and salvation of the Gentiles (third hour), martyrs (sixth hour), confessors (nineth hour), our own age (eleventh hour). (Wailes, 143–44). Mary Raschko, who has surveyed late-medieval, Latin and Middle English sermons on the Parable of the Workers in the Vineyard in *Rendering the Word*, makes the point that virtually all of these sermons focus on the "ages of the world" interpretation. Only one sermon, which appears in both BL, MS Harley 2247 and BL, Royal MS B.xxv, does not; instead, it focuses on explicating the allegorical significance of other details in the parable (Raschko, 82n).
19. Wailes, 142.
20. Wailes, 143.
21. Wailes, 143. For further discussion, see Lynn Staley, "*Pearl* and the Eleventh Hour," in *Text and Matter: New Critical Perspectives of the Pearl-Poet*, ed. Robert Blanch, Miriam Youngerman Miller, and Julian Wasserman (New York, NY: Whitston Publishing Company, 1991), 1–11.
22. For discussion, Lynn Staley, "The Dreamer and the Eleventh Hour," in Robert J. Blanch, Miriam Youngerman Miller and Julian N. Wasserman, eds., *Text and Matter: New Critical Perspectives of the Pearl-Poet*. Troy, NY: Whitston, 1991. 3–15.
23. For discussion of the relevance of this to *Pearl*, see chap. 2, "Allegorical Meaning."
24. See Raschko, *Rendering the Word*, 80. See also Siegfried Wenzel, *Latin Sermon Collections from Later Medieval England* (Cambridge: Cambridge University Press, 2005) and Spencer, *English Preaching in the Late Middle Ages* (Oxford: Clarendon, 1993), 22.
25. Mary Raschko, *Rendering the Word: Vernacular Accounts of Parables in Late-Medieval England* (Chapel Hill, NC: University of North Carolina, diss., 2009), 80.
26. Matt. 20:16 (emphasis added).
27. See chapter 2, "Allegorical Meaning."
28. Battacharjee, Santha, "*Pearl* and the Liturgical Common of Virgins," *Medium Aevum* 64 (1995), 37–50.
29. I use the term "Aesopian fables" (rather than "Aesop's fables") because although medieval audiences associated fables with Aesop, many fables that circulated cannot be traced back to ancient Greek or Latin sources. My term embraces the concept of a fable tradition rather than attribution to a specific author, whose *vita* (in Aesop's case) may have been largely invented. On the received biography of Aesop, see Edward Wheatley, *Mastering Aesop: Medieval Education,*

Chaucer, and His Followers (Gainesville, FL: University of Florida Press, 2000), esp. chaper 1 "Figuring the Fable and its Father." Several examples of fables ostensibly attributed to Aesopian tradition, but originating definitively later in time or having been significantly changed in translation, can be found in the fable collection of Marie de France. For an introductory discussion, see Jane Beal, "Marie de France," *British Writers Supplement,* Vol. 20, ed. Jay Parini (New York, NY: Charles Scribner's Sons, An Imprint of the Gale Group, 2013), 135–56.

30. Richardt has considered these three animal metaphors in his essay, "Animal Similies in *Pearl*."
31. "Fable," *Middle English Dictionary* (online): http://quod.lib.umich.edu/cgi/m/mec/med-idx?size=First+100&type=headword&q1=fable&rgxp=constrained.
32. John Trevisa, the translator of Ranulf Higden's Latin *Polychronicon* into English, contrasts "lying fable" with "the truthfulness of history." Chaucer, in the Physician's Tale, uses a similar contrast: "for this is no fable, but knowen for historial thyng notable." (Both quotes are cited in the MED entry on "fable.") The Dreamer's objection to the Pearl-Maiden's "fable," however, seems to be less concerned with history than theology.
33. However, since the term "fable" cannot shed its negative connotation in Middle English or present-day English, it might be fairer to compare *Pearl* to a parable.
34. Evelyn S. Newlyn, "Robert Henryson and the Popular Fable Tradition in the Middle Ages," *Popular Culture in the Middle Ages*, ed. Josie Campbell (Bowling Green, OH: Bowling Green State University Popular Press, 1986), 77–87, esp. 77.
35. See Edward Wheatley, *Mastering Aesop*, esp. chapter 3, "Toward a Grammar of Medieval Fable: Reading in its Pedagogical Context." For the broader context and development of the fable tradition in medieval Europe and England, see Jan Ziwolkowski, *Talking Animals: Medieval Latin Beast Poetry, 750–1150* (Philadelphia, PA: University of Pennsylvania Press, 1993) and *Fairy-Tales from before Fairy-Tales: The Medieval Latin Past of Wonderful Lies* (Ann Arbor, MI: University of Michigan Press, 2007) as well as Jill Mann, *From Aesop to Reynard: Beast Literature in Medieval Britain* (Oxford: Oxford University Press, 2009). Note that Susan Crane's book, *Animal Encounters: Contacts and Concepts in Medieval Britain* (Philadelphia, PA: University of Pennsylvania Press, 2013), makes the relevant point that fables had distinct appeal because medieval people had daily contact with animals and lived with the realities of the animal world differently than most of today's urban dwellers do.
36. Wheatley, *Mastering Aesop*, 52.
37. Gail Ivy Berlin, "The Fables of the Bayeux Tapestry: An Anglo-Saxon Perspective," *Unlocking the Word Hoard: Anglo-Saxon Studies in Memory of Edward B. Irving, Jr.,* ed. Mark Amodio and Kathrine O'Brien O'Keefe (Toronto: University of Toronto Press, 2003), 191–216.
38. *Pearl*, line 181.
39. Remein comments, "The Dreamer, far from failing to be able to read figurally, as many critics allege (and is surely the case in other instances), is here *all too eager* to supply an allegorical reading, to reduce the complexity of thing to sign, to sublimate an encounter with decorative aesthetics into *significance*. A sign fully reducible to (spiritual) significance would be easier to take in, but the Maiden appears as perceptible in terms of a phenomenon of unavoidable complexity." See Daniel C. Remein, "'Pygt': Ornament, Place, and Site—A Commentary on the Fourth Fitt of *Pearl*," *Glossator 9* (2015): 61–90, esp. 71.

40. *Pearl,* line 186.
41. J.J. Anderson, *Language and Imagination,* 29.
42. The Dreamer hopes for this vision to have "gostly ... porpose"—another claim in the poem hinting to readers that there is not only a literal but an allegorical or spiritual sense of the dream vision.
43. Spearing, "Symbolic and Dramatic Development in *Pearl,*" 132.
44. Reichardt, "Animal Similes," 18–19.
45. Ramein, "Pygt," 69–71.
46. Bogdanos, *Pearl: Image of the Ineffable,* 73.
47. Phaedrus, "Luscinia et Accipiter," in *Aesopica,* ed. Ben Edwin Perry (Champagne, IL: University of Illinois Press, 1952), 612. This fable appears in Greek fable collections, attributed to Aesop, that antedate the Phaedrus translation; it also appears in Hesiod's *Works and Days.* It is included in the *Fables* of Marie de France and printed in English in Caxton's *Aesop* as well.
48. Jacqueline de Weever, *Aesop and the Imprint of Medieval Thought: A Study of Six Fables as Translated at the End of the Middle Ages* (Jefferson, NC: McFarland, 2011), esp. chapter 5, which focuses on late-medieval redactions of this Aesopian fable.
49. De Weever, *Aesop and the Imprint of Medieval Thought,* 126.
50. Indeed, de Weever points out that medieval commentators on the fowler's use of birdlime was glossed as a type of deception since the lime was thought to be invisible to the birds captured by it: *Aesop and the Imprint of Medieval Thought,* 137.
51. Reichardt comments, "Both human beings and the quail of Exodus 16 and Numbers 11 seem naturally drawn toward death and destruction ... The carnal appetites of the Israelites [were] transferred in traditional commentary to the fleshy little birds on whom these people fed ... The dreamer, like the quail with which he has been compared, becomes an animated emblem of *voluptas carnales* [carnal desire]" ("Animal Similies," 23).
52. *Pearl,* line 336. Note that "doel" and "do" may be another example of the poet's wordplay.
53. Consider, for example, the well-known scripture verse, "My grace is sufficient for you; my strength is made perfect in weakness" (2. Cor. 12:9). The idea received from this was that a Christian's weakness was the perfect opportunity for Christ's strength to be made manifest.
54. For this Latin version, along with several, later versions in English, see "Fables of Aesop: A Complete Collection," http://fablesofaesop.com/the-one-eyed-doe.html. It is indexed in Perry's *Aesopica* as "#075: Cervus Oculo Captus." Note that "cervus" in this Latin version is a masculine noun, and would be translated "stag," but the ancient Greek version attributed to Aesop used "doe." Later versions and translations in English usually prefer the feminine noun "doe." See "The Hind Afflicted by Deformity," in *Aesop: The Complete Fables,* trans. Olivia and Robert Temple (New York, NY: Penguin Books, 1998), 82, included here:

> A hind, rendered congenitally disabled by being born with only one eye, went to the seashore to browse, turning her good eye to the land to watch out for hunters and the blind eye toward the sea, from whence she expected no danger. But some boatmen poachers were sailing along that part, and caught sight of her, adjusted their course, and mortally wounded her. While

rendering up her life, she said to herself: "Truly I am wretched; I was watching the land, which I believed was full of danger and expected no harm from the sea, which has been much more perilous." *It is thus that often our anticipation is mistaken: the things which seem troublesome to turn to our advantage, and those things which we hold beneficial show themselves to be injurious.*

The Temples translate from the 1927 bilingual, Greek-French edition-translation of Émile Chambry.

55. The English translation provided here is my own.
56. Romans 10:17.
57. Phaedrus, "The Wolf and the Lamb," in *Babrius and Phaedrus*, ed. and trans. Ben Edwin Perry, Loeb Classical Library (Cambridge, MA: Harvard University Press, 1965), 190–93. This fable is indexed in Perry's *Aesopica* as #155. This fable exists in Greek that antedates the Phaedrus translation. It is included in the late-medieval, vernacular fable collections of Marie de France, John Lydgate, and Robert Henryson; it was printed in English in Caxton's Aesopian fable collection as well.
58. See John 10:12 and cf. Matt. 10:16, Luke 10:3, and Acts 20:29.
59. Marie de France, *Fables*, ed. and trans. Harriet Spiegel, Medieval Academy Reprints for Teaching (Toronto: University of Toronto Press, 1994, repr. 2000), 34–35.
60. On the Pearl-Maiden's discourse recalling Christ's suffering before his passion, see Jane Beal, "The Jerusalem Lamb of *Pearl*," *Glossator* 9 (2015): 264–85.
61. Antti Aarne developed the "tale type" index, one part based on fairy-tale motifs and the other on plots, and published the initial work in 1910. This was translated into English by Stith Thompson in 1928. It became known as the Aarne-Thompson Tale Type Index, a standard resource for folklorists. Likewise, Vladimir Propp, a Russian structuralist, criticized the indices for ignoring the *functions* of fairy-tales. In *The Morphology of the Folktale* (1928; trans. into English 1958), he identified 31 functions and seven broad character types.
62. For a detailed overview beginning in 1970, see Donald Haase, "Feminist Fairy-tale Scholarship: A Critical Survey and Bibliography," *Marvels & Tales* 14 (2000): 15–63.
63. See Harold Neemann, *Piercing the Magic Veil: Toward a Theory of the Conte*, Biblio 17 (Tübingen: Narr, 1999), esp. chapter 5 "Psychoanalitical Approaches to Fairytales," 143–70.
64. Bruno Bettelheim, *The Uses of Enchantment: The Meaning and Importance of Fairy Tales* (New York, NY: Vintage Books, 1977), 5.
65. In his Master's thesis, Roger Andrew Amy uses the theories of Hans Robert Jauss and the "horizon of expectations" to argue that the *Pearl*-poet deliberately resisted conforming to generic standards for one genre because he was creating a new one and because he "carefully chooses elements of many familiar genres in order to manipulate the audience's reactions at crucial points in the poem. With these manipulations, the poet succeeds in making the experience of the poem personal for the reader, not merely literary" (ii). See Roger Andrew Amy, "Genre and Audience Response in the Middle English *Pearl*," (Vancouver: University of British Columbia, M.A. Thesis, 1992). Available online: https://circle.ubc.ca/bitstream/handle/2429/3615/ubc_1995-0192.pdf?sequence=3. Cynthia Kraman has made a similar point in her essay, "Body and Soul."

66. *Pearl*, line 163.
67. Arlyn Diamond, "Meeting Grounds: Gardens in Medieval Romance," *The Exploitations of Medieval Romance*, ed. Laura Ashe et al. (Cambridge: D.S. Brewer, 2010), 125–38.
68. Edward Vasta comments in his introduction to Sister Mary Vincent Hillmann's edition, "*The Pearl* is also a love vision of the type found in *The Romance of the Rose*. Here the speaker's vision takes the form of a dream in which he wanders through a lovely May world of singing birds and flowering meadows. He comes upon a stream flows so clearly that the bright stones of its bed are shimmeringly visible. He follows the stream until he comes upon a walled garden at whose gate he is met by lady. Within the garden he discovers a new life, the life courtly love. Again, parallels to *The Pearl* will be obvious … " (ix).
69. For a detailed explanation of this process, see chapter 3, "Moral Purpose."
70. On the Cupid and Psyche myth as a primal fairy-tale that influenced many later fairy-tales, see James Gollnick, *Love and the Soul: Psychological Interpretations of The Eros & Psyche Myth* (Waterloo, ON: Wilfrid Laurier University Press, 1992) See also Erich Neumann, *Amor and Psyche: The Psychic Development of the Feminine* (Princeton, NJ: Princeton University Press, 1956).
71. Cf. 1 John 4:8.
72. In *Pearl and Contemplative Writing*, Lagerholm recalls Bernard of Clairvaux and the four stages of loving God from the *Liber de diligendo Deo*: 1) when man loves himself for his own sake, 2) when man loves God for his own good, 3) when man loves God for God's sake, and 4) when man loves himself for the sake of God. She suggests that, at the conclusion of the poem, the Dreamer has attained only the second degree of love. "The second degree of love involves less self-interest than the first, but the motivating factor still remains one's own benefit rather than loving God for God's sake, which is the chief characteristic of the third degree. The highest form of love is the fourth degree, the perfection condition wherein 'man loves himself for the sake of God' only. However, St. Bernard is uncertain of whether the last stage is possible to attain in this life … In *Pearl*, the Dreamer begins on the first level … There can be little doubt that the Dreamer's loss makes him open to spiritual growth … In terms borrowed from St. Bernard, he 'starts loving God for his own benefit, because he learns from frequent experience that he can do everything that is good for him in God and that without God he can do nothing good.' This is a delineation of St. Bernard's second degree, and it where the Dreamer's interior journey ends in the narrative" (70–71). Against the conclusions of Ann Astell in *The Song of Songs in the Middle Ages* (121), Lagerholm states that the Dreamer's soul never achieves the mystical union with God. I agree that only the Pearl-Maiden is depicted as having experienced spiritual marriage to Christ; in the course of the poem, the Dreamer does not. I agree that, at the end of his vision of the New Jerusalem, plunging into the stream against the prohibition and seeking to reunite with the Pearl-Maiden, his progress is arrested at the second degree (if not rendered retrograde). However, by the end of the poem, he is acknowledging the goodness of God (line 1204) without specific expectation of God doing good to him. So he may be in the third degree of loving God, about which St. Bernard writes:

> This love is acceptable because it is given freely. It is chaste because it is not made up of words or talk, but of truth and action. It is just because it gives

back what it has received. For he who loves in this way loves as he is loved. He loves, seeking in return not what is his own, but what is Jesus Christ's, just as he has sought not his own good but our good, or rather, our very selves. He who says, "We trust in the Lord for he is good" (Ps. 117:1), loves in this way. He who trusts in the Lord because he is good to him but simply because he is good, truly loves God for God's sake and not for his own. (Bernard of Clairvaux, *Liber de diligendo Deo*, 194).

If he is not in the third degree of loving God, certainly the Dreamer is growing in that direction. The very brevity of the conclusion of *Pearl*, the end of a multitude of words, and the focus on the action of receiving the Eucharist, may reinforce this conclusion.

73. There are many versions of this essay available online and in print. This chapter relies on J.R.R. Tolkien, "On Fairy-Stories," in *Tales from the Perilous Realm* (London: HarperCollins, 1997; repr. Boston and New York: Houghton Mifflin Harcourt, 2008), 313–400.
74. Tolkien writes, "Fantasy remains a human right: we make in our measure and in our derivative mode because we are made, and not only made, but made in the image and the likeness of a Maker" ("On Fairy-Stories," 371).
75. Tolkien, "On Fairy-Stories," 361.
76. Tolkien, "On Fairy-Stories," 373. For a similar point made and developed with direct application to *Pearl*, see Santha Battacharjee, "The Middle English Poem *Pearl*: A Study in the Unfamiliar," *Dynamics of Difference: Christianity and Alterity*, ed. Ulrich Schmeidel and James Matarazzo (London and New York: Bloomsbury, 2015), 285–92.
77. Tolkien, "On Fairy-Stories," 375–76.
78. Tolkien, "On Fairy-Stories," 381.
79. Tolkien, "On Fairy-Stories," 384.
80. *Pearl*, line 1147.
81. Examples include many of the most famous fairy-tales: Beauty and the Beast, Cinderella, and Sleeping Beauty, among others.

Conclusion
Remembering

At the center of *Pearl* is the Dreamer's memory of trauma: the death of his beloved Pearl-Maiden. In the garden, his loss of a physical pearl cues the memory of his greater loss, the Pearl-Maiden's death and departure from earthly life and from him. The Dreamer's dream enables him to remember many things, including the appearance and character of the Pearl-Maiden herself. As he talks with her, he experiences memory-within-dream-memory: their discussion prompts his recollection of their prior, mutually shared experiences. Then, as his dream nears its conclusion, the Dreamer has a vision that is essentially memorial in character, a vision of the Lamb, the 144,000 virgins in procession, and the New Jerusalem that he recalls from his reading or hearing the biblical book of Revelation. He is actually, according to his Christian world-view, remembering the future! Upon waking, he remembers his dream and what transpired in it: another memorial layer. He then relates his individual memory to communal memory as it is experienced in the Eucharistic rite of the church, the "forme of bred and wyn" (line 1208). His emotional memory of the power of Christ's death, the atoning sacrifice that makes the resurrection of the body and reunion with the saints in heaven possible, enables him to move from anger (and rejection of his loss of the Pearl-Maiden) to grief (and acceptance of his loss) because he enters into Christ's sufferings just as Christ enters into his. He recognizes Christ as his God, his Lord, and his friend (line 1204).

In order to understand the memorial process in *Pearl* better, it is worthwhile to consider how memory works from some modern and medieval perspectives. These perspectives can provide a context for seeing the metaphoric comparisons of the Pearl-Maiden to "pearl," "seed," and "rose" as cues to memory with significance greater than their function. In turn, these metaphors in their context can provide an entry into further discussion of communal memory. For the *Pearl*-poet did a truly interesting thing when he depicted the Dreamer's vision of the New Jerusalem and its consequence, his sudden impulse to plunge into the stream before the Lamb of God: he put the Dreamer's memory of his beloved Pearl-Maiden in the context of communal Christian memory of the promises of Revelation.

Whereas at the beginning of the poem, the Dreamer's memory is darkened by the contemplation of his great loss, at the end his memory is illuminated by the hope of life beyond death. In the light, he conceives a desire, not only for reunion with his beloved, but also for more of God's "mysteries" (l. 1194). Light enters his mind, and his memory is changed. For the Dreamer's spiritual problem has not been remembering, which he is called to do, but rather remembering rightly. At the end of the poem, he can do so with greater clarity and hope.

The Memorial Process:
Some Medieval and Modern Perspectives

Mary Carruthers, in her admirable study *The Book of Memory*, notes that, traditionally, the metaphors for memory in the Middle Ages were two: *tabula memoriae* and *thesaurus sapientiae*, meaning the "writing-tablet of the memory" and the "treasure-chest (or storage-box) of wisdom" respectively. In the case of the first metaphor, "memory is a process most like reading written characters"[1] while the second metaphor refers to "the contents of such a memory and its internal organization ... equally visual, equally spatial."[2] *Pearl*, as a memorial poem preserved in writing, may externalize what medieval people conceived of as an internalized process: memory-as-metaphoric-writing (an idea that was certainly related to writing practices in their manuscript cultures). The highly visual and spatial organization of the Dreamer's journey in *Pearl*—rising as it does from the ground into space, through a marvelous dreamscape, and finally to a vision of the New Jerusalem—readily connects to the second idea about memory. Although all of the Dreamer's senses are affected by the dream, the effects on his sight (and therefore on his memory) are the most pronounced.

In his *Confessions*, Augustine comments on the perceptions of the five senses, noting that each enters "by their own various gates to be stored in memory. Nor indeed do the things themselves enter: *only the images of the things* perceived by the senses are there for thought to remember them."[3] This medieval notion of memory being impressed or written upon by images perceived by the eyes and organized in an internal storehouse of the soul had profound implications for medieval culture and Christian devotional practices. As a regular habit, monastic and lay folk prayerfully meditated upon images, icons, and symbols until, at length, they became written on their hearts and could be recalled without bodily sight in memory, in dreams, and in visions. Repeated rehearsal led to ready retrieval, sometimes even without conscious deliberation. This experience is represented as happening to the Dreamer in *Pearl* in the context of his grief.

In his *De Trinitate*, Augustine wrote of *memoria* in critically significant theological terms: as the third part of the soul (the other parts being reason and volition or the will). Thus, from his perspective, the human soul is Trinitarian in nature just as God is: Father, Son, and Holy Spirit. For medieval people, then, memory was tied to their eternal nature: a part of them that would continue after death and, when the body was resurrected, one that would work in and with the body and its sensory perceptions once again.

Medieval ideas about memory bear an interesting resemblance to modern ideas about memory. Today, the understanding of how memory works often rests on three basic concepts: encoding, storage, and retrieval. The Atkinson and Shriffin Information Processing Model (also called the Modal model) gives us one way of understanding how these concepts operate in human experience.[4] Graphically, the model can be represented like this:

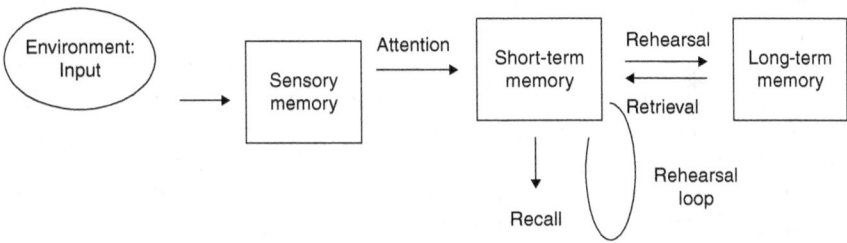

Figure C.1 Layers of Memory in *Pearl*

In this model, input from the environment enters the mind through the five senses of the body, is stored in sensory memory, short-term memory, and possibly long-term memory. At the short-term memory stage, input undergoes processes that may allow the memories-in-formation to enter long-term memory and be retrieved. Coding is the process whereby the mind seeks to recognize patterns in the input and associate the input with other information in long-term memory. Rehearsal is the repeated review of input in the conscious mind, which may involve assigning a verbal narrative to a lived experience, a process that makes input more memorable. Retrieval is, of course, the process of pulling memory from long-term storage in response to stimuli (i.e., triggers or cues). Human beings respond to happenings in their environment based on these internal, memorial processes.

It is certainly possible to explain *Pearl* in terms of modern memory theory. For the Dreamer, the input that has affected him so deeply is the Pearl-Maiden's death while his dream is, in itself, the retrieval process made possible by prior coding and rehearsal. He actually commits to further rehearsal by associating the trauma of the Pearl-Maiden's death with the trauma of Christ's death, which he remembers each day in the Eucharistic rite. By the poem's conclusion, because he has connected profoundly to compassion—his for Christ, Christ's for him—the emotional pain of his memory is lessened and lightened. The process depicted in *Pearl* suggests how deeply memory is affected by trauma and grief and, simultaneously, how memory can be healed over time through extraordinary demonstrations of love.

In her book, *On Death and Dying*, Elizabeth Kübler-Ross famously argued that there are five stages of grief: denial, anger, bargaining, depression, and acceptance.[5] The metaphor of "stages" implies a progression from one level to the next, but Kübler-Ross asserts that people experiencing loss move between these stages and might not experience all of them. In his studies, George Bonanno has argued that there is little evidence to support the Kübler-Ross model: there are certainly individual and cross-cultural exceptions to it.[6] Yet it remains a powerful tool for understanding something about grieving the death of a loved one, a process that is both mysterious and painful.

The Dreamer's experience of grief in *Pearl*, for example, seems to follow the five stages of grief rather closely. Although he has lost his pearl, he seems to live in denial that she is lost forever, and he wants to recover her for himself permanently. He expresses his deep depression, frustration, and even anger in his conversation with the Pearl-Maiden. Through his series of questions and objections, he bargains with her in an attempt to bring her closer to him or to be allowed to come closer to her. It is only upon waking that he expresses an acceptance of the loss of his beloved and the will of God. Some modern readers have found his acceptance to be both sudden and unsatisfying.[7] Psychologists who argue for seven stages (or more) of grief seem to want to see a longer process that involves working through the issues more thoroughly, after awakening, before they can accept the Dreamer's internal transformation as plausible or genuine. The Dreamer's brief vision of the bleeding Lamb seems too quick.

Nevertheless, it is powerful in effect. The Dreamer's vision of the Lamb with the bleeding side has definite parallels with medieval devotional and memorial practices. His vision has connections to the meditations of Christians viewing the Stations of the Cross in church during Lent as well as to the viewing of Passion Plays staged before Easter, to private contemplation of icons of Christ, and to other visual consideration medieval people gave to crucifixes, books, sculptures, and paintings, many of which featured the human Christ with a lamb or represented Christ himself as a lamb. The image of the Lamb is an image of atonement, and atonement, in medieval Christian thinking, is directly linked to the Cross.

While the Pearl-Maiden's death is the trauma in the center of the Dreamer's thought, there is for both the Dreamer and the Pearl-Maiden a greater trauma that stands in the center of Christian history: the Crucifixion of Jesus. Even before the Dreamer met the Pearl-Maiden, he reflected on the comfort Christ had made known to him (ll. 54–55), but that comfort clearly has not lessened his grief. When the Pearl-Maiden meets the Dreamer, one of the first things she says to him is that if he thinks his pearl is completely taken away, he has misunderstood his own tale: she lives forever in her own garden (lines 257–60). This promise is already inherent in the image of the seed that the Dreamer meditated on before sleeping. Yet the Pearl-Maiden's encouragement does not lessen the Dreamer's grief, either. Theological knowledge of Christ's comfort and the hope of a future life are not enough to mitigate the Dreamer's memory of trauma. Like most survivors of trauma, the Dreamer needs someone to enter into his suffering with him in order to heal.

In one sense, the Pearl-Maiden enters into the Dreamer's suffering with him because she comes to him in a dream when he is grieving and listens

Conclusion 141

to him and talks to him. Yet ultimately, it appears that the Dreamer cannot really hear what the Pearl-Maiden says or what she means. She cannot comfort him because the comfort he desires from her is herself, restored to him, not her hand pointing toward Christ in the Parable of the Vineyard, in her explanation of her spiritual marriage to Christ, or in her recollections of how her Lord the Lamb was slain in Jerusalem (l. 640, l. 700, l. 740, l. 800, l. 805). When the Dreamer asks to see the Pearl-Maiden's inner chamber, he is still pursuing her, not Christ. Naturally, she refuses his request, but she does reveal that she has requested permission from the Lamb for the Dreamer to see a sight (ll. 965–68).

When the Dreamer sees the Lamb, he sees him wounded. He sees him with blood pouring out from his side. Through this vision, the Dreamer perceives that someone, the Lamb, has entered into the experience of suffering that the Dreamer himself has known all too well. Someone else has experienced pain and loss. The Dreamer witnesses the wide, wet wound near the Lamb's heart, torn through his skin, and he sees the blood spraying out of his white side. He wonders who caused it. The orthodox answer for medieval Christians was, of course, that God became man in the form of Jesus, Jesus who lived a perfect life, and he offered himself as an atoning sacrifice on the Cross so that sinful humanity could be reconciled to God. But the Dreamer does not give this doctrinal statement in response to his own question. Instead, he says that "Ani breste for bale a3t haf forbrent / Er he þerto hade had delyt" (ll. 1139–40). In other words, the Dreamer feels that anyone who sees the Lamb's pierced side, any heart that witnesses his suffering, should burn with sorrow. Thus the theological knowledge that did not comfort the Dreamer is superseded by an experience of profound empathy: the Dreamer enters into the suffering of the Lamb just as the Lamb has entered into his.

This does not stop the Dreamer from trying to cross the stream in order to reunite with his beloved Pearl-Maiden. But when he awakens after his failed attempt to cross the water, and after he has a chance to reflect on his vision, the Dreamer reflects on the meaning of his experience:

> Ouer þis hyul þis lote I la3te,
> For pyty of my perle enclyin,
> And syþen to God I hit byta3te
> In Kryste3 dere blessyng and myn,
> Þat in þe forme of bred and wyn
> Þe preste vus schewe3 vch a daye. (1205–10)

The Dreamer, now awake, specifically recalls the memorial of the death of Jesus and the elements of the Eucharist. He recalls two items from the natural world, the bread and the wine that can be perceived with the senses—seen, smelled, touched, tasted, even faintly heard—and these function as the cues that call to his mind the memory of the trauma at the center of Christian history: the Crucifixion of Jesus. Only this memory does not make him mad with grief. It moves to the center of his thought, where the memory of the trauma of the Pearl-Maiden's death had been, and it brings him peace.

Medieval devotional and memorial practices were reinforced by the Eucharistic rite. The reference to the Eucharist at the conclusion of *Pearl* opens up the embrace of the poem's purpose to console not only the Dreamer but also the readers who have journeyed with him through his memorial dream. It opens up the experience of reading *Pearl* to the communal memory of the audience. The abrupt conclusion of the dream is intentionally meant to leave impressed upon readers' minds the *image* of the Lamb, bleeding but full of joy. The memory of that image has power. It stands as a kind of invitation to everyone who has experienced traumatic loss to step into the remembrance of Christ's death along with the Dreamer and into the hope that Christ's redemption brings for life on earth and the life to come in heaven. Furthermore, the bleeding Lamb is supposed to be remembered through the Eucharist. Just as Christ's death should be remembered, just so can human beings remember their own individual experiences of trauma, death, loss, and sorrow. They can remember rightly, in the light of the eternal significance of the bread and the wine.

Those elements are cues to memory at the end of *Pearl*. But they are not the only key image-cues in *Pearl* that appeal to the communal memory of the poet's audience. There are three that come before it: pearl, grain, and rose.

Metaphoric Memory Cues: Pearl, Seed, Rose

The metaphors for the Pearl-Maiden's death are three: the first image is of a lost pearl, the second of a buried seed, and the third of a failed rose. While it is clear from the poetic context that these metaphors refer to the death of the Pearl-Maiden, the exact nature and circumstances of the Pearl-Maiden's death are never specified. The readers of the poem, overhearing the personal reflections of the Dreamer and his later conversation with the Pearl-Maiden, are never invited into the sanctuary of silence that holds the mystery of exactly how the Pearl-Maiden died. What is suggested by these metaphors, however, is that tangible things in nature, things that can be perceived by the senses, are acting as cues to remind the Dreamer of the Pearl-Maiden's death. Thus pearl, seed, and rose take on significance that is not only natural, biblical, and literary, but also psychological and emotional. For the Dreamer in particular, these items in nature, which can be perceived by the senses, have become associated with his pain over the Pearl-Maiden's death, and the memory of one cues the memory of the other.

The first image, that of the lost pearl, is by far the most predominant, appearing repeatedly throughout the poem, but first in the opening stanza:

> Pearle plesaunte ... Allas! I leste hyr in on erbere
> Þurgh gresse to grounde hit fro me yot. (l.1, 9–10)
>
> (Pleasant pearl ... Alas! I lost her in a one garden
> Through the grass to the ground it fell from me.)

Modern people reading of pearls think of how they are formed within oysters: by an irritating grain of sand around which the oyster forms layers and layers of protective nacre, a mineral substance, until an iridescent pearl is produced. But medieval lapidaries, including the influential *De lapidibus* of Marbode, the eleventh-century Bishop of Rennes, revealed that medieval people believed that the pearl was formed when rays from the stars, moon, and sun entered the oyster with the dew of morning, and from the combination of these came the pearl. This conception of the pearl's natural origins went back to Pliny the Elder, in his first-century *Natural History*, and it was transmitted through the seventh-century *Etymologies* of Isidore of Seville. From Marbode, it was picked up by later twelfth- and thirteenth-century lapidary writers and compilers, including those translated into English, notably the one produced for King Philip IV the Fair, *De proprietatibus rerum* of Bartholomaeus Anglicus, and *Secreta Secretorum*.[8] It became an allegorical picture of the Virgin Mary's immaculate conception of Jesus.[9]

The idea of the pearl in nature was thus intimately connected to biblical exegesis and the Bible itself, where the pearl had two key incarnations for contemplation: the Parable of the Pearl of Great Price and the pearly gates of the New Jerusalem in Revelation. Jesus also forbade his disciples to cast their pearls before swine.[10] The pearl's associations with salvation and heavenly places in scripture contributed to its reputation for healing power. Medieval lapidaries advise that, when the pearl is ground up and drunk in an infusion, it has the power to heal all diseases—except death.

The pearl also had a shining place in medieval literature, especially saints' legends and lyrics. The pearl, or *margarita* (in Latin), was connected primarily to the legends of St. Margaret. Jacobus de Voragine recounts a version of her story in the *Legenda aurea*, in which he notes that just as the pearl is shining white, so Saint Margaret was shining in virginity; just as it is small, so she was small in her humility; and just as it is powerful in the performance of miracles, so she was, for she was constant in martyrdom and "overcame the devil."[11] He adds that she "strengthened the spirit by her doctrine, since her doctrine strengthened the spirits of many and converted them to the faith of Christ."[12] When this holy interpretation of the pearl's qualities is considered beside sacred lyrics referring to the Virgin Mary, the significance is clear. But medieval Latin and Middle English lyrics are both sacred and secular. Secular love lyrics compare the white body of the pearl to the white body of the beloved woman, its smallness to hers, its power to heal to her power to succor the lover.[13]

The pearl of *Pearl* appears in the contexts of natural, biblical, and literary texts that suggest a full range of possible meaning—and the loss of such a pearl has enormous emotional and psychological implications. Within the wide range of connotations associated with the pearl's intertextual significance, the Dreamer's loss of his pearl represents, symbolically, the loss of the union of the light of sun, moon, and stars with the dew of morning; the loss of that which has the power to heal him; the loss of salvation and access to the heavenly City. On the one hand, it represents the loss of virgin purity, tender humility, and the power to overcome the devil, and on the other, the loss of a woman's white body, her smallness next to him, and her power to relieve him from the sufferings of love. No wonder his memory is darkened, when the poem begins, by the shadows of a devastating grief.

The image of the lost pearl, which stands for the Pearl-Maiden, is complemented by the second image of the buried seed. It occurs in the third stanza of the poem:

> For vch gresse mot grow of graynez dede.
> No whete were ellez to wonez wonne. (l.30–31)
>
> (For each grass must grow from dead grains.
> No wheat otherwise could be brought home.)

Like the pearl, the grain of wheat (or seed) had natural, biblical, and literary contexts that would have been known to the *Pearl*-poet's audience. In medieval England, as well as France and Germany, August was the primary month for harvesting grain: the winter crops, wheat and rye, and then the spring grains, barley and oats. Wheat was harvested from high up with a sickle, other grains from low down with a long-handled scythe.[14] The image of death as a Grim Reaper, which modern people have inherited, emerges from this agricultural context: the grain being cut by the scythe of the harvester.

August is, in fact, the month and the "high season" in which the Dreamer of *Pearl* falls asleep: the agriculturally busy time of the wheat harvest, the liturgically significant season between Lammas (August 1st) and the celebration of the Assumption of the Virgin (August 15th), which included not only the celebration of the Transfiguration of Christ (August 6th) but also the octave of St. Anne (August 3rd). It is not coincidental that the poet, in the Dreamer's voice, meditates not only on a lost pearl, but on "dead grains," grains that become buried seeds, from which spring up the next crop for harvesting.

These lines from the third stanza of *Pearl* have more than agricultural connotations consonant with the rhythms of the natural world. They clearly allude to the famous biblical passage in 1 Corinthians 15, which concerns the resurrection of the body:

> tu quod seminas non vivificatur, nisi prius moriatur: et quod seminas, non corpus, quod futurum est, seminas, sed nudum granum.
>
> (What you sow does not come to life again unless it first dies: and what you sow is not the body that is to be but a bare kernel.)[15]

The "bare kernel" is, in the Latin, a *nudum granum*. In the *Pearl*-poet's translation, it becomes "graynez dede," dead grains of wheat. By alluding specifically to wheat, the poet immediately invokes familiar biblical images of wheat and harvest from the words of Jesus, including John 12:24, "Truly, truly, I say to you, unless a grain of wheat falls into the ground and dies, it remains alone, but if it dies, it bears much fruit." This saying was later understood to refer to Christ's death and resurrection and to the fruit of Holy Spirit and the Church.[16]

But the *Pearl*-poet's subsequent line, about wheat being gathered into barns, would have brought to mind the words of Jesus in the Parable of the Wheat and the Tares from Matthew 13 (a chapter in which the Parable of the Pearl of Great Price and the Parable of the Merchant also appear), and the words of John the Baptist, which foreshadow the parable, in Matthew 3:

> Ego quidem baptizo vos in aqua in pœnitentiam: qui autem post me venturus est, fortior me est, cuius non sum dignus calceamenta portare: ipse vos baptizabit in Spiritu Sancto, et igni. Cuius ventilabrum in manu sua: et permundabit aream suam: et congregabit triticum suum in horreum, paleas autem comburet igni inextinguibili.[17]
>
> (I baptize you with water for repentance, but he who is coming after me is mightier than I, whose sandals I am not worthy to carry. He will baptize you with the Holy Spirit and fire. His winnowing fork is in his hand, and he will clear his threshing floor and gather his wheat into the barn, but the chaff he will burn with unquenchable fire.)

According to the gospel-writer, John the Baptist here contrasts water with fire and fire with fire: the fire of God's Spirit, which ignites those who repent, as opposed to the unquenchable fire, which consumes the chaff.

It is worth noting that medieval Bible commentators connected John's reference to his unworthiness to carry the Messiah's sandals to the action of the kinsman depicted in the fourth chapter of Ruth (a story set in the time of the barley and wheat harvests): the kinsman took off his sandal to signify that he was ceding to Boaz his right to the land of Naomi as well as a marriage to Ruth.[18] Indeed, the kinsman was seen as a type foreshadowing John the Baptist, who called himself, "the friend of the Bridegroom,"[19] the bridegroom being Jesus.

It seems that the words and character of John the Baptist may well have been on the *Pearl*-poet's mind, as a context for several passages in *Pearl*, including the early lines 30–31, concerning the "dead grains," and the later lines with his reflections on baptism and innocence, and also some of the concluding lines toward the end of the poem. When the Dreamer recognizes God as his friend (l. 1204), he suggests a new identity for himself: like John the Baptist, the Dreamer has become the friend of God. The Dreamer never calls himself the Bridegroom nor does he identify himself, as the Pearl-Maiden and many medieval contemplatives (both male and female) did, as the Bride. This reluctance may reflect the limits of the Dreamer's progress in his journey into God, being illuminated and purged but not yet unified with the divine, but it may also align him with the role of John the Baptist—but only after he awakens.

It is highly significant that the Dreamer cannot set foot in the stream that separates him from the Pearl-Maiden and from the Lamb of God in heaven. John the Baptist, by contrast, was waist-deep in the Jordan baptizing the bodies of repentant sinners in the water. But the implication of the Dreamer's transformation at the end of the poem, and his willingness to submit to the incomprehensible but nevertheless glorious will of God, makes him more like John the Baptist and clearly implies that he will, one day, at the right time, cross over the water into heavenly places.

The biblical contexts for the poet's allusion to "dead grains," especially wheat grain, certainly had metaphoric resonance in the larger realm of medieval English literature. As the Wife of Bath's rather crass (but nevertheless, conventional) comparison of wives to barley ("barly-breed") and virgins to wheat ("pured whete-seed") implies, wheat was seen as finer and the bread it produced, obviously, whiter.[20] The whiteness of wheat bread connected it, symbolically, to the purity of virginity. This also provides a context for understanding the *Pearl*-poet's wheat, the grain that is a cue to the Dreamer's memory of his beloved, virginal Pearl-Maiden.

The emotional and psychological significance implied by the burial of a wheat-seed is distinctly different from the loss of a pearl. The wheat-seed has within it the germ of resurrection. A lost pearl may be gone forever, but a buried wheat-seed can sprout and grow. If it does, despite the Dreamer's fear that it will not (line 34), it will be utterly transformed by its death and subsequent growth process. When the Dreamer mourns the death of the wheat-seed, he mourns what was, but the comparison alone suggests that there is hope for what will be, even if the Dreamer does not yet dare to imagine it.

While it is the Dreamer who first compares the Maiden to pearl and wheat-seed, it is the Maiden who first compares herself to a rose and her death to a rose that bloomed and withered:[21]

"For þat þou lestez watz bot a rose
Þat flowred and fayled as kynde hyt gef." (l. 269–70)

(For what you lost was but a rose
that flowered and failed as nature gave it [to do].)

The image of the rose is naturally more connected to the wheat-seed than to the pearl, for it, too, is alive: it begins as a seed, which sprouts and forms a bud, eventually blooms and perfumes the air, participates in the pollination process with the help of bees (and so spreads its life into the world while yet living), and finally withers and fades, losing its petals and its scent.[22] In these lines, the Pearl-Maiden acknowledges that the Dreamer's loss is real, but her choice of metaphor—of memory cue—draws the Dreamer (and the reader) into a complex association of meanings involved in medieval rose imagery.

Perhaps the most famous rose in scripture is the one in the Song of Songs: "ego flos campi et lilium convallium" ("I am the flower of the field [*or* the rose of Sharon], and the lily of the valleys").[23] Origen identified the rose as Christ himself, the Bridegroom speaking in the ancient epithalamium, but other commentators sometimes interpreted the rose as the Bride. In the latter case, the flower was frequently taken to stand for Mary, the mother of Jesus.[24] But the flower that the Pearl-Maiden invokes here seems more to do with the flowers of the field that Jesus speaks of when telling his disciples not to worry:

> Et de vestimento quid solliciti estis? Considerate lilia agri quomodo crescunt: non laborant, neque nent. Dico autem vobis, quoniam nec Salomon in omni gloria sua coopertus est sicut unum ex istis. Si autem fœnum agri, quod hodie est, et cras in clibanum mittitur, Deus sic vestit, quanto magis vos modicæ fidei?[25]
>
> (And why do you worry about your clothes? Consider the lilies of the field, how they grow: they neither labor nor sew. Truly I say to you, that not even Solomon in all of his glory was dressed like one of these. If, moreover, God so clothes the grass of the field, which is here today, and tomorrow sent into the oven, how much more you, O you of little faith?)

The Pearl-Maiden's comparison of herself to a rose highlights her personal beauty but also the transitory and temporary nature of her life. Yet, in the context of Christ's words in Matthew's gospel, this is nothing to worry about. It is part of the natural cycle of a flower's life. It can also be understood in a related passage from Paul in 1 Corinthians 15:53: "For this perishable body must clothe itself with the imperishable, and the mortal body with immortality." Although the rose of the Pearl-Maiden's body failed on earth, the picture she portrays of herself to the Dreamer in *Pearl*—in heavenly places with Jesus—is of a new-bought bride whose clothes are washed in the Lamb's blood, only to become not red, but shining white as a representation of the cleanness of her virginity (lines 765–69).

The plethora of medieval literary uses of rose imagery is worthy of its own book, but suffice it to say, simply, that the rose stood for the beloved. In contemplative writings, the sacred rose was the Virgin Mary. In romance and *aventure*, the secular rose was the lady beloved by the knight who pursued her. From the *Romance of the Rose* to Dante's *Divine Comedy*, the image of the rose was elevated and became ever more allegorically significant, until even heaven itself was pictured as a rose of light. In the fourteenth century, when the *Pearl*-poet was writing, the rose had not become a cliché but remained a powerful—indeed, iconic—idea that held spiritual and emotional power.

The Pearl-Maiden's comparison of herself to a failed rose, unlike the Dreamer's comparisons of her to pearl and wheat-seed, implies both personal humility and a natural course of life that unfolds in time: first flourishing, then dying. The loss of a flower so beautiful, whose perfume is at once that of Christ, his Mother, and his Bride, the Church, and that of the irresistibly beloved woman, is terribly painful. The Pearl-Maiden acknowledges that this is a real loss for the Dreamer, in one sense, on earth, but as her ongoing discourses reveal, not necessarily the loss he perceives it to be: one permanently darkening memory. Instead, in the light, she tries to show him that as a rose, she was beloved not only to him, but to God, and she has been transformed into the "perle of prys" (line 272): the Bride of Christ.

For the Dreamer, pearl, seed, and rose are all vivid images, word-pictures, and memory-cues with which his emotional responses to the Pearl-Maiden's death are bound up—almost inextricably bound to pain. Indeed, the depth and intensity of the Dreamer's emotional response to the loss of the Pearl-Maiden cannot be overstated. His memory needs to be cleansed and healed. That is why he takes his journey from earth, through space and time and dream, to look up to the vision of the New Jerusalem. His memory needs to be illuminated.

The Illumination of Memory

Light gradually dawns on the Dreamer's mind as he journeys from the garden through the dreamscape to behold the vision of the New Jerusalem. In the garden, he sees the interplay of light and shadow, light and dark. In his dream, the landscape around him becomes brighter and more beautiful, shining around him, reflected in blue trees with silver leaves and crystal cliffs and jewels shimmering in the streambed, until he reaches the focal point of the Pearl-Maiden herself—and she is "blysande whyt" (l. 197) or *blazing white*. It almost does not seem as if the light could get any brighter, but after being in the Pearl-Maiden's bright presence a long while, the Dreamer then beholds the shining white Lamb of God in the resplendent New Jerusalem. This is the climax of the light imagery of the poem, for the Lamb is brighter than the sun or moon! It remains for the awakened Dreamer, whose memory has been illuminated in this process, to become more fully enlightened through meditation and memorial rehearsal of his experience.

The use of light in *Pearl* emerges from the use of light in scripture and the medieval Christian contemplative tradition. In the Bible, light symbolizes God himself, and by extension, his dwelling place in heaven (Pss. 4:6, 27:1, 1 John 1:5). His *Shekinah* glory is made manifest in light. Light also suggests moral goodness and holiness, especially in contrast to moral darkness, and to "walk in the light" is to listen to God's voice and do what God says.[26] Light stands for salvation: "The Lord is my light and my salvation; whom shall I fear?"[27] It is closely linked to the redeeming power of God in Christ Jesus, who calls himself "the Light of the World."[28] In scripture, light symbolizes truth and understanding, as opposed to deception and ignorance, and it is related to the fulfillment of justice at the end of time. Light also stands for life, God's favor in life, and grace as well as joy.[29] Medieval Christian contemplatives, who meditated on the scriptures night and day and ruminated on their meaning, were highly influenced by the use of light imagery in the Bible, so much so that light profoundly shaped their inner lives, experience in prayer, and the writings that they passed on to others. As Bonaventure says in his *Itinerarium mentis in Deum*:

> ... we receive light to discern the steps of the ascent into God. In relation to our position in creation, the universe itself is a ladder by which we can ascend into God. Some created things are vestiges, others images; some are material, others spiritual; some are temporal, others everlasting; some are outside us, others within us. In order to contemplate the First Principle, who is most spiritual, eternal and above us, we must pass through his vestiges, which are material, temporal and outside us. This means to be led in the path of God. We must also enter into our soul, which is God's image, everlasting, spiritual and within us. This means to enter in the truth of God. We must go beyond to what is eternal, most spiritual and above us, by gazing upon the First Principle. This means to rejoice in the knowledge of God and in reverent fear of his majesty.[30]

For the contemplative yearning to draw close to God, experience in the light was essential to making spiritual progress.

Applied to *Pearl*, this passage from Bonaventure, which exemplifies key concepts from the broad but well-established tradition of medieval Christian contemplative devotion, resonates with meaning. First, the Dreamer receives *light* at all three stages of his journey, as he is transported up the *ladder* of divine contemplation *into the mysteries of God*. Created things around him, material and spiritual, are *images* he perceives that lead him to the place where he can *gaze upon the Lamb*, God himself (the First Principle), and experience both *awe* and *joy*. Light enables his sight.[31] Sight, in turn, shapes his memory. As Mary Carruthers has observed, summarizing a key aspect of medieval thought on sight and memory formation, "Our memories store "likenesses" of things as they were when they appeared to and affected us ... all memory-images have an emotional component, acquired during the process of their formation."[32]

The relationship of light, sight, and the process of the illumination of the Dreamer's memory is worth considering from the point of view of medieval science, for the poet appears to be aware of late-medieval optical theory. The Greeks originated key ideas that the Middle Ages later inherited: Plato bequeathed the idea of *extramission*, the idea that a beam of light came from the eyes of the viewer and enabled sight while Aristotle bequeathed the idea of *intramission*, the idea that objects had light in and of themselves, which enabled them to project their image into the eyes of the beholder. By the eleventh century, Avicenna noted the independence of light from eyes and objects, rejecting the Platonic explanation and leaning on the Aristotelian concept of light and sight, saying: "when light falls on the visible object, it projects the image of the object onto the eye."[33] By the end of the fourteenth century, the period of time in which the *Pearl*-poet lived, a kind of fascination with light and optical science of optics had developed. This may be best exemplified by Grosseteste's *De Luce*, in which he distinguished between *lux,* the uncreated first light, which is God, and *lumen*, the created light of the natural world, and he wrote of light's power of diffusion from a single point throughout the entire universe.

While medieval science explored the interaction of natural light and literal sight, theology questioned it: for Augustine, relying on Paul and influencing later medieval thinkers, corporeal sight was unreliable.[34] The human spirit had eyes, with which to love the neighbor even in the neighbor's absence, and the mind had interior sight with which to look at Love itself and understand.[35] These forms of spiritual sight, enabled by inward illumination, were more trustworthy. In *Pearl*, the Dreamer relies on his sight, but the Pearl-Maiden questions that tendency (lines 301–302), basically saying that he thinks she is present because he sees her with his eyes. Bodily sight, can be deceived. The Pearl-Maiden wants the Dreamer's interior vision to be illuminated so he can see truly.

The Dreamer's journey in the light is one of gradual elevation and ever-brightening progress. The first light by which he sees, in the garden, seems to represent natural light; the second, in the dream, the inner light of the Dreamer's reason or growing (but still limited) understanding; the third, in the *visio*, the *prima lux* of God, for "God is light" and Jesus is "the Light of the World."[36] The light gradually illuminates the Dreamer's memory of the past (his loss) and his shared Christian communal memory of the future: the promises of Revelation. Certainly this upward progress can be understood as one from humility to illumination to purification, a purification that not only affects the mind (reason), but the heart (feeling). For in the key context for his vision, Revelation 21, are these promises:

> Et ego Joannes vidi sanctam civitatem Jerusalem novam descendentem de cælo a Deo, paratam sicut sponsam ornatam viro suo. Et audivi vocem magnam de throno dicentem: Ecce tabernaculum Dei cum hominibus, et habitabit cum eis. Et ipsi populus ejus erunt, et ipse Deus cum eis erit eorum Deus: et absterget Deus omnem lacrimam ab oculis eorum: et mors ultra non erit, neque luctus, neque clamor, neque dolor erit ultra, quia prima abierunt. Et dixit qui sedebat in throno: Ecce nova facio omnia.[37]

(And I, John, saw the holy city, the new Jerusalem, descending from heaven from God, prepared as a bride adorned for her husband. And I heard a loud voice from the throne, saying, "Behold, the Tabernacle of God is with man, and he will live with them and they will be his people, and God himself will be with them as their God. He will wipe away every tear from their eyes, and death shall be no more, neither shall there be mourning, nor crying, nor sorrow anymore, for the former things have passed away." And he who was seated on the throne said, "Behold, I make all things new.")

Conclusions

So at the end of *Pearl*, readers realize that the story has been about the Dreamer's memory (at least in part) from the very beginning. In fact, the entire poem is structured around his memory just as a pearl develops around a grain of sand in shining layers of nacre. A simple illustration shows this clearly:

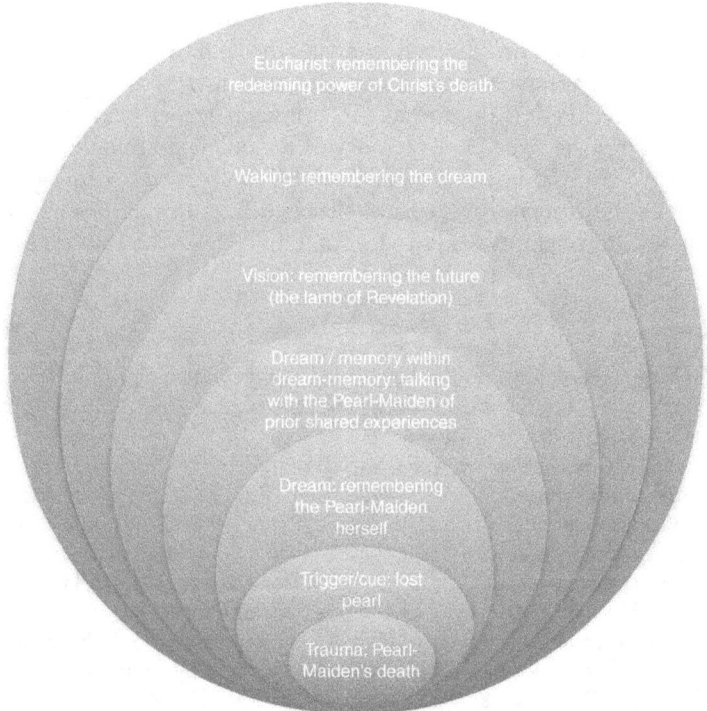

Figure C.2 Memorial Processes

To show how every memorial layer connects to the others and to the originary trauma of loss, the final lines of the poem echo the opening ones, bringing the poem and the nature of the memory depicted full-circle. It is a cliché of *Pearl* scholarship, but it is true nonetheless: the poem is circular.

Like a pearl, the form of the poem suggests roundness, wholeness, perfection, eternity, and luminescent purity. At the end, the poet returns to the beginning, and the process of remembering again can generate deeper and deeper understanding of the Dreamer's past experience and future hope. For the awakened Dreamer does have hope at the conclusion of the poem—a real hope, not a doctrinal cliché—a hope based on witnessing the suffering of the Lamb of God, in a vision of the New Jerusalem, and realizing that Jesus entered into his suffering not only long ago on the Cross, but again, through this vision intended to console him and to change, not just his mind, but his heart. Unlike the allegory of Plato's cave, in which a man must climb with his own effort to reach the light of truth, the Dreamer is elevated by supernatural intervention, and when he reaches the place beyond which he can go no further, the Light of heaven descends into his darkness and illuminates him more and more. The Dreamer later accepts that his Pearl-Maiden is in the company of the holy, and trusting in his Lord and Friend, who has revealed to him again the promises of Revelation, he knows that he will see her again and be joined with all the saints, angels, and Christ himself in heavenly places.

Indeed, by participating in the Eucharist—through the communal Christian memory of Christ's past sacrifice as well as Christ's future return—that hope can be recalled again and again, bringing deeper healing to his soul each time. Thus the Dreamer's memory of trauma is illuminated, redeemed, and restored. So, the poet suggests, may be the sorrows of the readers of his poem as they journey with whole-hearted humility deeper into Christ's redemptive suffering and God's redeeming love.[38]

Notes

1. Mary Carruthers, *The Book of Memory: A Study of Memory in Medieval Culture* (Cambridge: Cambridge University Press, 1990, repr. 2004), 21.
2. Carruthers, *The Book of Memory*, 33.
3. Augustine, *Confessions*, trans. F.J. Sheed (Indianapolis, IN and Cambridge, MA: Hackett Publishing Company, 1942, repr. 1993), 179. Atkinson and Shriffin emphasize two kinds of memory storage, iconic (visual) and echoic (auditory), but Augustine emphasizes earlier in his *Confessions* that there are particular memory storage processes for information from all five senses. All three memory analysts agree on the primacy and importance of images.
4. Richard Atkinson and Richard Shiffrin, "Human Memory: A Proposed System and Its Control Processes," in *The Psychology of Learning and Motivation*, Vol. 2, ed. K.W. Spence and J.T. Spence (New York, NY: Academic Press, 1968), 89–195.
5. Elizabeth Kübler-Ross, *On Death and Dying* (New York, NY: Macmillan, 1969). The five stages of grief were later expanded by others to seven: shock and denial, pain and guilt, anger and bargaining, depression and loneliness, the upward turn, reconstruction and working through, acceptance and hope.
6. George Bonanno, *The Other Side of Sadness: What the New Science of Bereavement Says about Life after Loss* (New York, NY: Basic Books, 2009). Bonanno emphasizes the human quality of resilience in the face of loss.
7. See, for example, Aers, "*Pearl*: The Self Mourning" and Watson, "The Gawain-Poet as Vernacular Theologian."
8. For an overview of the development of lapidaries in the Middle Ages, see George Keiser, "Lapidaries," in *Medieval Science, Technology, and Medicine: An Encyclopedia*, eds. Thomas Glick, Steven Livesey, and Faith Wallis (New York and London: Routledge / Taylor and Francis Group, 2005), 306–307.
9. Marbode of Rennes, *De Lapidibus*, trans. C. W. King and John M. Riddle (Wiesbaden: Franz Steiner Verlag GMBH, 1977). See also "Pearl," *Medieval Bestiary* http://bestiary.ca/beasts/beast548.htm (accessed 7 March 2015) and

http://www.wheaton.edu/Academics/Departments/English/Majors/Resources/Medieval-Lit-Bibliography/Stones.
10. Matt. 7:6.
11. Jacobus de Voragine, *The Golden Legend: Readings on the Saints*, Vol. I, trans. William Granger Ryan (Princeton, NJ: Princeton University Press, 1993), 368. Note the allusion to Rev. 12:11.
12. Ibid., 368.
13. Two specific, female, "pearl" figures from late-medieval literature, contemporaneous with *Pearl*, are Queen Alceste from Chaucer's *Legend of Good Women* and Margarite from Thomas Usk's *Testament of Love*. For further discussion of the *marguerite* literary tradition, and especially its possible connection to Richard II's Queen Anne, see chap. 8 "Courtly Love: From Elegy to Epithalamium," in John Bowers, *The Politics of Pearl*, esp. 155–59.
14. See Andy Staples, "The Medieval Farming Year (Version 1.0)," *Witheridge: The Centuries in Words and Pictures*, (1999): http://www.witheridge-historical-archive.com/medieval-year.htm/. The emphasis on the harvest in August in abundantly clear in background of the month of August depicted in the *Très Riches Heures du Duc de Berry*. See http://publicdomainreview.org/collections/labors-of-the-months-from-the-tres-riches-heures/.
15. 1 Cor. 15:36–37.
16. For further discussion of the development of seed images as metaphoric for death and resurrection in medieval Christian thought, see Caroline Walker Bynum, *The Resurrection of the Body in Western Christianity, 200–1336* (New York, NY: Columbia University Press, 1995). See also chap. 3, "Images of Transformation," in P.M. Kean, *The Pearl: An Interpretation* (New York, NY: Barnes & Noble, Inc., 1967), esp. 76–83, which focus on "seed," "root," and "wheat."
17. Matt. 3:11–12.
18. For a discussion and examples from the medieval commentary tradition, see *Medieval Exegesis in Translation: Commentaries on the Book of Ruth*, trans. with introduction and notes by Lesley Smith, TEAMS Commentary Series (Kalamazoo, MI: Medieval Institute Publications of Western Michigan University, 1996). Boaz and Ruth came to be viewed a typological precursors of Christ and the Church.
19. John 3:29.
20. See lines 143–44 from Geoffrey Chaucer, "Wife of Bath's Prologue," *The Riverside Chaucer*, 3rd ed., ed. Larry D. Benson (Oxford: Oxford University Press, 1987), 107.
21. The Pearl-Maiden accepts the Dreamer's designation of her as his "pearl" but shifts the emphasis from his possessiveness to her salvation through Christ as a "perle of prys" (line 272). Likewise, the Dreamer accepts the Pearl-Maiden's self-designation of herself as rose, but "so ryche a reken rose" (line 906), which attempts to shift the emphasis from failure to complement, as the adjective "reken" connotes loveliness, nobility, fitness, piety, and worthiness as well as the special courtesy of courtly circles. They are using similar words but meaning different things by them.
22. In medieval botany, the rose was prized for its many healing virtues in the various phases throughout its life-cycle. See Mia Touw, "Roses in the Middle Ages," *Economic Botany* 36 (1982): 71–83.
23. Song of Songs 2:1.

24. See Richard A. Norris, Jr., trans. and ed., *The Songs of Songs Interpreted by Early Christian and Medieval Commentators*, The Church's Bible (Grand Rapids, MI: William B. Eerdmans Publishing Company, 2003), 90–97. See also Mary Dove, trans., *The Glossa Ordinaria on the Song of Songs*, TEAMS Commentary Series (Kalamazoo, MI: Medieval Institute Publications of Western Michigan University, 2004), 35–36.
25. Matt. 6:28–30; cf. Luke 12:27–28.
26. 1 Sam. 2:5.
27. Ps. 27:1.
28. John 8:12.
29. See Leland Ryken and David Jeffrey, "Light," *A Dictionary of Biblical Tradition in English Literature,* ed. David Lyle Jeffrey (Grand Rapids, MI: William B. Eerdmans Publishing Company, 1992), 451–52.
30. Bonaventure, *The Soul's Journey into God*, trans. Ewert Cousins, The Classics of Western Spirituality Series (Mahwah, NJ: Paulist Press, 1978), 54.
31. Others have considered light and sight in *Pearl*. See, for example, Josephine Bloomfield, "Aristotelian Luminescence, Thomistic Charity: Vision, Reflection, and Self-Love in *Pearl*," *Studies in Philology* 108 (2011): 165–88; Barbara Newman, "The Artifice of Eternity" (2005); and Sarah Stanbury, *Seeing the Gawain-Poet* (1991).
32. Carruthers, *The Book of Memory*, 54.
33. Cited from Avicenna, *Compendium of the Soul*, 51 in Lucy Anderson, *The Architecture of Light: Color and Cathedral as Rhetorical Ductus in the Middle English "Pearl,"* (New York University: diss, 2009), 11. See chap. 1, "A Short History of Color in Medieval Optics," for more detail on light, sight, and medieval science. Mary Carruthers supervised this dissertation.
34. 2 Cor. 5:7 conveys the quintessential Pauline thought on this matter: "For we walk by faith and not by sight."
35. Augustine, *The Literal Meaning of Genesis*, XII.6.15.
36. 1 John 1:5 and John 8:12.
37. Rev. 21: 2–5.
38. The actual last words of the poem are "Amen, amen." Assuming that these words are authorial, and not a scribal addition affirming agreement with the poet's final points, the words suggest another genre for the poem as a whole: that of prayer. As Lagerholm remarks in *Pearl and Contemplative Writing*, "The epilogue summarizes the moral lesson and echoes the beginning of the narrative, as critics have observed, and in a manner resembling the rhetorical closure of a prayer addressed to God, it ends with 'Amen. Amen'" (43). I would only add that, while Christians who are praying do often indicate the end of any particular prayer with the word "Amen," prayer itself is an on-going, repeated process—with diverse genres, many of which are meant to be habitually repeated throughout life ("Our Father," "Hail Mary," etc.)—and so the implication of closure in the words "Amen, amen" may actually suggest the necessity of repetition. Thus, by invoking the idea of prayer at the conclusion, the poet invites readers to re-read *Pearl*, perhaps aloud, as a prayer with all that a genre of prayer requires: humility on the part of the petitioner and an awareness that God is listening.

Bibliography

Andrew, Malcolm. *The Gawain-Poet: An Annotated Bibliography, 1839–1977*. New York, NY: Garland Publishing, 1979.

Beal, Jane, "Materials: Classroom Texts and Teacher's Library." In *Approaches to Teaching the Middle English Pearl*. Edited by Jane Beal and Mark Bradshaw Busbee. New York, NY: MLA, 2017.

Blanch, Robert. "The State of *Pearl* Criticism." *Chaucer Yearbook* 3 (1996): 21–33.

Blanch, Robert J. "Supplement to the Gawain-Poet: An Annotated Bibliography, 1978–85." Chaucer Review 25.4 (1991), 363–86.

Cotton Nero A.x Project.

Courtney, Charles Russell. "The Pearl Poet: An Annotated International Bibliography, 1955–1970." Diss. University of Arizona, 1975. Print.

Eldredge, Laurence. "The State of *Pearl* Studies since 1933," *Viator* 6 (1975): 171–94. London, British Library, Cotton Nero A.x.

Foley, Michael. "The Gawain-Poet: An Annotated Bibliography, 1978–85." Chaucer Review 23.3 (1989), 250–82.

McGillivray, Murray, ed. "London, British Library MS Cotton Nero A.x. (art.3): A Digital Facsimile." London, British Library MS Cotton Nero A.x. (art. 3): A Digital Facsimile and Commented Transcription. Calgary: Cotton Nero A.x. Project, 2012. http://people.ucalgary.ca/~scriptor/cotton/CottonNeroBiblio.pdf

Welleck, René. *The Pearl: An Interpretation of the Middle English Poem*, Studies in English by Members of the English Seminar of the Charles University, Prague. Praze, Czech Rep.: Riváce, 1933.

Primary Sources

Aesop, *The Complete Fables*, trans. Olivia and Robert Temple. New York, NY: Penguin Books, 1998.

Anderson, J. J. and A. C. Cawley, eds., *Sir Gawain and the Green Knight, Pearl, Cleanness, and Patience*, Rev. ed. London: Everyman, 1996.

———. *Sir Gawain and the Green Knight, Pearl, Cleanness, and Patience*, rev. ed. London: Dent, 1962, 1976; rev. ed. London: Everyman, 1996.

Andrew, Malcolm, and Ronald Waldron, ed., *The Poems of the Pearl Manuscript: Pearl, Cleanness, Patience, Sir Gawain and the Green Knight*. Berkeley and Los Angeles: University of California Press, 1978.

———. *The Poems of the Pearl Manuscript: Pearl, Cleanness, Patience, Sir Gawain and the Green Knight*, 5th ed. Exeter: Liverpool University Press, 2007.

Augustine, *Confessions*, trans. F.J. Sheed. Indianapolis, IN and Cambridge, MA: Hackett Publishing Company, 1942, repr. 1993.

Augustine, *The Literal Meaning of Genesis*, XII.6.15.

Avicenna, *Compendium of the Soul*.

Babrius and Phaedrus, ed. and trans. Ben Edwin Perry, Loeb Classical Library. Cambridge, MA: Harvard University Press, 1965.

Beal, Jane, *Pearl: A Medieval Masterpiece in Middle English and Modern English* (forthcoming): medievalpearl.wordpress.com.

Bernard of Clairvaux, *Selected Works*, trans. and forward by G.R. Evans, introduction by Jean LeClercq, Classics of Western Spirituality. New York: Paulist Press, 1987.

Biblia pauperum. Albert C. Labriola and John W. Smeltz, eds., *The Bible of the Poor: A Facsimile and Edition of BL Blockbook C.9 d.2*. Pittsburgh, PA: Dusquesne University Press, 1990.

Boccaccio, "Olympia." In *Pearl: An English Poem of the XIVth Century, Edited, with Modern Rendering, Together with Boccaccio's Olympia*, ed. and trans. Sir. Israel Gollancz. London: Chatto and Windus, 1936.

Boethius, *Boethius: The Theological Tractates; The Consolation of Philosophy*, trans. and ed. H. F. Stewart, E. K. Rand, and S. J. Tester, Loeb Classical Library 74. Cambridge, MA: Harvard University Press 1973.

———. *Consolation of Philosophy*, trans. by W.V. Cooper, The Temple Classics. London: J.M. Dent and Company, 1902.

Bonaventure, *The Soul's Journey into God*, trans. Ewert Cousins, The Classics of Western Spirituality Series. Mahwah, NJ: Paulist Press, 1978, 54.

Borroff, Marie, trans., *The Gawain Poet: Complete Works; Sir Gawain and the Green Knight, Patience, Cleanness, Pearl, Saint Erkenwald*. New York: Norton, 2011. Print.

———, trans., *Pearl: A New Verse Translation*. New York, NY: W.W. Norton, 1977.

Brown, Carleton, ed., *Religious Lyrics of the XIVth Century*. Oxford: Clarendon Press, 1952, 234–37.

Canticum Canticorum in B. Fischer, et al., ed. *Biblia Sacra Iuxta Vulgata Versionem*. Stuttgart: Deutsche Bibelgeseschaft, 1994.

Chaucer, Geoffrey, "House of Fame," "Parliament of Fowls," and "Wife of Bath's Prologue." In *The Riverside Chaucer*, 3rd ed., gen. ed. Larry D. Benson. Boston: Houghton Mifflin Company, 1987.

Dante, *Purgatorio*, trans. A.S. Kline. http://www.poetryintranslation.com/PITBR/Italian/DantPurg29to33.htm, 2000.

Dove, Mary, trans., *The Glossa Ordinaria on the Song of Songs*, TEAMS Commentary Series. Kalamazoo, MI: Medieval Institute Publications of Western Michigan University, 2004.

Finch, Casey, trans., *The Complete Works of the Pearl Poet with Translation and Introduction*, with facing-page Middle English Texts. Edited by Malcolm Andrew, Ronald Waldron, and Clifford Peterson. Berkeley and Los Angeles, CA: University of California Press, 1993.

"Fowles in the frith" http://www.luminarium.org/medlit/medlyric/fowles.php - accessed 4 February 2014.

Gollancz, Israel, ed. and trans., *"Pearl": An English Poem of the Fourteenth Century; with a Modern Rendering* 1891. Rev. ed. London: Privately Printed, 1897.

Gordon, E. V., ed., *Pearl*. New York: Oxford University Press, 1953.

Guigo II. "*The Ladder of Four Rungs*: Guigo II on Contemplation," trans. Julia Bolton-Holloway http://www.umilta.net/ladder.html - accessed 25 March 2014.

Guigo II the Carthusian, "Ladder of Monks" and "Twelve Meditations," trans. Edmund Colledge and James Walsh. In *Cistercian Studies Series 48*. Kalamazoo, MI: Cistercian Publications, 1979.
Hillmann, Mary Vincent, trans. *The Pearl: A New Translation and Interpretation*. Notre Dame, IN: University of Notre Dame Press, 1961.
Jacobus de Voragine, *The Golden Legend: Readings on the Saints*, Vol. I, trans. William Granger Ryan. Princeton, NJ: Princeton University Press, 1993.
Jewett, Sophie, trans. *Pearl: A Middle English Poem—A Modern Version in the Metre of the Original*. New York, NY: Thomas Crowell & Co., 1908.
Julian of Norwich. *A Revelation of Love*, ed. Marion C. Glasscoe. Exeter: University of Exeter Press, 1993.
Luria, Maxwell S., and Richard L. Hoffman, eds. *Middle English Lyrics*. New York, NY: W.W. Norton, 1974.
Mann, Jill. *From Aesop to Reynard: Beast Literature in Medieval Britain*. Oxford: Oxford University Press, 2009.
Map, Walter. *De Nugis Curialum*, ed. and trans. M.R. James, C.N.L. Brooke, and R.A.B. Mynors. Oxford: Clarendon Press, 1983.
Marbode of Rennes. *De Lapidibus,* trans. C. W. King and John M. Riddle. Wiesbaden: Franz Steiner Verlag GMBH, 1977.
Marie de France. *Fables,* ed. and trans. Harriet Spiegel. Toronto: University of Toronto Press, 1994, rpt. 2000.
———.*The Lais of Marie de France*, trans. Robert Hanning and Joan Ferrante. Grand Rapids, MI: Baker Books, 1978, repr. 2004.
———. *The Lais of Marie de France*, trans. Glyn S Burgess and Keith Busby. London: Penguin Books, 1986, repr. 2003.
Molinet, Jean. *La Roman de la Rose Moralisé*. Lyons: Guillaume Balsarin, 1503.
Moorman, Charles. *The Pearl-Poet*. New York: Twayne, 1968.
Morris, Richard, ed. *Early English Alliterative Poems in the West-Midland Dialect of the Fourteenth Century*. EETS, OS 1. Oxford: Oxford University Press, 1864, rev. ed. 1869.
Norris, Richard A., Jr., trans. and ed. *The Songs of Songs Interpreted by Early Christian and Medieval Commentators*, The Church's Bible. Grand Rapids, MI: William B. Eerdmans Publishing Company, 2003.
Origen: The Song of Songs: Commentary and Homilies, ed. R.P. Lawson. Westminster, MD: Newman Press, 1957.
Origène: Commentaire sur le Cantique des Cantiques, ed. Luc Brésard. Paris: Editions du Cerf, 1991.
Osgood, Charles, ed. *The Pearl: A Middle English Poem*. Boston and London: D.C. Heath & Co., 1906.
Ovid. *Metamorphoses*, unidentified translator http://www.thelatinlibrary.com/ovid/ovid.met15.shtml - accessed 14 October 2013.
———. *Metamorphoses,* trans. A.S. Kline http://www.poetryintranslation.com/PITBR/Latin/Metamorph15.htm#_Toc64106008 - 2000.
———. *Metamorphoses*, trans. Frank Justus Miller, Loeb Classical Library Vol. II. Cambridge, MA: Harvard University Press, 1916, repr. 1939.
———. *Metamorphoses*, translated by Rolfe Humphries. Bloomington, IN: Indiana University Press, 1955, 1983.
Ovide moralisé: poème du commencement du quatorième siècle, ed. C. de Boer, 5 vols. Amsterdam: Johannes Müller, 1915–38.

"Pearl." *Medieval Bestiary* http://bestiary.ca/beasts/beast548.htm accessed 7 March 2015.
Phaedrus. "Luscinia et Accipiter." In *Aesopica*. Edited by Ben Edwin Perry. Urbana, IL: University of Illinois Press, 1952.
Putter, Ad, and Myra Stokes, eds. *The Works of the Gawain-Poet: Pearl, Cleanness, Patience, Sir Gawain and the Green Knight.* London: Penguin Classics, 2014.
Robbins, R.H., ed. *Secular Lyrics of the XIVth and XVth Centuries*, 2nd ed. Oxford: Clarendon Press, 1955.
Rudel, Jaufré. "Lanquan li jorn son lonc en may," 4 June 2002 //perso.wanadoo.fr/moulin.veste/rudel.htm.
———. *The Songs of Jaufré Rudel.* Edited by Rupert T. Pickins. Toronto: Pontifical Institute of Mediaeval Studies, 1978.
Stanbury, Sarah, ed., *Pearl*, TEAMS: Teaching Middle English Text Series. Kalamazoo, MI: Medieval Institute, 2001.
Stanton, Bill, *This Being a Translation in Verse of the Middle English Poem* Pearl *by an Unknown Poet* (1995) - http://www.billstanton.co.uk/pearl/pearl_old.htm.
Tolkien, J.R.R., trans., *Sir Gawain and the Green Knight, Pearl and Sir Orfeo.* New York, NY: Ballantine Books, 1975.
Vantuono, William, ed. and trans. *Pearl: An Edition with Verse Translation.* Notre Dame, IN: University of Notre Dame Press, 1995.
Virgil, *Georgics*, trans. H. Rushton Fairclough. Loeb Classical Library Vol. 63. Cambridge, MA: Harvard University Press, 1999.

Secondary Sources

Ackerman, Robert, "The Pearl-Maiden and the Penny." In *The Middle English Pearl: Critical Essays.* Edited by John Conley, 149–62. Notre Dame, IN: University of Notre Dame Press, 1970.
Aers, David, "The Self Mourning: Reflections on *Pearl*," *Speculum* 68 (1993): 53–73.
Amy, Roger Andrew, "Genre and Audience Response in the Middle English *Pearl*." Vancouver: University of British Columbia, M.A. Thesis, 1992. Available online: https://circle.ubc.ca/bitstream/handle/2429/3615/ubc_1995-0192.pdf?sequence=3.
Anderson, J.J., *Language and Imagination in the Gawain-Poems.* Manchester: Manchester University Press, 2005.
Anderson, Lucy, *The Architecture of Light: Color and Cathedral as Rhetorical Ductus in the Middle English Pearl.* Diss., New York University, 2009.
Andrew, Malcolm. "Theories of Authorship." In *A Companion to the Gawain-Poet.* Edited by Derek Brewer and Jonathan Gibson. Woodbridge: D.S. Brewer, 1997, rpt. 1999.
———. "*Pearl*, Line 161." *The Explicator* 40/1 (1981): 4–5.
Astell, Ann. *The Song of Songs in the Middle Ages.* Ithaca, NY: Cornell University Press, 1990.
Atkinson, Richard, and Richard Shiffrin. "Human Memory: A Proposed System and its Control Processes," In *The Psychology of Learning and Motivation*, Vol. 2. Edited by K.W. Spence and J.T. Spence, 89–195. New York, NY: Academic Press, 1968.
Auerbach, Erich. *Scenes from the Drama of European Literature*, trans. Ralph Manheim. Minneapolis, MN: University of Minneapolis Press, 1984.
Backhouse, Janet. *Medieval Rural Life in the Luttrell Psalter.* Toronto: University of Toronto Press, 1989.

Beal, Jane. "The Relationship between the Pearl-Maiden and the Dreamer." In *Approaches to Teaching the Middle English Pearl*. Edited by Jane Beal and Mark Bradshaw Busbee. New York, NY: MLA, 2017.
———. "The Jerusalem Lamb of *Pearl*," *Glossator* 9 (2015): 264–85.
———. *John Trevisa and the English Polychronicon*. Tempe, AZ: ACMRS & Turnhout: Brepols, 2012.
———. "Marie de France." In *British Writers Supplement*, Vol. 20. Edited by Jay Parini, 135–56. New York, NY: Charles Scribner's Sons, An Imprint of the Gale Group, 2013.
———. "Medieval Pearl" – http://medievalpearl.wordpress.com.
———. "Moses and the Christian Contemplative Devotion." In *Illuminating Moses: A History of Reception from Exodus to the Renaissance*. Edited by Jane Beal, 305–52. Leiden: Brill, 2014.
———. "The Pearl-Maiden's Two Lovers." *Studies in Philology* 100 (2003): 1–21.
———. "The Signifying Power of *Pearl*," *Quidditas: A Journal of the Rocky Mountain Medieval Association* 33 (2012): 27–58.
——— and Ann Meyer. "Symbolism and Allegory in *Pearl*." In *Approaches to Teaching the Middle English Pearl*. Edited by Jane Beal and Mark Bradshaw Busbee. New York, NY: MLA, 2017.
Berlin, Gail Ivy. "The Fables of the Bayeux Tapestry: An Anglo-Saxon Perspective," In *Unlocking the Word Hoard: Anglo-Saxon Studies in Memory of Edward B. Irving, Jr.* Edited by Mark Amodio and Kathrine O'Brien O'Keefe, 191–216. Toronto: University of Toronto Press, 2003.
Bettelheim, Bruno. *The Uses of Enchantment: The Meaning and Importance of Fairy-Tales*. New York: Vintage Books, 1977.
Bhattacharji, Santha. "The Middle English Poem *Pearl*: A Study in the Unfamiliar." In *Dynamics of Difference: Christianity and Alterity*. Edited by Ulrich Schmeidel and James Matarazzo, 285–92. London and New York: Bloomsbury, 2015.
———. "*Pearl* and the Liturgical 'Commons of Virgins.'" *Medium Aevum* 64 (1995): 37–51.
Bishop, Ian. *The Pearl in Its Setting* (Oxford: Blackwell, 1968).
Blanch, Robert. "Color Symbolism and Mystical Contemplation in *Pearl*." *Nottingham Medieval Studies* 17 (1973): 58–77.
Blanch, Robert, and Julian Wasserman. *From Pearl to Gawain: Forme to Fynisment*. Gainesville, FL: University of Florida Press, 1995.
Boffey, Julia. *Fifteenth-Century English Dream Visions: An Anthology*. Oxford: Oxford University Press, 2003.
Bogdanos, Theodore. *Pearl: Image of the Ineffable*. University Park and London: The Pennsylvania State University Press, 1983.
Bonanno, George. *The Other Side of Sadness: What the New Science of Bereavement Says about Life after Loss*. New York, NY: Basic Books, 2009.
Borroff, Marie. "The Literary Background." In *The Gawain Poet: Complete Works*. Edited by Marie Borroff, 118–19. New York, NY: W.W. Norton, 2011.
Bowers, John. *An Introduction to the Gawain-Poet*. Gainesville, FL: University Press of Florida, 2012.
———. *The Politics of Pearl: Court Poetry in the Age of Richard II*. London: Boydell and Brewer, 2001.
Brown, Peter. *Reading Dreams: The Interpretation of Dreams from Chaucer to Shakespeare*. Oxford: Oxford University Press, 1999.

Búllon-Fernández, María. "'Beyond the Water': Courtly and Religious Desire in *Pearl*," *Studies in Philology* 91 (1994): 35–49.
Burrow, J.A. *The Gawain-Poet*. Tavistock: Northcote House, 2001.
Bynum, Caroline Walker. *Holy Feast and Holy Fast: The Religious Significance of Food to Medieval Women*. Berkeley and Los Angeles: University of California Press, 1987.
Camille, Michael. *The Gothic Idol: Ideology and Image-Making in Medieval Art*. Cambridge: Cambridge University Press, 1991.
Carruthers, Mary. *The Book of Memory: A Study of Memory in Medieval Culture*. Cambridge: Cambridge University Press, 1990; repr. 2003, 2004; 2nd ed. 2008.
———. *The Craft of Thought: Meditation, Rhetoric, and the Making of Images, 400–1200*. Cambridge: Cambridge University Press, 1998, repr. 2000, 2003.
———. "Invention, Mnemonics, and Stylistic Ornament in *Psychomachia* and *Pearl*." In *The Endless Knot: Essays on Old and Middle English in Honor of Marie Borroff*. Edited by M. Teresa Tavormina and R.F. Yeager, 201–14. Cambridge and Rochester, NY: D.S. Brewer, 1995.
———, and Jan Ziolkowski, eds. *The Medieval Craft of Memory: An Anthology of Texts and Pictures*. Philadelphia, PA: University of Pennsylvania Press, 2002.
Carson, Mother Angela. "Aspects of Elegy in the Middle English *Pearl*." *Studies in Philology* 62 (1965): 17–27.
Casey, Michael, *Sacred Reading: The Ancient Art of Lectio Divina*. Liguori, MI: Liguori/Triumph Publications, 1996.
Cavallo, Guglielmo, and Robert Chartier, eds. *A History of Reading in the West*. Oxford: Blackwell Publishing Ltd., 1999.
Cawley, A.C., and J.J. Anderson. "Introduction." In *Pearl, Cleanness, Patience, Sir Gawain and the Green Knight*, vii–xxviii. London: Dent, 1962, 1967.
Chagnati, Seeta. *The Medieval Poetics of the Reliquary: Enshrinement, Inscription, Performance*. New York: Palgrave Macmillan, 2008.
Chance, Jane. "Allegory and Structure in *Pearl*: The Four Senses of the *Ars praedicandi* and Fourteenth-Century Homiletic Poetry." In *Text and Matter: New Critical Perspectives of the Pearl-Poet*. Edited by Robert J. Blanch, Miriam Youngerman Miller, and Julian N. Wasserman, 31–59. Troy, NY: Whiston, 1991.
———. *Medieval Mythography: From Roman North Africa to the School of Chartres, A.D. 433–1177*. Gainesville, FL: University of Florida Press, 1994.
———. *The Mythographic Chaucer: The Fabulation of Sexual Politics*. Minneapolis, MN: University of Minnesota Press, 1995.
Cherniss, Michael. *Boethian Apocalypse: Studies in Middle English Vision Poetry*. Norman, OK: Pilgrim Books, 1987.
Chism, Christine. *Alliterative Revivals*. Philadelphia, PA: University of Pennsylvania Press, 2002.
Ciccione, Nancy. "*Pearl* and the Bleeding Lamb." In *Approaches to Teaching the Middle English Pearl*. Edited by Jane Beal and Mark Bradshaw Busbee. New York, NY: MLA, 2017.
Clark, James G., Frank T. Coulson, and Kathryn L. McKinney. *Ovid in the Middle Ages*. Cambridge: Cambridge University Press, 2011.
Clark, Willene, and Meredith McMunn. *Beasts and Birds of the Middle Ages: The Bestiary and Its Legacy*. Philadelphia, PA: University of Pennsylvania Press, 1991.
Clopper, Lawrence. "*Pearl* and the Consolation of Scripture," *Viator* 25 (1992): 231–46.

Condren, Edward I. *The Numerical Universe of the Gawain-Poet: Beyond Phi.* Gainesville, FL: University Press of Florida, 2002.
Conlee, John, ed. *Middle English Debate Poetry: A Critical Anthology.* East Lansing, MI: Colleagues Press, 1991.
Conley, John. "Pearl and a Lost Tradition." *Journal of English and Germanic Philology* 55 (1955): 332–47; repr. in *The Middle English Pearl: Critical Essays.* Edited by John Conley, 50–72. Notre Dame, IN: University of Notre Dame Press, 1970.
Cox, Catherine. "'My Lemman Swete': Gender and Passion in *Pearl.*" In *Intersections of Sexuality and the Divine in Medieval Culture.* Edited by Susannah Chewning, 75–86. Surrey: Ashgate, 2005.
Crane, Susan. *Animal Encounters: Contacts and Concepts in Medieval Britain.* Philadelphia: University of Pennsylvania Press, 2013.
Croft, Claire M. "Pygmalion and the Metamorphosis of Meaning in Jean Molinet's *Roman de la Rose Moralisé.*" *French Studies* 59, 4 (2005): 453–66.
Curley, Michael, ed. and trans. *Saint Patrick's Purgatory: A Poem by Marie de France.* Binghamton, NY: Medieval and Renaissance Texts and Studies, 1993, repr. 1997.
Davenport, William. "Desolation, not Consolation: *Pearl* 19–22." *Review of English Studies* (1974): 421–23.
Davis, Norman. "A Note on *Pearl.*" *Review of English Studies* 16 (1965), 233–34; repr. in *The Middle English Pearl.* Edited by John Conley, 325–34. Notre Dame, IN: University of Notre Dame Press, 1970.
De Weever, Jacqueline. *Aesop and the Imprint of Medieval Thought: A Study of Six Fables as Translated at the End of the Middle Ages.* Jefferson, NC: McFarland, 2011.
Diamond, Arlyn. "Meeting Grounds: Gardens in Medieval Romance." In *The Exploitations of Medieval Romance.* Edited by Laura Ashe et al., 125–38. Cambridge: D.S. Brewer, 2010.
Dronke, Peter. *The Medieval Lyric.* London: Hutchinson University Library, 1968.
———. "The Song of Songs and Medieval Love-Lyric." In *The Bible and Medieval Culture.* Edited by W. Lourdaux and D. Verhelst, 236–62. Leuven: Leuven University Press, 1979.
Dunn, Charles, and Edward Byrnes, eds. *Middle English Literature.* New York: Harcourt, Brace, and Jovanovich, Inc., 1973.
Dyer, Joseph. "The Psalms in Monastic Prayer." In *The Place of the Psalms.* Edited by Nancy van Deusen, 59–89. Albany, NY: SUNY Press, 1999.
Earl, James. "Saint Margaret and the Pearl-Maiden." *Modern Philology* 70 (1972): 1–8.
Edmondson, George. "*Pearl*: The Shadow of the Object, the Shape of the Law." *Studies in the Age of Chaucer* 26 (2004): 29–63.
Eldredge, Laurence. "Imagery of Roundness in William Woodford's *De Sacramento Altaris* and Its Possible Relevance to the Middle English *Pearl.*" *Notes & Queries*, N.S. 24 (1978): 3–5.
———. "The State of *Pearl* Studies since 1933." *Viator* 6 (1975): 171–94.
Emmerson, Richard, and Bernard McGinn, ed. *The Apocalypse in the Middle Ages.* Ithaca, NY: Cornell University Press, 1993.
Evans, G.R. "Saint Anselm's Analogies." *Vivarium* 14 (1976): 81–93.
Fanning, Steven. *Mystics of the Christian Tradition.* London: Routledge Press, 2001.
Fein, Susanna Greer. "Twelve-line Stanza Forms in Middle English and the Date of *Pearl.*" *Speculum* 72 (1997): 367–98.

Field, Rosalind. "The Heavenly Jerusalem in *Pearl*." *Modern Language Review* 81 (1986): 7–17.
Finlayson, John. "*Pearl*: Landscape and Vision." *Studies in Philology* 71 (1974): 314–43.
Fletcher, Alan J. "*Pearl* and the Limits of History." *Studies in Late Medieval and Early Renaissance Texts in Honour of John Scattergood.* Edited by Anne Marie D'Arcy and Alan J. Fletcher, 148–70. Dublin: Four Courts, 2005.
Friedl, Jean-Paul and Ian J. Kirby. "The Life, Death, and Life of the *Pearl-Maiden*." *Neuphilologische Mitteilungen* 103 (2002): 395–98.
Friedman, John Block. *Orpheus in the Middle Ages.* Syracuse, NY: Syracuse University Press, 1970, repr. 2000.
Fulton, Rachel. *From Judgment to Passion: Devotion to Jesus and the Virgin Mary, 800–1200.* New York: Columbia University Press, 2005.
Furlong, Monica. *Visions and Longings: Medieval Women Mystics.* Boston: Shambala, 1997.
Garbáty, Thomas. *Medieval English Literature.* Ann Arbor, MI: University of Michigan Press, 1984.
Gardiner, Eileen. *Visions of Heaven and Hell before Dante.* New York: Italica Press, 1989.
Garrett, Robert. *Pearl: An Interpretation*, Publications in English. Seattle, WA: University of Washington Press, 1918.
Garrison, Jennifer. "Liturgy and Loss: *Pearl* and the Ritual Reform of the Aristocratic Subject." *Chaucer Review* (2010): 294–322.
Gatta, John. "Transformation Symbolism and the Liturgy of the Mass in *Pearl*." *Modern Philology* 71 (1974): 243–56.
Gilbert, Jane. "Gender and Sexual Transgression." In *A Companion to the Gawain-Poet.* Edited by Derek Brewer and Jonathon Gibson, 53–69. Rochester, NY: Boydell & Brewer, 1999.
Ginsberg, Warren. "Place and Dialectic in *Pearl* and Dante's *Paradiso*." *English Literary History* 55 (1988): 731–53.
Girard, René. *Violence and the Sacred*, trans. Patrick Gregory. Baltimore, MD: Johns Hopkins University Press, 1977.
Goldsmith, Elizabeth Edwards. *Sacred Symbols in Art.* New York, NY: G.P. Putnam's Sons: The Knickerbocker Press, 1911.
Gollnick, James. *Love and the Soul: Psychological Interpretations of the Eros & Psyche Myth.* Waterloo, Ontario: Wilfrid Laurier University Press, 1992.
Griffiths, Paul. *Religious Reading: The Place of Reading in the Practice of Religion.* Oxford: Oxford University Press, 1999.
Gross, Charlotte. "Courtly Language in *Pearl*." In *Text and Matter: New Critical Perspectives of the Pearl-Poet.* Edited by Robert J. Blanch, Miriam Youngerman Miller, and Julian N. Wasserman, 79–91. Troy, NY: Whiston, 1991.
Haase, Donald. "Feminist Fairy-tale Scholarship: A Critical Survey and Bibliography." *Marvels & Tales* 14 (2000): 15–63.
Hamilton, Marie Padgett. "The Meaning of the Middle English *Pearl*." *PMLA* 70 (1955): 805–24; repr. in *Middle English Survey: Critical Essays.* Edited by Edward Vasta, 117–45. Notre Dame, IN: University of Notre Dame Press, 1965.
Harwood, Britton. "Pearl as Diptych." In *Text and Matter: New Critical Perspectives of the Pearl-Poet.* Edited by Robert J. Blanch, Miriam Youngerman Miller, and Julian N. Wasserman, 61–78. Troy, NY: Whitston, 1991.
Haskell, Ann Sullivan, ed. *A Middle English Anthology.* Detroit, MI: Doubleday and Co., 1969, rpt. 1985.

Hatt, Cecilia. *God and the Gawain-Poet*. Woodbridge: Boydell and Brewer, 2015.
Hillmann, Sister Mary Vincent. "Interpretation." In *The Pearl: A New Translation and Interpretation*, trans. Hillmann, xix–xxi. Notre Dame, IN: University of Notre Dame Press, 1961, 1967.
Hoenen, Maarten J.F.M., and Lodi Nauta, ed. *Boethius in the Middle Ages: Latin and Vernacular Traditions of the Consolatio Philosophiae*. Leiden: Brill, 1997.
Howes, Laura L., ed. *Place, Space, and Landscape in Medieval Narrative*. Knoxville, TN: University of Tennessee Press, 2007.
Jack, Kimberly. "What is the Pearl-Maiden Wearing, and Why?" *Medieval Clothing and Textiles*, vol. 7. Edited by Robin Netherton and Gale R. Owen-Crocker, 65–86. Woodbridge: Boydell Press, 2011.
Jaeger, C. Stephen, "Orpheus in the Eleventh Century," *Mittellateinisches Jahrbuch* 27 (1992): 141–68.
Jarrott, C. A. L. "Erasmus' 'In Principio Erat Sermo': A Controversial Translation," *Studies in Philology* 61:1 (1964): 35–40.
Johnson, Lynn Staley, "*Pearl* and the Contingencies of Love and Piety." In *Medieval Literature and Historical Inquiry: Essays in Honor of Derek Pearsall*. Edited by David Aers, 83–112. Woodbridge: D.S. Brewer, 2000.
———. "The Pearl Dreamer and the Eleventh Hour." In *Text and Matter: New Critical Perspectives of the Pearl-Poet*. Edited by Robert Blanch, Miriam Youngerman Miller, and Julian Wasserman, 3–15. Troy, NY: The Whitson Publishing Company, 1991.
Keiser, George, "Lapidaries." In *Medieval Science, Technology, and Medicine: An Encyclopedia*. Edited by Thomas Glick, Steven Livesey, and Faith Wallis. New York and London: Routledge/Taylor and Francis Group, 2005.
Kline, Dan. "The *Pearl*, A Crayon, and a Lego." *Essays in Medieval Studies* 15 (1999): 119–22.
Kraman, Cynthia. "Body and Soul: *Pearl* and Apocalyptic Literature." In *Time and Eternity: The Medieval Discourse*. Edited by Gerhard Jaritz and Gerson Moreno-Riaño, 355–62. Turnhout: Brepols, 2003.
Kruger, Stephen. *Dreaming in the Middle Ages*. Cambridge: Cambridge University Press, 1992.
Kübler-Ross, Elizabeth. *On Death and Dying*. New York, NY: Macmillan, 1969.
Lagerholm, Annika Sylén. *Pearl and Contemplative Writing*, Lund Studies in English. Stockholm: Almqvist and Wiksell International, 2005.
Leach, Elizabeth Eva. *Sung Birds: Music, Nature, and Poetry in the Later Middle Ages*. Ithaca, NY: Cornell University Press, 2007.
Leclercq, Jean.*The Love of Learning and the Desire for God: A Study of Monastic Culture*, trans. Catharine Misrahi, 3rd ed. New York, NY: Fordham University Press, 1982.
Lee, Jennifer. "The Illuminating Critic: The Illustrator of Cotton Nero A.x." *Studies in Iconography* 3 (1977): 17–46.
Lefebvre, Henri. *The Production of Space*, trans. Donald Nicholson-Smith. Oxford: Blackwell Publishing, 1974.
Lisco, Friedrich Gustav. *The Parables of Jesus*. Philadelphia, PA: Daniels and Smith Publishers, 1850.
Lubac, Henri de. *Medieval Exegesis: The Four Senses of Scripture*, Vol. I, trans. Mark Sebanc. Grand Rapids, MI: Eerdmans, 1998; Vol. II, trans. E.M. Macierowski. Grand Rapids, MI: Eerdmans, 2000; Vol. III, trans. E.M. Macierowski. Grand Rapids, MI: Eerdmans, 2009.

Lucas, Peter. "The Pearl-Maiden's Free-Flowing Hair." *English Language Notes* 15 (1977–78), 94–95.

Lynch, Kathryn L., *The High Medieval Dream Vision: Poetry, Philosophy and Literary Form*. Stanford, CA: Stanford University Press, 1988.

Madeleva, Sister Mary. *Pearl: A Study in Spiritual Dryness*. New York, NY: D. Appleton and Co, 1925.

Marti, Kevin, "The Dream Vision." In *A Companion to Old and Middle English Literature*. Edited by Laura Lambdin, et al. Westport, CT: Greenwood Press, 2002.

Matter, E. Ann. *The Voice of My Beloved*. Philadelphia, PA: University of Pennsylvania Press, 1990.

McClung, William Alexander. *The Architecture of Paradise: Survivals of Eden and Jerusalem*. Berkeley and Los Angeles: University of California Press, 1983.

McGinn, Bernard. *The Flowering of Mysticism, 1250–1350*. New York, NY: Crossroad Publishing Company, 1998.

McNamer, Sarah. *Affective Piety and the Invention of Medieval Compassion*. Philadelphia, PA: University of Pennsylvania Press, 2010.

Medieval Bestiary. http://bestiary.ca/beasts/beast256.htm - accessed 16 October 2013.

Meyer, Ann. *Medieval Allegory and the Building of the New Jerusalem*. Woodbridge: D.S. Brewer, 2003.

Minnis, Alastair. "Unquiet Graves: *Pearl* and the Hope of Reunion." In *Truth and Tales: Cultural Mobility and Medieval Media*. Edited by Fiona Somerset and Nicholas Watson, 117–34. Columbus, OH: Ohio University Press, 2015.

——— and Ian Johnson. *The Cambridge History of Literary Criticism*, Vol. II: The Middle Ages. Cambridge: Cambridge University Press, 2005.

Mitchell, J. Allan. "The Middle English *Pearl*: Figuring the Unfigurable." *Chaucer Review* 35 (2000): 86–111.

Morris, Richard. "On *The Pearl*, an Excerpt." Repr. in *The Middle English Pearl: Critical Essays*. Edited by John Conley, 3. South Bend, IN: University of Notre Dame Press, 1970.

Neemann, Harold. *Piercing the Magic Veil: Toward a Theory of the Conte*, Biblio 17. Tübingen: Narr, 1999.

Nelson, Ingrid, and Shannon Gayk. "Introduction: Genre as Form-of-Life." *Exemplaria* 27 (2015): 3–17.

Neumann, Erich. *Amor and Psyche: The Psychic Development of the Feminine*. Princeton, NJ: Princeton University Press, 1956.

Newhauser, Richard. "Sources II: Scriptural and Devotional Sources." In *A Companion to the Gawain-Poet*. Edited by Derek Brewer and Jonathan Gibson, 257–76. Woodbridge: D.S. Brewer, 1997.

Newlyn, Evelyn S. "Robert Henryson and the Popular Fable Tradition in the Middle Ages." In *Popular Culture in the Middle Ages*. Edited by Josie Campbell. Bowling Green, OH: Bowling Green State University Popular Press, 1986.

Newman, Barbara. "The Artifice of Eternity: Speaking of Heaven in Three Medieval Poems." *Religion and Literature* 37 (2005): 1–24.

———. "What Did It Mean to Say "I Saw"? The Clash between Theory and Practice in Medieval Visionary Culture." *Speculum* 80 (2005): 1–43.

Nolan, Barbara. *The Gothic Visionary Perspective*. Princeton, NJ: Princeton University Press, 1977, repr. 2016.

O'Daly, Gerard. *The Poetry of Boethius*. Chapel Hill, NC: University of North Carolina Press, 1991.

Parmelee, Alice. *All the Birds of the Bible: Their Stories, Identifications, and Meaning.* New Canaan, CT: Keats Publishing, Inc., 1959.
Pearsall, Derek. "The Alliterative Revival: Origins and Social Backgrounds." In *Middle English Alliterative Poetry and Its Literary Background: Seven Essays.* Edited by David Lawton Cambridge: D.S. Brewer, 1982.
———. "The Origins of the Alliterative Revival." In *The Alliterative Tradition in the Fourteenth Century.* Edited by Bernard S. Levy and Paul Szarmach, 1–24. Kent, OH: Kent State University Press, 1981.
——— and Elizabeth Salter. *Landscapes and Seasons of the Medieval World.* Toronto: University of Toronto Press, 1973.
Peck, Russell A. "Jacob's Ladder." In *A Dictionary of Biblical Tradition in English Literature.* Edited by David Lyle Jeffrey, 388–90. Grand Rapids, MI: William B. Eerdmans Publishing Company, 1992.
Petroff, Elizabeth Alvilda, ed. *Body and Soul: Essays on Medieval Women and Mysticism.* Oxford: Oxford University Press, 1994.
———. "Landscape in 'Pearl': The Transformation of Nature." *The Chaucer Review* 16 (1981): 181–93.
Phillips, Heather. "The Eucharistic Allusions in *Pearl*." *Mediaeval Studies* 47 (1985): 474–86.
Pilch, Herbert. "The Middle English *Pearl*: Its Relation to the *Roman de la Rose*." *Neuphilologische Mitteilungen* 65 (1964): 427–46 or as translated by Heide Hyprath in *The Middle English Pearl: Critical Essays.* Edited by John Conley, 163–84. Notre Dame, IN: Notre Dame University Press, 1970.
Ployd, David. "The Unity of the Dove: The Sixth Homily on the Gospel of John and Augustine's Trinitarian Solution to the Donatist Schism." *Augustinian Studies* 21:1 (2011): 57–77.
Prior, Sandra Pierson. *The Fayre Formez of the Pearl Poet.* East Lansing, MI: Michigan State University Press, 1996.
Putter, Ad. *An Introduction to the Gawain-Poet.* London: Pearson Education Limited, 1996; rpt. New York: Routledge, 2014.
Raschko, Mary. *Rendering the Word: Vernacular Accounts of Parables in Late-Medieval England.* Chapel Hill, NC: University of North Carolina, diss., 2009.
Reed, Teresa. "Mary, the Maiden, and Metonymy in *Pearl*." *South Atlantic Review* 65:2 (2000): 134–62.
Reichardt, Paul. "Animal Similes in *Pearl*." In *Text and Matter: New Critical Perspectives of the Pearl-Poet.* Edited by Robert J. Blanch, Julian N. Wasserman, and Miriam Youngerman Miller, 17–30. Troy, NY: Whitston, 1991.
———. "'Several Illuminations, Coarsely Executed': The Illustrations of the *Pearl* Manuscript." *Studies in Iconography* 18 (1997): 119–42.
Reid, Heather. "Female Initiation Rites and Women Visionaries: Mystical Marriage in the Middle English Translation of 'The Storie of Asneth.'" In *Women and the Divine in Literature before 1700.* Edited by Kathryn Kerby-Fulton, 137–52. Kelburn, Wellington, NZ: University of Victoria Press, 2009.
Remein, Daniel C. "'Pygt': Ornament, Place, and Site – A Commentary on the Fourth Fitt of *Pearl*." *Glossator* 9 (2015): 61–90.
Rhodes, Jim. *Poetry Does Theology: Chaucer, Grosseteste, and the Pearl-Poet.* South Bend, IN: University of Notre Dame Press, 2001.
Robertson, D.W. "The Pearl as Symbol." *Modern Language Notes* 65 (1950): 155–61.

———. *A Preface to Chaucer: Studies in Medieval Perspectives*. Princeton, NJ: Princeton University Press, 1969.
Rowland, Beryl. *Birds with Human Souls*. Knoxville, TN: University of Tennessee Press, 1978.
Russell, J. Stephen, *English Dream Vision*. Columbus, OH: Ohio State University Press, 1988. Available online (https://ohiostatepress.org/index.htm?/books/book%20pages/russell%20 english.htm).
Saenger, Paul. "Silent Reading: Its Impact on Late Medieval Script and Society." *Viator* 13 (1982): 367–414.
Salter, Elizabeth. "The Alliterative Revival I." *Modern Philology* 64 (1966): 146–50.
———. "The Alliterative Revival II," *Modern Philology* 64 (1966–67): 233–37.
Schirmer, Elizabeth Kate. "Genre Trouble: Spiritual Reading in the Vernacular and the Literary Project of the Pearl-Poet." Diss., University of California Berkeley, 2001.
Schofield, W.H. "Symbolism, Allegory, and Autobiography in *The Pearl*." PMLA 24 (1909): 585–675.
Shea, Colleen Erin. *Early Modern Women's Dream Visions: Male Literary Tradition and Female Authorial Voice*. M.A. Thesis, Dalhousie University, 1999. Available online: http://www.collectionscanada.gc.ca/obj/s4/f2/dsk1/tape9/PQDD_0023/MQ50096.pdf.
Singleton, Charles. "Appendix: Two Kinds of Allegory." In *Commedia: Dante Studies I*. Cambridge, MA: Harvard University Press, 1965.
———. *Commedia: Elements of Structure*. Baltimore: Johns Hopkins University Press, 1977.
Sklute, Larry. "Expectation and Fulfillment in *Pearl*." *Philological Quarterly* 52 (1973): 663–79.
Smalley, Beryl. *The Study of the Bible in the Middle Ages*. South Bend, IN: University of Notre Dame Press, 1964, repr. 1978.
Spearing, A.C. *The Gawain-Poet: A Critical Study*. Cambridge: Cambridge University Press, 1971.
———. *Medieval Dream Poetry*. Cambridge: Cambridge University Press, 1976.
———. "Symbolic and Dramatic Development in *Pearl*." *Modern Philology* 60 (1962–3): 1–12.
Spyra, Piotyr. *The Epistemological Perspective of the Pearl-Poet*. London: Ashgate, 2014.
Stanbury, Sarah. "The Body and the City in *Pearl*." *Representations* 48 (1994): 30–47.
———. "Feminist Masterplots: The Gaze on the Body of the *Pearl's* Dead Girl." In *Feminist Approaches to the Body in Medieval Literature*. Edited by Sarah Stanbury and Linda Lomperis, 96–115. Philadelphia: University of Pennsylvania Press, 1993.
———. *Seeing the Gawain-Poet: Description and the Art of Perception*. Philadelphia: University of Pennsylvania, 1991.
Steffler, Alva William. *Symbols of the Christian Faith*. Grand Rapids, MI: Eerdmans, 2002.
Swanson, R. N. *Religion and Devotion in Europe, c. 1215–c.1515*. Cambridge: University of Cambridge Press, 1995, repr. 1997.
Thorpe, Douglas. *A New Earth: The Labor of Language in Pearl, Herbert's Temple, and Blake's Jerusalem*. Washington, DC: Catholic University Press, 1991.

Tolkien, J.R.R. "Introduction III: *Pearl*." In *Sir Gawain and the Green Knight, Pearl, and Sir Orfeo*, 10–19. New York, NY: Ballantine Books, 1975.

———. "On Fairy-Stories." In *Tales from the Perilous Realm*, 313–400. London: HarperCollins, 1997; rpt. Boston and New York: Houghton Mifflin Harcourt, 2008.

Trotter, D.A. "The Anglo-Norman Inscriptions at Berkeley Castle." *Medium Aevum* 59 (1990): 114–20.

Turville-Petre, Thorlac. *The Alliterative Revival*. Woodbridge: Boydell & Brewer, 1977.

Vasta, Edward "Introduction." In *The Pearl*, trans. Sister Mary Vincent Hillmann. South Bend, IN: University of Notre Dame Press, 1961), vii–xiii.

Wailes, Stephen L. *Medieval Allegories of Jesus' Parables*. Berkeley and Los Angeles: University of California Press, 1987.

Watson, Nicholas. "The *Gawain*-Poet as Vernacular Theologian." In *A Companion to the Gawain-Poet*. Edited by Derek Brewer and Jonathan Gibson, 293–313. Woodbridge: D.S. Brewer, 1997.

———. "Middle English Mystics." In *The Cambridge History of Medieval English Literature*. Edited by David Wallace, 539–65. Cambridge: Cambridge University Press, 1999.

Watts, V.E. "*Pearl* as a Consolatio." *Medium Ævum* 32 (1963): 34–36.

Weiser, Francis. *Easter Book*. New York, NY: Harcourt, Brace, and Company, 1954) and online at http://www.fisheaters.com/septuagesima.html (accessed 18 May 2010).

Wenzel, Siegfried. *The Art of Preaching: Five Medieval Texts and Translations*. Washington, DC: Catholic University of America Press, 2013.

Wheatley, Edward. *Mastering Aesop: Medieval Education, Chaucer, and his Followers*. Gainesville, FL: University of Florida Press, 2000.

Whitaker, Muriel A. "*Pearl* and Some Illustrated Apocalypse Manuscripts." *Viator* 12 (1981): 183–96.

White, Hugh. "Blood in *Pearl*." *The Review of English Studies* 38 (1987): 1–13.

Wimsatt, James. *Allegory and Mirror: Tradition and Structure in Middle English Literature*. New York, NY: Pegasus, 1970.

Windeatt, Barry. *English Mystics of the Middle Ages*. Cambridge: Cambridge University Press, 1994.

Winstead, Karen A., ed. *Chaste Passions: Medieval English Virgin Martyr Legends*. Ithaca: Cornell University Press, 2000.

Ziwolkowski, Jan. *Fairy-Tales from before Fairy-Tales: The Medieval Latin Past of Wonderful Lies*. Ann Arbor: University of Michigan Press, 2007.

———. *Talking Animals: Medieval Latin Beast Poetry, 750–1150*. Philadelphia, PA: University of Pennsylvania Press, 1993.

Index

Abraham 112
Adam 49, 61, 112
Aesop 9, 107, 117–118, 128–132
Aesopian 9, 107, 115–117, 119–122, 129–133
Aesopica 117, 132–133
affective piety 11, 86, 89, 92–93, 97–98, 100, 104
Against Jovinian 91
Agnus et Lupus 121
allegoresis xviii, 4, 8, 43, 45
allegorical significance 8, 11, 44, 57, 109, 130
allegory iii, xviii, xx–xxii, 2–8, 17–18, 20, 39, 43–49, 52, 56, 60–64, 66, 78, 80, 85, 87, 100–101, 107, 112–113, 129, 152
alliterative revival xx, 80–81, 87
allusion/s xix, 6, 9, 20, 25, 32, 35, 36, 44, 47, 48, 50, 55, 62, 79, 81–82, 97, 100, 105–106, 108, 115, 117, 120, 128, 146, 153
Amans 69, 80, 125
Ambrose 49, 89
Amor 126, 134
amour courtois 28, 69
anima 29, 120
Andersen, Hans Christian 107, 123
angel/s 10, 13, 35, 43, 54, 83, 84, 111, 152
Angela of Foligno 92
anger/s 35, 95, 99, 119, 137, 139, 140, 152
animal characters 107, 115
Anne, St. 144
anthropomorphize/d/s 9, 86
Apocalypse 9, 29, 48, 61, 85, 88, 100, 102, 105
Apocalypse manuscripts 9, 85, 88, 100, 105

Aquinas, Thomas 110
Arabia 71, 72, 77
archetype/s 124
architecture xv, xvii, xx, 8, 13, 76, 84, 101, 107, 154
Aristotle 36, 50, 63, 149
Arnobius the Younger 110
Ars praedicandi 10, 17, 129
atone / atonement 63, 97, 98, 140
August 44, 57, 58, 124, 144, 153
Augustine xvii, xxii, 26, 41, 45–46, 79, 87, 89, 91, 92, 113, 138, 150, 152, 154
Aulnoy, Madame d' 107, 123
author/s 17, 20, 34, 47, 52, 56, 76, 79, 88, 103, 130
authority 27, 88
avian metaphors 8, 68, 71, 77
avian imagery 5, 11, 67, 69, 79
Avicenna 149, 154
awaken / awakened 12, 25, 44, 55, 62, 66, 69, 70, 76, 86, 94, 99, 100, 125, 141, 145, 148, 151
awakening 11, 76, 86, 94, 140

Babrius 117, 133
baptism 68, 145
beauty xx, 1, 13, 32, 36, 42, 55, 56, 82, 94, 97, 125, 135, 147
bees 146
beloved xi, xvi, 7, 9, 12–13, 20, 22, 24, 26, 27, 29–34, 38–39, 41–44, 47, 50, 58–59, 63, 68–69, 71–72, 74, 93–94, 99–100, 102, 104, 124–127, 137–138, 140–141, 143, 146–148
Benedict 90
Bernard of Clairvaux 92, 104, 134–135
bestiary 75, 79, 81, 83, 118–119, 152

170 Index

Bible 14, 42, 44–46, 50, 61, 64, 68–69, 79, 87–88, 91, 96, 103, 109, 143, 145, 148–149, 154
biblical iv, xvi, xviii, xx, 4–5, 19, 45–48, 58, 60, 70–71, 79, 85, 88–90, 98, 100, 108, 112, 114, 116, 137, 142–144, 146, 154
bird/birds xviii, 8, 67–71, 73, 74–79, 81, 105, 118–119, 123, 132, 134
birdlime 122, 132
bird-watching 70, 81
Birgitta of Sweden 5, 92, 103
bleeding 8, 12, 19, 44, 67, 77–78, 85–86, 94, 99, 126–128, 140, 142
blessed/ness 49, 110, 125–126
blood 14, 19, 24, 96–97, 99, 101, 105, 125, 141, 147
blue xvi, xxvi, 26, 27, 47, 124, 148
Boaz 145, 153
Boccaccio 26, 40
body xv, xvi, xxi, 11, 16–18, 21, 26, 28, 30, 39, 48, 50–52, 61–62, 73, 79, 81, 88, 100, 104–105, 125, 133, 137–139, 143–144, 147, 153
Boethius 5, 17, 46–47, 49–52, 61–62, 67–69, 80
Bonaventure 149, 154
bread 44, 57, 105, 125, 141–142, 146
bride/s 9, 13–14, 29, 31, 36–37, 53–54, 56, 61, 74–75, 77, 89, 100, 103, 108, 111, 147, 150
Bride of Christ 53, 56, 97, 100, 105, 111, 126, 148
bridegroom 9, 11, 29, 39, 89, 97, 99–100, 103, 105, 145, 147
Brothers Grimm 107, 123
Bruno of Segni 111

calendrical time 8
canto 69, 79
Cassian 89
Catherine of Siena 92
Cervus Oculo Captus 120, 132
charity 30, 43, 113, 154
Chaucer, Geoffrey 42, 55, 73, 77, 80, 82, 84, 101, 117, 153
Cheshire 71
child 7, 20, 21, 23–26, 31, 33, 40, 53, 124
childhood 112
children 23–26, 30, 117, 124, 126, 128
Christ xi, xvi, 5, 8, 9, 13–14, 21, 24, 27, 29, 36–38, 41, 43, 45, 49, 52–54, 56–57, 61–62, 68–69, 73, 77–78, 82, 84–86, 89, 91–100, 102–103, 105–106, 108–115, 122, 125–127, 130, 132, 133–135, 137, 139–143, 145, 147–148, 151–153
Christian 1, xix, xxiii–xxv, 5–6, 11, 17, 22, 27, 29, 32, 43–44, 46–47, 49–50, 52, 56–57, 62–63, 66, 73–79, 83–84, 88–93, 95, 98–100, 102, 104, 108, 111, 115–116, 119–120, 126, 128, 132, 137, 138, 140–141, 148–150, 152–154
Christianity xxii, 29, 46, 86, 104, 113, 135, 153
Chrysostom 109
Church xvi–xviii, xxvi, 5, 10, 29, 43, 56–57, 59–60, 65, 68, 75–76, 89, 91–92, 97, 100, 103–104, 107, 109, 111, 114, 126, 128–129, 137, 140, 145, 147, 153–154
circle 133
circular 151
city 10, 16, 18, 61, 73, 75–76, 79, 87, 98, 100, 104, 143, 150
City of God / *De Civitate Dei* 26, 41
Clara visio 13
clean / cleanness 1, 14–15, 21, 60, 97, 122, 126, 147
cloisters 90, 91
collective unconscious 124
commentary 15, 29, 41, 52–55, 56, 87–88, 111, 117, 122, 131–132, 153–154
commentator/s 28–31, 44–45, 73, 110, 113, 119, 122, 129, 132, 145, 147, 154
Common of Virgin-Martyrs 115
compassion 92–94, 98–99, 104–105, 139
concatenation xv, xxi, 58, 61
Confessions 138, 152
consolatio/n iii, xviii, 5–8, 17–18, 46, 49, 61–62, 66–71, 75–78, 80, 83, 85, 95, 101, 107, 126, 127
Consolation of Philosophy 5, 17, 46, 61–62, 67–68, 70, 80
contemplation 11–12, 90–92, 99, 103, 113, 137, 143, 149
contemplatives xviii, 3, 89–90, 93, 98–99, 102, 111, 145, 148
context xix, 4–5, 7–9, 11, 14, 17, 22, 24, 26, 28–29, 34, 39, 44, 47, 50, 55, 58, 64, 67, 68, 71, 74, 76,

86, 91, 94, 100–101, 104, 106, 107, 113, 116, 118–120, 122, 125, 128, 131, 137, 138, 142, 144–147, 150
conte du fee 123
contra-consolatio 18, 66, 83, 85
Cotton Nero A. x xiii, xx, 9, 16, 22, 26, 40, 64, 111, 108
courtly love 3, 21, 26, 28, 85, 134, 153
creed 24
Cross xvi, 14, 49, 63, 77, 91–93, 98–99, 100, 105, 122, 127, 140–141, 151
crown xv, xxi, 13, 65
Crucifixion 37, 45, 94, 97–98, 100, 105, 140–141
crux 66, 74, 86
cue xvii, 146, 151
culture/cultural iv, xv, xviii, 10, 18, 21, 42, 46, 63, 84, 103–104, 107, 116–117, 128–129, 131, 138
Cupid and Psyche iv, v, xvii, xviii, xx, xxii, 2, 3, 17, 47, 86, 88, 93, 100, 101, 104, 106

Dante 4, 8, 17, 46–47, 49–50, 52, 61, 67–69, 77, 79, 80, 84, 87–88, 102, 147
dark 26, 27, 28, 51, 77, 123, 148
darkness 152
daughter 3, 7, 20–26, 28, 38, 40, 55
death xxv, 7, 13–14, 20, 22–24, 28, 38, 43, 47, 50–52, 58, 61, 63, 65–66, 72, 77–78, 80, 85, 88, 91, 94–95, 98, 102, 111, 119–120, 122, 127, 132, 137–146, 148, 150–153
debate/*debatio* vii, 15, 20, 34, 36, 55, 66, 78, 85, 125
decalogue 113
delight 37, 77–78
depression 140, 152
desire xvii, 7, 10, 13, 21–22, 26, 33, 34–36, 38–40, 53, 67, 72, 78, 81, 92, 94, 103, 105, 117–118, 125, 132, 138
devil iv, 9, 53, 75, 81, 118–122, 143, 144
devotion xxv, 6, 17, 30, 34, 92–93, 98, 100, 102, 104, 149
dialogue 12, 13, 22, 46, 74, 85, 89, 114
Disney, Walt 107

divine 4, 6, 8–9, 11, 17–18, 43, 46–47, 49, 56, 61, 64, 67, 69–70, 80, 84, 87–88, 89, 91–93, 99–100, 104, 106, 114, 126, 128, 145, 147, 149
Divine Comedy 4, 8, 17, 46, 47, 49, 61, 67, 69–70, 87–88, 147
doctrine xix, 43, 100, 143
doe 9, 79, 81, 115–116, 119–120, 122, 132
double-entendre xviii, 47–48, 74, 77, 82
doubt 3, 9, 23, 63, 73, 77, 128, 130,134
dove 68, 79, 80, 154
drama 29, 44, 49, 57, 62, 93
drede 71, 94, 117, 118
Dreamer xiii–xxv, 3, 5–9, 11–29, 32–41, 43–44, 47–50, 53–67, 69–82, 85–89, 91, 93–101, 104, 105–112, 114–120, 122, 124–128, 130–132, 134–135, 137
dreamscape xvi, 12–13, 70–71, 75, 86–87, 91, 138, 148
dream vision iii, xviii, xxiii, 6, 9, 11, 14, 20, 26, 38, 43, 60, 66, 68–69, 76, 80–81, 83, 85–89, 91, 101–102, 107, 120, 122, 125–126, 132

eagle 8, 67–69, 76–77, 80, 83–84
earth xvi, xvii, xxii, 8, 11–13, 24, 30, 33–34, 36–38, 44, 47, 51, 55, 57, 58, 62, 65–66, 70, 74–76, 81, 84, 88, 90–91, 105, 128, 137, 142, 147–148
Easter 5, 44, 57, 58, 60, 64–65, 83, 114, 140
eating 90–91, 105
ego 124, 145–146, 150
Elecktra complex 7
elegy iii, xviii, 2–3, 6–7, 16, 18, 20, 39–40, 43, 66, 78, 85, 101, 107, 153
Elijah 68
emotion 84, 88, 94, 117, 124
emotional xviii, xix, 3, 5, 8, 9, 11–13, 24, 25, 66–67, 69, 70–71, 75–78, 80–81, 91–93, 95, 98–100, 115, 118, 125–126, 137, 139, 142–143, 146–149
empathy 78, 95, 141
encoding 139
England xviii, xx, 24, 50, 58, 71, 74, 98, 104, 107, 116–117, 128, 130–131, 144

172 Index

English iii, iv, xviii, xx–xxi, xxiii–xxv, 1–2, 4, 6, 9–11, 14–20, 23, 30, 38–43, 48, 52, 59, 60–64, 66, 68, 73–74, 78–85, 87, 96, 101–105, 107–109, 115–117, 123–133, 135, 143, 146, 153
epithalamion 92
erber 12, 57, 142
escape 88, 118, 126, 127
eternal life 43, 45, 110–111, 113
eternity 18, 57, 66, 98, 100–101, 126, 151, 154
eucatastrope 127–128
Eucharist xix, 44, 57, 62, 86, 98–100, 105–106, 125–126, 135, 137, 139, 141–142, 151–152
Eurydice 8, 44, 46, 50–55, 60–61, 63
Evangelist/s 67, 76–77, 83
eventyr 123
exegesis 6, 45–46, 60, 62, 92, 129, 143, 153
exegetical tradition 92
exempla 17, 68, 116
extramission 149

fable iii, xviii, xix, 6–7, 9–11, 16, 21, 107–108, 115–123, 128–133
fable motifs 9, 115, 128
Färie 123–125
fail/s 127
failure 127, 130, 153
fairy-tale iii, xviii, xix, 6–7, 9, 11, 107–108, 122–129, 131, 133–135
faith 1, 11, 36, 41, 44, 61–62, 78, 83, 113–114, 120, 143, 147, 152, 154
fantasy 94, 125, 126, 135
fantasies 87–88, 123
father 3, 7, 18, 20–22, 26, 28, 38–39, 53, 56, 62, 65–66, 68, 73, 89, 121, 131, 138, 154
faunt 22–23, 25
fear 26, 53, 69, 71, 94–95, 107, 117, 120, 124, 146, 148–149
feast 44, 57, 58, 65, 98, 100, 105–106
feminist criticism 21
fertility symbol 27
figure/*figura* xvi, 3, 5, 8, 27, 29, 32, 36, 41, 43, 46, 48–50, 52–56, 59–60, 68, 71, 83, 87–89, 107, 119, 12–122, 124–125, 139, 151, 153
fire xx, 69, 73, 75, 145
First Principle 149
fish 27–28, 41, 47, 105, 111
flame 71, 74, 77, 80

Flood 68
flower 12, 26–27, 31, 53, 63, 69, 104, 146–147
foliage 26
foreshadowing 100, 145
form xv–xvi, xviii–xxi, 7–8, 17, 22–23, 29–30, 43, 45–46, 48, 55, 68–69, 81, 83–85, 87–88, 97, 99–102, 104, 108, 115, 117, 129, 134, 137, 141, 143, 146, 150–151
fortune 95
fourteenth century iii, xviii, xxiii, 6–7, 16–17, 20, 26, 30, 41, 43, 52, 55, 58, 65–66, 71, 80–82, 85, 103, 107, 109–110, 129, 147
fowler vii, xxiv, 119, 121–122, 132
fox 115
frame narrative 87, 101
French 20–21, 23, 46, 52, 63–64, 69, 81–82, 87, 108–109, 113, 116, 123, 133
Freud 11, 39, 66, 79, 124
friend 3–4, 9, 11, 14, 39, 78, 96, 112, 116, 120, 125, 137, 145, 152
friendship 3, 38, 95, 99
future xix, 7, 11, 49, 78, 98, 124, 137, 140, 150–152

Galatea 8, 44, 50, 54–56, 60, 63
garden xvi, xxiii, 12–13, 26, 28, 34, 41, 44, 48, 50, 57, 69–70, 76, 80, 86–87, 91, 124–125, 134, 137, 140, 142, 148, 150
Garden of Love 69, 80
gaze 18, 21, 27, 39, 50, 62, 77, 84, 149
gender 16, 18, 21, 33, 39, 93, 105, 124
gender inequality 124
Genesis 68, 90, 154
genre iii–v, vii, xi, xvii, xviii, xix, 3–7, 9–11, 15, 17, 20, 25, 30, 66, 78, 85–89, 101, 102, 107, 118, 123, 125–126, 128, 133, 154
God xvi–xvii, xix, xxiii, xxv–xxvi, 5–14, 16, 19, 22–23, 25, 29, 30–31, 35–41, 46, 48, 50, 53, 55–56, 58, 63, 68, 76, 78, 84–86, 88, 89–95, 97–101, 103–106, 109, 113–116, 119, 121–122, 126, 128, 134–135, 137–138, 140–141, 145–146, 147–152, 154
God's lovers 90–91, 93, 100
gold/en xv, 14, 27–28, 51, 101, 153
goose 115
Gottfried of Admont 111, 130

grace 25, 35, 55, 57, 72, 76, 81, 114–115, 132, 148
grain 13, 58, 142–146, 151
Greek 41, 45, 88, 108–109, 117, 130, 132–133, 149
Gregory the Great 109–110, 112
grief, five stages of 139–140, 152
grieving iii, xix, 11, 38, 51, 57, 140
griffin 68–69, 84
grim Reaper 144
Grosseteste, Robert 82, 150
Guigo II 90, 103

Haimo of Auxerre 110
hagiography / hagiographical account 85
hand/s 3, 19, 21, 26–28, 41, 43, 53, 55, 72, 74, 97, 106, 117, 127, 141, 143, 145
happy ending 122–123, 125, 127, 128
hawk 9, 71, 72, 75, 77, 79, 81, 115–116, 118–119, 122
healing xix, 5, 11, 143, 152–153
heaven/s xvi, xix, xxiii, 8, 11–14, 19, 24, 26, 30, 32, 35, 43, 46–47, 54, 57–58, 62, 66, 69–72, 74–75, 77–79, 85, 88–91, 98, 100–102, 105, 109–112, 114, 128, 137, 142, 146–148, 150, 152
heart/s xi, xv, xxi, 8, 12, 28, 51, 62, 66, 70, 71, 76, 90–94, 98, 108, 111, 117, 120, 124–126, 128, 138, 141, 150, 152
Henryson, Robert 63, 117, 131, 133
Herod 122
Herodis 125
Hilary of Poitiers 109–110
Holy Spirit 68, 80, 138, 145
homiletic purpose 10
homily 36, 49, 79, 130
hope/s xix, 7, 11, 44, 57, 71, 75–76, 81, 95, 107–108, 113, 117, 125, 128, 132, 138, 140, 142, 146, 151–152
Hortus conclusus 34, 70
Hosea 29
Hugh of Saint-Cher 110
human/humanity xv–xvi, xix–xx, 8–9, 14, 26, 30, 32, 34, 36, 43–44, 52–53, 56, 63–64, 66, 68–69, 78–80, 83–87, 93, 97–98, 100, 104–105, 107–111, 114–115, 120, 124, 126, 132, 135, 138–142, 150, 152

humilitas 99
humility 12, 89, 113, 143–144, 147, 150, 152, 154
humus 12

ichthus 27, 41
icon/iconic xvii, 8, 12, 14, 46, 67, 94, 115, 127, 138, 140, 147, 152
iconographic/iconography 27–28, 40–41, 76–77, 80, 83, 98, 121
id 29, 124
identity 14, 39, 72, 93, 114–115, 145
illumination 6, 12, 41, 76, 89, 91–92, 113–114, 148–150
illustrations (*see* Cotton Nero A.x) 7, 22, 26, 28, 40–41, 84, 108, 111, 129
Immaculate Conception 143
image xvii–xviii, xxi, xxv, 5, 8, 12, 14, 16, 27, 29, 36, 41, 43–44, 46, 57, 63, 67, 69, 80, 81, 84, 97–98, 103, 107–109, 126, 129, 132, 135, 138, 140, 142, 144, 146–149, 152–153
imagery xxii, 5, 9, 11–12, 14, 16, 22, 30, 57, 64, 67, 69, 79, 89, 96, 105, 108, 146–149
imagination xxiii, 5, 36, 61, 73, 84, 87, 107, 124, 129, 130, 132
Incarnation 48–49, 82, 110, 130, 143
incest/uous 7, 11, 16, 18, 21–22, 39, 40
Inferno 79
Information Processing Model (modal model) 139
inheritance 34, 95
injustice 107, 115, 119, 127
intramission 149
inner consistency of reality 126
innocence 10, 35, 43, 96, 115, 121–122, 145
interpretation iii, xviii–xix, xxi, xxiv, 2–5, 7–11, 13, 16–18, 20, 22, 26–29, 31, 33–34, 39–41, 43–47, 49–50, 52, 54, 56, 60, 64, 66, 78, 82–83, 85–86, 89, 92, 101–102, 105, 108–113, 115, 118, 122, 130, 134, 143, 153
intimacy 9, 24, 25, 89, 95
Isaac of Stella 113–114
Isidore of Seville 143
Israel 29, 40, 65, 68, 97–98, 100, 103, 132
Italian 1, 15, 23, 26, 69, 80, 87
Itinerarium mentis in Deum 149

174   Index

Jacob's Ladder 12, 19, 91
Jerome 65, 89, 91, 109–110
Jesus xxiii, 13, 23, 27, 31–32, 41, 45, 49, 54, 61, 63, 68, 77, 91–93, 98, 103–105, 107, 108, 109, 115–116, 122, 128–129, 135, 140–141, 143–145, 147–148, 150–151
jewel/s 148
Jeweler xxi, xxii, 66, 86, 124
Jezebel 68
Joachim of Fiore 89, 102
John (gospel-writer) eight, 13, 67, 76–77, 79, 83, 97–98
John the Baptist 103, 145, 146
John's gospel 45, 65, 76, 79
John's Apocalypse 48
journey xvi–xvii, xix, 5, 8, 11, 12, 44, 46–47, 57, 62, 75, 79, 88–89, 93, 114, 122–125, 134, 138, 142, 145, 148–150, 152, 154
joy xxv, 5, 8, 11, 22, 25, 42, 48, 57, 60, 64–65, 67, 70, 77–79, 97, 105, 114, 127–128, 142, 148–149
Jung / Jungian 11, 124
justice 115, 148

kernel 144
kingdom of God 13, 58, 109, 115
kingdom of heaven xxiii, 13–14, 57, 110, 112
kinsman 145
kiss 28, 92

Lacan / Lacanian 11, 39
ladder 12, 19, 89–91, 99, 103, 149
Lady Philosophy 68
Lady White 73
Lamb xvi, xix, xxv, 7–9, 12–14, 19, 27, 37, 44, 53–54, 56, 63, 67, 69, 72, 74–78, 85–86, 93–101, 105, 108, 115–117, 121–122, 125–128, 133, 137, 140–142, 146–149, 151
landscape 12, 47, 69–71, 76, 87, 91, 94, 98, 101, 124–125, 128, 148
language xviii, xxiii–xxiv, 1, 3, 7, 8, 11, 15–18, 20–22, 26, 28–34, 38–39, 41, 44, 47, 52, 60–61, 65, 68, 74, 89, 92–93, 105, 107, 108, 111, 116, 130–132
lapidary 143

Last Judgment 105, 111–113
Latin xxii, 6, 9, 19, 29–30, 40, 48, 50, 52, 59, 61–63, 80, 82, 89–90, 96, 107–109, 116, 117–118, 120–121, 130–132, 143–144
lesson 44, 58, 66, 90, 107, 154
Lectio divina 89–90, 92, 98, 103
letter/s 4, 16, 25, 45, 90
levels of meaning iii, xi, xviii, 6–7, 9–11, 50, 91, 101, 107–135
Literal, allegorical, moral, anagogical (literal) xi, xvi, xviii, 5, 7–8, 10, 13–14, 17, 19, 48, 50, 53–54, 60, 76, 81, 90–92, 103, 114, 128, 132, 150, 154
light iii, xvi, xx, 6, 12–13, 19, 33, 51, 54, 56, 60, 92, 98, 114–115, 138, 142–143, 147–150, 152, 154
Light of the World 148, 150
lily 32, 146
literary analysis 11
literary tradition 71–72, 80, 102, 153
liturgy xv, xvii, xviii, xxi, 5, 57–60, 105, 115
liturgical time 6, 44, 46–47, 56–58, 60
London xxi, 14–17, 40, 42, 60, 71, 80–82, 104, 135, 152
longing xvi, xvii, 12, 34, 38, 62, 95, 104, 109, 125
Lord vii, xvii, 11–12, 27, 35–39, 55–56, 78, 95, 97, 99, 106, 112–113, 116, 119, 122, 125, 135, 137, 141, 148, 152
Lorris, Guillaume 46–47, 50, 68–69, 87
loss xvi, xix, 1, 8, 12, 19–20, 22, 38, 44, 46–47, 50–51, 53, 58, 66–67, 70, 72, 76, 86, 93–94, 99, 105, 119, 127, 134, 137, 139, 140–144, 146–148, 150–152
love xi, xvii, xviii, xx, 3, 5–11, 17, 21–22, 26, 28, 29, 30–36, 38–39, 42, 44, 46–47, 49, 50–56, 60, 63, 68–69, 80, 85, 87, 93, 95, 98–100, 103, 108, 119, 123, 125–126, 128, 134, 139, 143–144, 150, 152–154
lover 3, 16–17, 21–22, 24, 26–27, 28–29, 31, 34, 39, 41–42, 46, 50–51, 54–55, 63, 68, 72, 78–79, 81, 90–91, 93, 96, 98, 100, 105, 124, 126, 143
love-song 93
Luce, De 150
Ludoph of Saxony 110

luf-daungere 34
Luscinia et accipiter 118, 132
Lydgate, John 102, 117, 133
lyric vii, xviii, 7, 21–22, 28, 30–34, 38–39, 42, 68, 80, 82, 92, 143

magic 107, 123, 128, 133
man 19–20, 25–28, 30–33, 38, 45, 47, 50–53, 58, 78, 82, 84, 86–88, 92, 110–112, 120, 125–127, 129, 134, 141, 150, 152
Marbode, Bishop of Rennes 143, 152
märchen 123
Margaret, Saint 64, 80, 104, 143
margarita 19, 110, 143
Margery Kempe 5–6, 92
Marian hymns 7, 22, 28, 30, 33–34
marriage xi, xxi, 5, 7, 8–9, 12, 21, 29, 35, 37, 52–53, 56, 72, 75, 77, 85, 89, 91, 92–93, 95, 96, 97–100, 103, 104–105, 134, 141, 145
Mary, the Virgin 29, 32, 57, 104, 143, 147
Matilda 69
Matthew 13 108, 109, 111, 145
Matthew's gospel xxiii, 13, 81, 147
maturity 123, 125, 126
meditation xvii, 30, 36, 47–48, 50, 90–93, 97, 99, 103, 129, 140, 148
memory ix, xiii, xv–xxi, 5, 11, 13, 44, 50, 54, 60, 84, 131, 137–142, 144, 146, 148–154
mercy / merciful 31, 86, 93, 100, 129
Messiah 145
Metamorphoses 35, 42, 51–55, 62–63, 72, 82
Methodius 89
Meun, Jean de 55, 61, 63, 68–69, 87
Middle Ages xvi, 3–5, 7, 16, 29–30, 41–42, 44, 46, 49–50, 52, 54, 60, 62, 68, 79, 81–82, 85, 87–89, 91, 92, 100–104, 118, 129–132, 134, 138, 149, 152–153
monastery 113
monastic life 90, 114
Mons Veneris 28
moon 143, 148
Moses xxv, 6, 17, 45, 102, 112
mother xxv, 3, 18, 22, 24, 31, 32, 40, 75, 81, 93, 123, 147
mystic/s 6, 21, 89, 102–104
mysticism 102, 104

nacre 143, 151
Naomi 145
natural 55, 100, 141–144, 147, 150
Nature 6, 8, 9, 27–28, 30, 35, 50, 53–56, 63, 69, 71, 75, 79–80, 84–86, 88, 89–98, 100–102, 108–109, 125, 138, 142–143, 146–147, 151
New Jerusalem xvi–xxii, 8, 12–13, 18, 37, 44, 48, 56, 60–61, 67, 75–78, 85–86, 89, 91, 94, 98, 100, 125, 134, 137–138, 143, 148, 150–151
net 10, 108–109, 111–112
nightingale 118–119, 122
Noah xvi, xxi, 68, 112

Odo of Morimond 113
Olympia 26, 40
optical theory 149
optics 150, 154
Origen 29, 41, 89, 91, 110, 112, 146
Orfeo 15, 52, 60, 62–63, 82, 101, 125, 128
Orpheus 8, 44, 46, 50–56, 60–64
other vi, xv–xvi, xviii–xx, xxiii, xxvi, 1, 3, 6, 8–11, 13–14, 18, 21, 23–24, 26–28, 31, 33, 35, 45–47, 49, 51–53, 55, 64, 66–67, 72–74, 76, 78, 79, 80, 84–86, 88, 90–91, 93–94, 105–106, 108, 109, 116–117, 122–125, 127, 129–131, 133, 138–142, 144, 147, 152
otherness 86
Ovid/Ovidian 6, 35, 36, 42, 44, 50–55, 60, 62–63, 72–73, 82

parable iii, xviii–xix, xxi, xxiii, 6–7, 9–11, 13, 32, 35, 36, 43, 48, 49, 56–61, 64, 65, 68, 81, 88, 98, 103, 107–116, 122–123, 128–131, 141–143, 145
Parable of the Growing Seed 58, 108
Parable of the Laborers in the Vineyard 9, 35, 48–49, 56, 58, 59, 81, 114
Parable of the Merchant xxi, 13, 56, 108, 145
Parable of the Seine Net 108, 111–112
Parable of the Sheep and the Goats 88
Parable of the Sower 108, 129
Parable of the Treasure Hidden in a Field 108
Parable of the Wheat and the Tares 145

Index

Paraclete 68
Paradise 44, 47, 67, 69, 70–71, 101, 110
Paradiso 61, 90–91
paraphrase xvii, 8–9, 48, 52, 58, 64, 91, 96, 98
passion 18, 42, 51, 52
Passion, Christ's 93, 97–99, 103–104, 133
Passion plays 140
Paternoster 24
patriarchy 124
Patrick's Purgatory 88, 102
Paul 41, 44–45, 61, 65, 79, 81, 88, 103, 110, 147, 150
pearl/s xxi, xxii, xxx, 10, 12–14, 19, 25, 37, 43, 47, 54, 56, 59, 65, 67, 70, 79, 86, 97, 99, 105, 109–111, 115, 124–126, 137, 140, 142–144, 146–148, 151, 153
pearlescent xvi, 13, 14, 26, 27, 99
Pearl-Maiden ix, xvi, xix, xxv, 3, 5, 7–14, 16–18, 20–29, 32, 34–41, 43–44, 48–50, 53–65, 67–69, 71–75, 77–82, 86, 89, 91, 93–106, 108, 110–122, 124–125, 128–129, 131, 133–134, 137, 139–142, 144–148, 150–153
Pearl-poet xvi, xviii, xix, xxi–xxiv, 1, 2, 4, 6, 7–8, 11, 15–17, 21, 24, 26, 38–41, 44, 47, 50, 53, 55, 57, 60, 63–65, 67, 69, 70, 73, 76–77, 79, 80–85, 91, 101, 103, 108–109, 114–115, 117, 128, 130, 133, 137, 144–147, 150
perception 2, 16, 78, 83, 93–96, 99, 138
perfection xvii, 28, 110, 113–114, 134, 151
perspective xx–xxi, 11, 15, 17, 21, 27, 39, 63–64, 72, 76–77, 79, 93, 95, 100, 120, 122, 127, 128, 130–131, 137–138
Peter iv, xxii, 15, 27, 41–42, 52, 83, 88, 102, 111
Peter Chysologus 111
Phaedrus 117, 132, 133
phallic symbol 27
Pharisees 122
philology xxi, 3, 11, 16–19, 40, 52, 64–65, 78, 81, 101, 104–105, 154
phoenix xxv, 71, 72–75, 77, 82
picture xxii, xxvi, 10, 26–27, 41, 48, 54, 56, 66, 75, 84–85, 87, 103, 111, 114–115, 143, 147–148, 153

Pilate 122
Pisces 27, 41
Plato 63, 88, 149
poetry xviii, xxi, xxiii, 15, 16–17, 43, 47, 49–50, 52, 61–62, 69–70, 79, 80–83, 89, 102, 106, 128–129, 131
possessiveness 126–127
post-traumatic stress xix, 11
prayer xviii, xxvi, 24, 33, 59, 89–92, 103, 114, 138, 149, 154
preacher 10, 36, 64, 114, 116
prey 50, 75, 119, 122
prison 46, 69, 81, 127
prisoner 127
procession xvi, 10, 37–38, 44, 59, 65, 86, 94
Prodigal Son 113, 129
progress 52, 57, 66–67, 71, 87, 89, 94, 114–115, 125, 134, 139
prohibition 123, 125, 127
promises 97, 137, 150
protagonist xxi, 3, 22, 39, 88, 123–124, 127
proverb 49, 79, 81, 107, 109
Providence/ providential 46, 100
Psalm xxii, 68, 79, 103
Psalmist 68
Psalter 41, 108
Pseudo-Bede 111
psychoanalysis 11, 39
psychological iii, xix, 11, 27, 104–105, 107, 134, 142–143, 146
psychology xix, xx, 152
Puella senex 26
pun xviii, xxii, 37, 74, 79, 81
purgation 12, 89, 91
Purgatorio 69, 77, 80, 84
purity 103, 143, 146
Pygmalion 8, 35–36, 44, 50, 54–56, 60, 63–64

quail 9, 71, 75, 77, 79, 81, 115, 119, 122
queen 30, 32, 35, 51, 58, 71–74, 77, 95, 105, 153
Queen of Heaven 30, 35, 58, 71, 72, 77
Quia amore langueo 30–31, 34, 38, 42

raven 68
reading iii, vii, xviii, xxv, 1, 3, 5, 7, 10–12, 14, 17–18, 20, 24–25, 29–30, 32, 39, 40, 44, 51–52, 56,

65, 76, 79, 83–84, 89–91, 101–103, 108, 111–112, 115, 127, 131, 137–138, 142–143, 153
reason xx, 4, 24, 32, 36, 42, 52–53, 76, 87, 117, 123, 128, 138, 150
recovery 126
red 14, 26–27, 147
redemption 77–78, 130, 142
regret 94–95
rehearsal 138–139, 148
relationship xv, xviii, 1, 3, 5–6, 9, 11, 16, 26, 28–29, 31, 32, 34, 39, 49, 57, 62, 68, 82, 85–86, 89, 91, 93, 99, 100, 103, 108, 109, 149
remembering xi, xviii, xxi, 44, 57, 84, 86, 98, 100, 137, 138, 151
Resurrection xvi, 26, 44, 47, 52, 57, 73, 78, 82, 88, 113, 137, 144, 145, 146, 153
retrieval vi, 138, 139
Revelation iii, xi, xviii, 6–9, 13–14, 18, 35, 42, 58, 64, 76, 79, 84–87, 89–107, 137, 143, 150–152
reward 10, 12, 35, 114, 116, 129
Richard/Ricardian xxi, 3, 16–18, 20, 39, 42, 71, 80–81, 100, 104, 106, 131, 152–154
righteousness xxiii, 13, 35
romance iv, 7–9, 17, 20, 26, 43, 46, 52, 61, 63, 67–72, 80, 82, 87, 108, 118, 123, 125, 128, 134, 147
Romance of the Rose 8, 17, 20, 43, 46, 61, 63, 67, 69, 70, 80, 82, 87, 134, 147
Roman de la Rose 34, 39, 55, 56, 61, 63, 64, 80, 125, 128
Rome 65, 89, 91, 109, 110, 116, 117
Romulus 117
Rose xv, 1, 8, 17, 20, 34, 39, 43, 46–47, 49, 55–56, 61, 63–64, 67, 69–70, 80–82, 87, 89, 117, 125, 128, 134, 137, 142, 146–148, 153
Rose of Sharon 146
Ruminate / ruminating / rumination xvii, 91, 148
Ruth xvi, xx, xxi–xxii, 1, 8–9, 44, 46, 78, 84, 87, 89, 91, 95, 103, 107, 108–109, 115–116, 120–122, 125–127, 129, 131, 134, 138, 145, 148–149, 152–154

sacrifice/d 8, 54, 62–63, 115, 137, 141, 152
sailor 120–122

saint/s xv, xvi, xxii, 2, 13, 15, 19, 64, 69, 78, 80, 83–84, 86, 90, 98–99, 102, 104, 110, 113, 127, 137, 143, 152–153
salvation xi, xxiii, 8, 11, 13–14, 43, 48, 56, 57, 63, 77, 98, 111, 114, 126, 130, 143, 148, 153
sand 13, 47, 143, 151
Savior 14, 41
Scala Paradiso / Scala claustralium 90, 91
science xv, 149–150, 152, 154
script 93, 103
Scripture xvii, xviii, 7, 17, 36, 43–46, 49, 53, 60, 62, 67–68, 70, 87, 89–92, 98, 115–116, 122, 128, 132, 143, 146, 148
scroll 5, 114
season 5, 44, 57, 59, 60, 65, 90, 101, 114–115, 124, 144
Second Coming of Christ 26
Secreta secretorum 143
seed 58, 108–109, 137, 140, 142, 144, 146–148, 153
senses 6, 17–18, 23, 45, 53, 60, 62, 89–90, 92, 98, 129, 138–139, 141–142, 152
sensual/ity 29–30, 33–34, 38, 42, 52–53, 92
servant/s 39, 85, 90, 99
sexual objectification 124
sexuality 18, 30
sight xvi, 76, 94, 117, 120–121, 132, 138, 141, 149–150, 154
silence 70, 89, 97–98, 105, 122, 142
sin iv, 8, 14, 19, 53, 56, 78, 97–98, 113–114, 141
sinners 14, 146
Sir Orfeo 15, 52, 60, 62–63, 82, 101, 125, 128
sister vii, xxv, 17–18, 20, 24, 31–32, 40, 60, 65, 134
sleep / sleeping 12, 26, 34, 44, 58, 86–88, 124, 135, 140, 144
Solomon 10, 29, 63, 92, 147
somnium 76
song xvii, 29, 30, 42, 52, 63, 68–70, 76, 80, 93, 96, 119
Song of Songs 7, 20–22, 25, 28–34, 36, 38–42, 68, 89, 91–93, 96, 102, 104, 134, 146, 153, 154
sorrow 1, 20, 25, 31, 60, 67, 69, 70, 71, 76–77, 85, 87, 95, 105, 124, 127–128, 141–142, 150, 152

soul xv–xvi, 4, 9–11, 18–19, 29, 43, 47, 50–54, 56, 63–64, 68, 79, 87–90, 92–93, 96–98, 100, 104, 106, 109, 111, 133–134, 138, 149, 152, 154
space xvi–xvii, xxi, 12–13, 27, 48, 86, 89, 101, 124, 138, 148
spirit xvi, 38, 43, 45, 48, 51, 68, 80, 86, 92, 120, 124, 138, 143, 145, 150
spiritual iii, xi, xvi, xviii, xxiii, 3–9, 11–13, 18, 20–21, 23, 25, 27, 29–30, 32–34, 36–38, 40, 44–49, 54, 57–58, 60, 62, 71, 76, 81, 85, 89–93, 95, 99, 101–102, 106–110, 114–117, 120, 122, 125–126, 128, 131–132, 138, 147, 149
spiritual growth 106, 112–113, 134
spiritual marriage xi, 5, 7–8, 12, 72, 74, 89, 91–93, 96–97, 104, 134, 141
spiritual quest 85
Sponsa Christi 5, 29, 44, 111, 150
spouse 33–34, 42, 106, 123
stag 120, 132
Stations of the Cross 140
Stephen 52, 63, 88, 102, 109, 129
storage 138–139, 152
stream i, xiii, xvi, 12, 27–28, 37–38, 41, 49, 58, 69, 78, 91, 99, 111, 117, 124–125, 127, 134, 137, 141, 146
submission 85, 100
suffering xix, 5, 8, 12, 34, 77–78, 86, 92–94, 98–100, 105, 122, 125, 128, 133, 137, 140–141, 144, 151–152
sun 10, 16, 53, 73, 80, 143, 148
superego 124
sweetheart 74
symbol xxiii, 6, 10, 13–14, 17–18, 20, 27, 41, 46–47, 60, 67, 73, 82–83, 87, 101, 109, 114–115, 123, 138
symbolism xxi, 2, 4, 6, 13, 17–18, 20, 22, 27, 30, 39, 60–61, 67, 69, 71, 76, 79, 105, 125
Synoptic gospels 23, 68, 103, 129

Teresa of Avila 92
theme xxi, xxvi, 22, 28, 52, 67, 73, 81, 108, 110, 119–120, 122–123
theologian 45–46, 64, 66, 78, 83, 85, 101, 152
theology xx, 62, 75, 77, 82, 92, 103, 131, 150
time vii, xv–xx, xxiii, xxv–xxvi, 1–3, 5–6, 8, 18, 20, 24, 26, 30, 32, 35, 38, 44, 46, 47, 49, 51, 54, 56–58, 60, 62, 64, 68, 71, 75, 77, 84, 87, 89–91, 94, 98, 100, 105–106, 111, 114–115, 119, 121–125, 128, 131, 139, 144, 145–148, 150, 152
Tolkien, J.R.R. xxiii, xxv, 15, 43, 60, 62, 74, 82, 87, 101, 107, 126–127, 135
topos 69
Transfiguration of Christ 57, 144
transfigured 125
translation xviii, xx–xxv, 1, 2, 9, 14–16, 19, 36, 39–40, 42, 52, 60–62, 65, 74, 79–80, 82–83, 96, 102–104, 107, 116–117, 131–133, 144, 153
translator xxiii, 74, 131
trauma iii, xix–xx, 5, 11, 137, 139, 140–142, 151–152
treasure 19, 64, 108–110, 126, 129, 138
trigger 139, 151
Trinitate, De 46, 138
Trinity 68
truth xvi, 1, 8, 44, 46, 78, 84, 87, 89, 91, 95, 107–109, 115–116, 120–122, 125, 126, 134, 148–149, 152
Two-year/s-old 7, 21, 22, 25, 28

understanding iii, xv, xvi–xviii, xx, 3–7, 9, 11, 12–13, 17–18, 28–30, 36, 43–45, 48–50, 52, 57, 60, 68–69, 76, 86, 89, 91–93, 100, 108–109, 114–116, 119, 122, 128, 139–140, 146, 148, 150–151
unification 6, 12, 89, 91–93, 98
unveil/ing 7, 88

vernacular xviii, 10–11, 52, 62, 64, 66, 78, 83, 85, 89, 101, 114, 116–117, 128, 130, 133, 152
vineyard 9, 35, 36, 43, 48–49, 56, 58, 59, 61, 81, 98, 108–109, 112, 114–116, 129–130, 141
virgin xvi, 29, 32, 36, 54, 57, 63, 91, 103–104, 115, 129, 130, 137, 143, 144, 146
virgin martyr 91, 104, 115
virginity 37, 43, 97, 110, 143, 146–147
vision iii, xvi, xviii, xxiii, 4–9, 11–14, 20, 26, 37–38, 43–44, 47, 48, 58, 60–62, 66, 68, 69–71, 75–76, 78, 80–81, 83, 85–89, 91–92, 94, 97–98, 101–102, 104, 107,

113–114, 120–122, 125–127, 132, 134, 137–138, 140–141, 148, 150–151, 154
Vision of Piers Plowman 8, 43, 101
Vulgate ix, 36, 96
vulnerability 119–121, 128

Walter of England 117
water 27, 37, 38, 40–41, 48, 59, 105, 121, 141, 145–146
wedding 50–51, 56, 97, 100
West Midlands 24, 104
wheat 57, 144–147, 153
wholeness 151
Wife of Bath 101, 146, 153
will of God 7, 12, 78, 140, 146
wine 31, 44, 57, 125, 141, 142
wings 8, 68, 70–71, 76, 83
wish-fulfillment fantasy 94, 125
witness/es / witnessing 44, 80, 109, 141, 151

white / whiteness 14, 19, 26–28, 36, 40, 54, 73, 99, 105, 125, 141, 143–144, 146, 147–148
wisdom 1–3, 48, 68, 110, 138
wolf 9, 121–122, 133
woman / ly 1, 7, 25–26, 28, 30, 32, 36, 38, 40, 46, 49–50, 53, 73–74, 79, 99, 125, 126, 143–144, 148
word xv–xvi, xviii, xxi, 5, 13–14, 23, 29, 30, 33–38, 41, 42, 45, 47–49, 58–61, 66, 76, 81–83, 92–94, 96, 97, 104, 108–114, 116, 128–132, 134–135, 141, 144–145, 147–148, 153–154
worry 68, 81, 147
wound xix, 8, 14, 77, 94, 99, 119, 125, 132, 141
Wycliffite Bible 108
wyrde 94, 99

Zion 97

For Product Safety Concerns and Information please contact our EU
representative GPSR@taylorandfrancis.com
Taylor & Francis Verlag GmbH, Kaufingerstraße 24, 80331 München, Germany

www.ingramcontent.com/pod-product-compliance
Lightning Source LLC
Chambersburg PA
CBHW070259230426
43664CB00014B/2585